About This Book

Why is this topic important?

Trainers, consultants, and facilitators depend on activities that are creative as well as practical and exciting as well as useful for their learners. This book is filled with activities that are road-tested and certain to work every time. It provides a wonderful array of tools you can use with confidence that they will achieve the results you desire.

What can you achieve with this book?

This book offers a selection of more than one hundred activities and trainer tools and techniques. Every activity has been used successfully by experienced training professionals, many of whom you may recognize as American Society for Training and Development (ASTD) colleagues and friends. Consider *The Book of Road-Tested Activities* as a trusted, rich source of practical classroom tools, approaches, and ideas that others in your profession find useful. Whether you spice up your long-distance learning events with some of the technology tools presented or use time tested classroom techniques, this book will add loads of learning and fabulous fun to your next training session. Each activity is accompanied by insider tips and observations provided by the activity designer to ensure you consider every detail to ensure success.

How is this book organized?

The book is divided into two sections and sixteen chapters. Section I, "Training Topics," includes ten of the sixteen chapters. Each chapter represents a specific training topic, such as communication, teamwork, and leadership. The activities are presented as complete and ready-to-use designs for working with groups. Facilitator instructions, lecturettes, handouts, and participant materials are included.

Section II, "Training Tools and Techniques," includes six chapters. Each of these chapters presents training techniques that may be incorporated into many training sessions, including icebreakers, training techniques, and technology tools. All will enrich your training design.

About Pfeiffer

Pfeiffer serves the professional development and hands-on resource needs of training and human resource practitioners and gives them products to do their jobs better. We deliver proven ideas and solutions from experts in HR development and HR management, and we offer effective and customizable tools to improve workplace performance. From novice to seasoned professional, Pfeiffer is the source you can trust to make yourself and your organization more successful.

Essential Knowledge Pfeiffer produces insightful, practical, and comprehensive materials on topics that matter the most to training and HR professionals. Our Essential Knowledge resources translate the expertise of seasoned professionals into practical, how-to guidance on critical workplace issues and problems. These resources are supported by case studies, worksheets, and job aids and are frequently supplemented with CD-ROMs, websites, and other means of making the content easier to read, understand, and use.

Essential Tools Pfeiffer's Essential Tools resources save time and expense by offering proven, ready-to-use materials—including exercises, activities, games, instruments, and assessments—for use during a training or team-learning event. These resources are frequently offered in looseleaf or CD-ROM format to facilitate copying and customization of the material.

Pfeiffer also recognizes the remarkable power of new technologies in expanding the reach and effectiveness of training. While e-hype has often created whizbang solutions in search of a problem, we are dedicated to bringing convenience and enhancements to proven training solutions. All our e-tools comply with rigorous functionality standards. The most appropriate technology wrapped around essential content yields the perfect solution for today's on-the-go trainers and human resource professionals.

Pfeiffer *Essential resources for training and HR professionals*
www.pfeiffer.com

About the American Society for Training & Development

The American Society for Training & Development (ASTD) is the world's largest professional association dedicated to the training and development field. In more than 100 countries, ASTD's members work in organizations of all sizes, in the private and public sectors, as independent consultants, and as suppliers. Members connect locally in 130 U.S. chapters and with 30 international partners.

ASTD started in 1943 and in recent years has widened the profession's focus to align learning and performance to organizational results and is a sought-after voice on critical public policy issues. For more information, visit www.astd.org.

For Mason
You're the Best-Tested!

—ebb

The Book of Road-Tested Activities

Elaine Biech

Editor

Pfeiffer

A Wiley Imprint

www.pfeiffer.com

An Imprint of Wiley
989 Market Street, San Francisco, CA 94103-1741
www.pfeiffer.com

For additional copies/bulk purchases of this book in the U.S. please contact 800-274-4434.

Pfeiffer books and products are available through most bookstores. To contact Pfeiffer directly call our Customer Care Department within the U.S. at 800-274-4434, outside the U.S. at 317-572-3985, fax 317-572-4002, or visit www.pfeiffer.com.

Pfeiffer also publishes its books in a variety of electronic formats. Some content that appears in print may not be available in electronic books.

Library of Congress Cataloging-in-Publication Data

The book of road-tested activities / [edited by] Elaine Biech.
    p. cm.
  ISBN 978-0-470-90544-9 (pbk.)
  1. Management games. 2. Business communication. 3. Teams in the workplace. 4. Leadership.
I. Biech, Elaine.
  HD30.26.B66 2011
  658.4'0353—dc22

                              2011005632

Acquiring Editor: Holly J. Allen
Director of Development: Kathleen Dolan Davies
Production Editor: Dawn Kilgore
Editor: Rebecca Taff
Editorial Assistant: Michael Zelenko
Manufacturing Supervisor: Becky Morgan
Printed in the United States of America

Printing 10 9 8 7 6 5 4 3 2 1

Road Map

Grateful Acknowledgments

This experience has been a real trip! Thanks to everyone along the way who helped us reach our destination.

A huge thanks to all the ASTD contributors to this book who took the time to share their road-tested activities. Trainers everywhere will thank you for fueling their tanks with new and exciting activities that work.

Thank you to the ASTD chapters (small, medium, and large) who put the word out. We are grateful for your willingness to drive the chapters-for-chapters call for activities.

Thank you to Mark Morrow, editor and spark plug for the creation of this book concept. I appreciate that you trusted me to test drive your model.

Thanks to Lisa Shannon, Kathleen Dolan Davies, Marisa Kelley, Michael Zelenko, Adam Chesler, and Jacki Edlund-Braun, publishers who helped to fast-track this book so that it would be ready for a 2011 ASTD-ICE release.

Thank you to Lorraine Kohart, ebb associates inc, who helped to race the final manuscript to the finish line, and Dan Greene, who adhered to a strict maintenance schedule. Thanks to Rebecca Taff for perfecting it.

Thank you, Dawn Kilgore, for detailing this book as only you can do.

Your Highway to Success

An Introduction to Road-Tested Activities

As workplace learning and performance (WLP) professionals, we are always looking for the best solutions. We want tried-and-true activities, ones that work every time, ones that always lead participants to learn what is required. We are looking for "road-tested" activities.

So when Mark Morrow came to me with this project that he had initiated with Pfeiffer, I did not hesitate to say "yes." I was sure it would both be fun and produce a practical product. Now how can you make a project better than that? By inviting ASTD members to participate. And thus ASTD and Pfeiffer partnered to create an exciting opportunity for ASTD members to be published.

Chapters-For-Chapters

A call went out to ASTD chapters everywhere. We were looking for activities that work—every time. ASTD held a Chapters-For-Chapters contest, giving away four books to the chapters that submitted the most road-tested activities in the large, medium, and small chapter-size categories. The winners with the most submissions were:

- Large Chapter—Metro Washington, D.C., Chapter
- Medium Chapter—Houston Chapter
- Small Chapter—Space Coast Chapter

We received a tremendous response, with excellent submissions from which to select. We had submissions from international chapters as well as chapter members living abroad. The book grew to be a bit larger than we intended, but we think that the result is worth it. Included are more than one hundred activities that your ASTD colleagues have taken to the finish line with excellent results every time.

A Powerful Design

This book has a special design. Like a high-powered engine that is finely tuned, it provides activities that will perform for you again and again, driving you to training success.

What is in a high-performing activity? What do trainers need?

- **Participation.** Activities should create a high degree of participant involvement, either physically (movement) or psychologically (visual or mental thought). Participants should "experience" something. In fact, that is the point of activities—they should be active!
- **Results.** Activities should ensure that learning occurs in every situation, every time. While they may be fun, that is not all that activities should produce. Participants need to learn something. They need to gain knowledge or skills or improve their attitudes. Activities should make your learners focus attention, think, react, and/or do something better than they did before their involvement in the activity.
- **Adaptability.** Activities should be able to be adapted to fit many situations and still retain their original character; allow trainers to modify them to meet many needs: needs of their companies, needs of the participants' career, participants' level in the organization, and the training topic.
- **Application.** Activities should have a "so what" factor. Learners should be able to connect the activity and what they learned to themselves and real life. Learners should be able to state or model what they will do differently as a result of the experience they had during the activity.
- **Proven.** Activities should be effective—every time. They should have completed a trial run, be road tested, and verified that they deliver what they promise. The trainer should have minimal risk when implementing an activity; trainers want to trust that the activity will work.

The true value of conducting activities comes when you use a thoughtful, bold debriefing. Don't be afraid to ask the hard questions. You want participants to confront their issues and to make the changes required. This debriefing for every activity is vital to the results you desire and the learning your participants will gain. Since your colleagues have road tested these activities, you can trust that, with an excellent debriefing discussion, you will be successful in your final "time trials" and that first lap around the classroom track.

What's in This Book?

The book is made up of two sections. The first section includes activities that address specific content and topics that trainers deliver to their customers. The second section provides training tools and techniques that trainers use to deliver the content. These activities will help you avoid wrong turns and potholes in your training travels.

Section I: Training Topics

The first section is a collection of activities geared toward specific workshop topics. Within the section, activities are grouped by topic into chapters. We did not predetermine topics, so we can only assume that the ten topics are those that are used most often by trainers.

It is important to note that many of the activities cross over to topics in other chapters. For example, many of the activities in the teamwork chapters are also focused on communication or could be adjusted slightly for opening icebreakers. Be sure to use the Activity GPS in the back of the book to locate activities that may be appropriate for your needs.

Selecting an Activity

First read the objectives. Then read the debriefing questions to determine whether the activity will accomplish the goals you desire. You may also find that you can expand or change, or even add new questions to facilitate the discussion. If necessary, review the guidelines for facilitating an experiential learning activity (ELA). You will find information in the Pfeiffer books and Pfeiffer *Annuals* or in *Training for Dummies.*

The ten chapters are

Chapter 1—Communication: The Most Vital Skill
Chapter 2—Listening: The Second Half of Communication
Chapter 3—Customer Service and Sales: Imperative for Organizations
Chapter 4—Creativity and Innovation: Most Important in a Complex World
Chapter 5—Diversity and Inclusion: Valuing Differences
Chapter 6—Teamwork: Get to Know Your Team
Chapter 7—Teamwork: Working Together
Chapter 8—Leadership: What It Takes to Make a Leader
Chapter 9—Solving Problems: Find Practical Solutions
Chapter 10—Professional Development: Skills for the Workplace

Section II: Training Tools and Techniques

The second section represents a collection of trainer tools and techniques such as icebreakers and review activities. We are excited to present the six activities that address online learning. One of the advantages of being the editor is that I have an opportunity to road test some of these tools myself before the book is published. I have tried several already and am more than pleased with their performance.

Five of the chapters in Section II address specific trainer skills:

Chapter 11—Icebreakers: Getting to Know You
Chapter 12—Openings: Start with a BANG
Chapter 13—Reviewing: Make It Fun
Chapter 14—New Tools: Add a Twist to Your Techniques
Chapter 15—Online Learning: Tools to Try

The last chapter, "Ideas for Your ASTD Chapter," provides ideas for your chapter to use during and between meetings,

Every time you pull this book from its parking space on your shelf and take it for a spin, you will have a great ride. You will find exciting yet practical activities you can build into your training events. I hope that you enjoy using this book as much as I have enjoyed compiling it for you.

Elaine Biech
ebb associates inc
April 2011

Section I

Training Topics

Chapter 1

Communication: The Most Vital Skill

As a consultant, I frequently tell my clients that if they all communicated perfectly, I wouldn't have any business. They chuckle, but they know the statement is very close to the truth. Everyone needs to improve communication with someone. Whether you are working with groups and teams or individuals, an opportunity to develop communication skills always exists.

As for my opening statement about perfect communication, I don't think I'm too far off. The late Peter Drucker often noted that more than 60 percent of all management problems are the result of faulty communication. I think if he were alive and intimately involved with the communication challenges facing our organizations today he would increase his estimate by a sizeable amount.

The number of books written about communication could fill a library, and still most of us would say that we are not as good at communicating as we could be, should be, or wish we were. There are many aspects of communication, and as trainers you need reliable maps in your console and as many tools as possible in your trunk to provide the support your learners need and desire.

The Communication chapter opens *The Book of Road-Tested Activities*. What better way to ignite your learners' engines than with one of the most critical learning skills every employee needs? The first activity, "Story, Song, Poem, Saying," helps participants understand one of the most basic, although little understood communication skills, behavioral style. Whether you call it communication style, personality characteristics, or behavioral style, Barbara Carnes presents an activity with a twist to help participants see that we demonstrate our style in everything we do.

Sharon Dera and Rodger Adair share ideas for helping your participants learn about how important perceptions are in the communication process from a visual and an audio perspective. Paul Signorelli gives us an activity that he saw in a small Italian village one warm summer evening. The activity demonstrates the value of inclusive conversations. The last activity in this chapter is short and powerful. Curtis Curry describes a simple way to demonstrate the importance of a win-win attitude.

Trainers are called upon more to help learners communicate than to practice any other skill. Try some of these road-tested activities. You won't be disappointed.

Story, Song, Poem, Saying

Submitted by Barbara Carnes

Overview
Participants identify their own personality styles and characteristics using a standard scale such as DiSC or Myers-Briggs Type Indicator (MBTI) before moving to a designated area of the training room set aside for that particular style or characteristic. The participants gathered in each designated area work together to construct and share or perform a story, song, poem, or saying that clearly describes the group's style or personality traits.

Objectives
- To demonstrate behavior style characteristics as defined in tools such as MBTI, DiSC, or other personality type assessments
- To energize participants by moving around the room

Audience
This activity works well with groups of ten up to one hundred or more. Managing extremely large groups can be a bit challenging, but it is still effective.

Time Estimate
15 to 30 minutes

Materials and Equipment
- No handouts, equipment, or materials are necessary. However, if you do provide handouts that describe the personality style or characteristic instrument you are using, encourage participants to refer to handouts and other materials to more accurately judge their own personality traits and styles.

Area Setup
There should be sufficient space at the perimeter of the room so people can congregate into small groups.

Preparation

Whichever personality assessment you use, participants should be briefed or provided with materials explaining personality styles, should know their particular style/profile, or have a basic understanding of the model before beginning this activity.

Process

1. After you have explained or given the participants an opportunity to study any handout you've provided on personality styles, ask the participants to raise their hands to identify their styles. For example, if you chose to use the DiSC tool, you might say, "How many of you came out with a high D?" (Regarding MBTI, this activity works best with E/I and/or P/J scales.)

2. Point to the specific corners of the room and ask the participants to "temporarily relocate" to an identified corner based on their own styles. For example, if using the DiSC, you would have four designated spots and might say, "Will all those who raised their hand for the D style move to the front, left corner of the room." Assign each of the groups to a location.

3. Once the participants have moved to their respective locations, ask them to work in groups to develop a story, a song, a poem, or (emphasize OR) a saying that best describes the group's style. State that each group will have 10 minutes to complete the activity. Tell them their groups will be asked to share or perform it.

4. As the groups work, observe how each group approaches their task and how this approach demonstrates the specific style of the group.

5. After 10 minutes, ask each group to demonstrate their results. Lead enthusiastic applause after each.

6. After all "performances" ask the groups to think back to their planning and design process. Ask how their processes modeled their styles. For example, extroverts typically begin the task by talking, whereas introverts begin by reviewing the materials and taking notes. You may need to provide a few examples of what you observed about the groups as they approached this task. Encourage contributions from all participants.

InSider's Tips

- Send the largest groups to the areas of the room where there is the most space.

- This activity works best if groups are allowed only a short time. After the first 4 minutes, apply gentle pressure to finish by reminding them they have "1 minute left." Don't allow any more than 10 minutes before you ask each group to deliver a short performance.
- Although initially they may push back, even the most serious participants get into this activity and enjoy it once they start.

Barbara Carnes, Ph.D., is a consultant, trainer, speaker, and writer in St. Louis, Missouri. She is the author of the book *Making Learning Stick* and co-author of the books *Making Training Stick* and *Making Training Stick: A Training Transfer Field Guide.* Formerly a trainer with Sprint, Barbara has her own learning and development consulting practice. She develops and delivers classroom learning programs as well as e-learning. She has a Ph.D. in human and organizational systems from The Fielding Graduate University and she is an adjunct professor for Webster University and for the University of Phoenix.

Barbara Carnes, Ph.D.
7251 Princeton Avenue
St. Louis, MO 63130
(314) 862.7733
Email: bcarnes@maketrainingstick.com
Website: www.MakeTrainingStick.com
ASTD Chapter: St. Louis

Personality Type Assessments

Personality type refers to the psychological classification of individual differences and behaviors displayed by people. Personality types distinguish and label traits individuals may exhibit. For example, according to one type theory, individuals might be introverts or extraverts. Introversion and extraversion are part of a continuum, with individuals exhibiting varying degrees of each from one end to the other. It is believed that all individuals are made up of a unique set of motivations that influence their behaviors in various situations. The idea of psychological types originated in the theoretical work of Carl Jung and William Marston in the early 20th century.

Two well-known instruments are used to assess individuals: the DiSC based on Marston's work and the Myers-Briggs Type Indicator (MBTI) based on Jung's work. Both of these assessments help individuals better understand their strengths and limitations. This knowledge can help individuals understand and accept others' behavior, communicate better, and adapt to the needs of others.

The DiSC Profile assessment is a tool developed to identify an individual's natural behavioral tendencies, displayed in various environments. The resulting report shows an individual's strengths, weaknesses, motivations, behavioral tendencies, along with strategies that could increase daily effectiveness in both personal and work situations. The results are displayed in a four-quadrant behavioral model classified as:

- Dominance (D)—relating to control, power, and assertiveness
- Influence (i)—relating to social situations and communication
- Steadiness (S)—relating to patience, persistence, and thoughtfulness
- Conscientiousness (C)—relating to structure and organization

These four dimensions can be grouped in a matrix with the vertical dimension represents a factor of "Assertive" (at the top) versus "Passive"(at the bottom). The horizontal represents "Guarded" (left side) versus "Openness" (right side). The "D" and "I" share the top row, representing extroverted aspects of the personality, and "C" and "S" below represent introverted aspects. "D" and "C" also share the left column and represent task-focused aspects, and "I" and "S" share the right column and represent social aspects.

The Myers-Briggs Type Indicator (MBTI) is a questionnaire designed to measure behavioral preferences in how people perceive the world and make decisions. These preferences were extrapolated from the personality type theories proposed by Carl Jung. The original developers of the personality inventory were Katharine Cook Briggs and her daughter, Isabel Myers. They began creating the indicator during World War II, believing that knowledge of personality preferences would help women who were entering the industrial workforce for the first time. The initial questionnaire grew into the Myers-Briggs Type Indicator (MBTI), first published in 1962. The self-assessment results in four dimensions:

- Flow of energy—extraverted (E) or introverted (I)
- How information is received—sensing (S) or intuitive (N)
- Preference for making decisions—thinking (T) or feeling (F)
- Preference for dealing with the outside world—judging (J) or perceiving (P)

The self-assessment presents one preference from each of the four categories. This is expressed as a four letter code, such as ENTJ. The sixteen personality MBTI combinations are often displayed in what is called a type table.

Do You See What I See?

Submitted by Sharon Dera

Overview

Participants explore the power of perception in this activity by providing their impressions and reactions to a set of images projected on a screen.

Objectives

- To define perception and discuss its importance
- To understand that others may see things differently

Audience

Twenty to fifty individuals

Time Estimate

20 to 35 minutes

Materials and Equipment

- Copies of various illusion images on PowerPoint slides or as large posters such as those found at www.123OpticalIllusions.com
- Projection capability for PowerPoint slides
- Flip chart and markers

Area Setup

Any room arrangement where all can see the images projected on a screen

Process

1. Ask participants for a definition of perception. Accept several comments and jot them down for reference later.
2. Project one of the illusion images provided or you may search for another example if you prefer. Ask participants for input on what they see in the image. Note the suggestions and offer one or two of the group's suggestions and ask "How many of you see X?" or "How many of you see Y?" Encourage each group to help others in the group see the image that they see.

3. Project another one of the images and conduct another large group discussion on what everyone sees. As before, discuss the different points of view and encourage the groups to help the others in their group see what they see.
4. Ask participants again for a definition of perception. This time write some of the words and phrases on flip-chart paper.
5. Summarize with questions such as these:
   - What happened during this exercise?
   - Why did some people see one thing and others see another?
   - How does this relate to real life?
   - What did you do to help others see what you saw?
   - How important are perceptions in real-life situations?
   - What will you do differently as a result of this exercise?
6. Wrap up the discussion by sharing the following quote from Tom Peters:
   "Perception is all there is. There is only one perceived reality; it is the way each of us chooses to perceive a communication, the value of a service, the value of a particular product feature, the quality of a product."
7. State that the perceptions of each individual are the only realities that matter and that we need to keep this human tendency foremost in our minds when we communicate, solve problems, or try to reach agreement.

InSider's Tips

- This activity is good for helping participants understand that there are different ways of looking at the same issue, problem, situation, or solution. This activity also reinforces the importance of communicating clearly, asking questions, paraphrasing, and gaining agreement on any transmitted message.

- Images for this activity can be found at the website www.123OpticalIllusions .com. This activity has been passed around the training profession for at least thirty-five years. It still brings "ah-ha's" to those experiencing it for the first time and is an excellent demonstration of perception and its importance in communication.

Sharon Dera, CPLP, has more than seventeen years of experience in needs assessment, human performance, process improvement, and organization development. Her broad experience was acquired by working in the retail, finance, healthcare, government, manufacturing, hospitality, and travel industries in operations, business management, customer service, sales, communications, marketing, succession planning, leadership, coaching, and training. Sharon is owner and CEO of The Proficience Group, Inc., working in partnership with organizations to identify the root cause of performance deficiencies and determine the best solutions/interventions that close the performance gap; lending a "fresh set of eyes" exposing possible blind spots. Sharon is currently serving on the National ASTD Chapter Recognition Committee. She holds an MBA from the University of Dallas.

Sharon Dera, CPLP
8948 Random Road
Fort Worth, TX 76179
(817) 236.7594
Email: sdera@charter.net
Website: www.proficiencegroup.com
ASTD Chapter: Fort Worth

Perception Reflection

Submitted by Rodger Adair

Overview
In this activity, participants discover how their perceptions are impacted when they hear only one side of a conversation and how conclusions they draw do not necessarily reflect reality.

Objective
- To better understand how we perceive communications

Audience
Any size

Time Estimate
10 to 20 minutes

Materials and Equipment
- Perception Reflection conversation sheet for the facilitator

Area Setup
No special room setup needed

Process
1. Ask the participants how many have experienced miscommunication due to a misperception of reality. Solicit examples if you wish.
2. Explain that to demonstrate this dynamic you will read one side of a telephone conversation and that the job of the participants is to imagine what the conversation is about based solely on what they hear.
3. Use the Perception Reflection conversation sheet and read only Part A. When you are finished, pause before engaging the audience in discussion.
4. Ask several participants to explain what they think might be happening in this conversation based on what they heard.
5. Ask for a volunteer to join you at the front of the room. Perform the Perception Reflection conversation again, but this time ask the volunteer

to read Part B of the conversation while you read Part A again. Pause for impact when you are finished.

6. Debrief the activity using the following questions:
   - How has your perception of this conversation changed? Why?
   - How did your perceptions differ from reality?
   - Have you ever gone into a situation with an incorrect perception? What happened?
   - How do perceptions cloud clear communication? What is often the result?
   - How can we prevent this from occurring? What tools do you have that you can use to prevent miscommunication due to incorrect perceptions (ask questions, listen, watch body language)?
   - What can you commit to doing in the future to ensure fewer misperceptions?

InSider's Tips

- Most people are surprised by how badly they misjudged the real story.
- Allow for reflection and learning before moving on.

For the last twenty years **Rodger Adair** has focused on organization development, industrial psychology, and corporate training, twelve of those years mainly in the Arizona market. He has a B.S. in adult/workforce education from Southern Illinois University. He has a master's in organizational management and an MBA from the University of Phoenix. He is in a Ph.D. program in I/O psychology with Northcentral University in Prescott Valley, Arizona. He serves as a director of continuous quality improvement with the University of Phoenix. He is a former member of the board of directors for the local Valley of the Sun ASTD chapter. He is also a former scholarship member interest group chair for the International Leadership Association (ILA). Rodger recently contributed a chapter on this topic to the book, *The Art of Followership: How Great Followers Create Great Leaders and Organizations.* He presented at ILA and the VOS chapter's Arizona annual convention. He consults with several non-profits.

Rodger Adair
4605 E. Elwood Street
Phoenix, AZ 85040
(602) 557.7035
Email: rodger.adair@apollogrp.edu
ASTD Chapter: Valley of the Sun

the circle. Invite the next participant to react or otherwise add to the discussion by stepping forward into the circle.

4. Advise the participants that the sharing will continue until the time limit has been reached or no one else shows any interest in stepping into the circle—whichever comes first.

5. At the end of the sharing activity, ask the participants to return to their seats for any further action, vote, or decision-making process you've established or simply summarize what has been accomplished or discussed during the activity.

6. Post the decision or highlights of the discussion if you wish.

InSider's Tips

- Keep the conversation moving; if someone goes over the six-sentence maximum, remind the participant of the limit.

- Do not discourage participants from stepping into the circle to share more than once, but be attentive to ensure that as many participants as possible contribute to the conversation.

- This is a variation of something I saw in a small Italian village one summer evening several years ago. Everyone stood in a semicircle outside the village coffee house in the town square. Each person who wanted to add to or build on the ensuing conversation took one step forward into the circle, made a few comments, then stepped back into the circle. You can find much more on this powerful technique through a simple "sharing circle" key word search using your favorite search engine.

Paul Signorelli is a writer, trainer, and consultant who has served as president-elect and president for the ASTD Mt. Diablo chapter and joined ASTD's National Advisors for Chapters for a three-year term effective January 2011. He explores uses, writes about, and helps others become familiar with new technology to creatively facilitate positive change within organizations. He also develops and manages workplace learning and performance programs; helps clients improve their face-to-face and online presentation skills; writes for a variety of print and online publications; and develops and delivers innovative online learning opportunities.

Paul Signorelli
1558 16th Avenue
San Francisco, CA 94122
(415) 681.5224
Email: paul@paulsignorelli.com
Website: http://paulsignorelli.com
Blog: http://buildingcreativebridges.wordpress.com
ASTD Chapter: Mt. Diablo

Go for the Win

Submitted by Curtis D. Curry

Overview

In this lively activity, participants engage in a game of "thumb wrestling" as the facilitator leads the group toward a lesson in "win-win" solutions.

Objectives

- To energize the group
- To introduce a topic such as conflict or negotiation

Audience

Any size

Time Estimate

10 minutes

Materials and Equipment

None required

Area Setup

Any room arrangement that allows participants to work in pairs

Process

1. Ask for a volunteer to come to the front of the room to help you demonstrate the activity.
2. Tell the volunteer that the activity involves wrestling and that the first lesson is how to get in a proper wrestling stance. Demonstrate the stance as you say, "feet about two feet apart, knees slightly bent, chest aligned evenly with your knees." For fun you might say, "Did I mention that I wrestled in high school?"
3. Invite your volunteer to mirror your wrestling stance. Once both of you have moved into the wrestling stance, only then tell the volunteer that you will be thumb wrestling.

4. Ask the volunteer to extend his or her right hand. Clasp each other's fingers leaving the thumbs free on top to wrestle. Show the rest of the participants the proper thumb wrestling "stance."

5. Tell the participants that you and your volunteer will demonstrate the activity. Say, "The objective of thumb wrestling is to 'pin' your partner's thumb."

6. With your hands remaining clasped, demonstrate, beginning by counting out loud "1—2—3—go." Raise and cross your thumb with your volunteer opponent's thumb as each number is counted and when you say "go" try for a quick "pin" of your opponent's thumb. If the volunteer pins your thumb that's OK, too.

7. Thank your volunteer and ask all the participants to stand up and find partners. Your volunteer may return to the audience to find a partner or, if you have an odd number of participants, you can continue to work with the volunteer.

8. Tell the group the activity will be timed, and that the goal is to "win as much as possible." Ask them to be careful not to bend the wrists of their partners, reminding them that the goal is to win, not to harm their partners.

9. Provide a beginning count of, "1—2—3—go." to begin the activity. The energy level in the room will increase within seconds and participants will be laughing and having a good time.

10. After 20 seconds, instruct the group to stop. Ask the group who had the most "pins" during the game. Typically, the best thumb-wrestler will have scored four or five pins. Tell the participants there will be one last round and that you think they can do much better, Remind the group that the goal is to "win as much possible." Count, "1—2—3—go" to initiate the second round.

11. If you are still working with a volunteer, quietly mention that the goal is for your *team* to win as much as possible and suggest that he or she pin *you* as many times as possible in the remaining time, then ask whether you can pin him or her as many times as possible. Whether working with a volunteer or not, after about 20 seconds call time.

12. Ask how many pins were made this time. If a pair of participants has a high number of "pins" between them, have the team demonstrate their technique in front of the group (they may or may not have figured out the win-win angle). If no team has more than five pins, ask the volunteer to come up again (if you are not still working with the volunteer) so that you can demonstrate the most effective thumb-wrestling technique for winning as many times as possible. Instruct the volunteer to pin you as many times as he or she can within the time limit and then ask whether you can pin him or her as many times as you can within the time limit.

13. Tell the group that the goal of the activity was in fact to win as much as possible, not as individuals, but as a team. Explain that a win-win strategy leads to everyone being able to "win as much as possible." Ask the participant what paradigm of human interaction they initially adopted (win-lose) and ask them why.

14. Transition into your presentation of conflict or win-win negotiating.

InSider's Tips

- This activity works best if the group members have already had worked together for a time.
- This is an excellent introductory activity to numerous classes, including negotiations training to demonstrate the win-win technique or conflict management to illustrate the collaborate style.

Curtis D. Curry has more than twenty years of leadership experience working with global organizations in HPI. He is the president of Quality Learning International. He has trained over 20,000 leaders and individual contributors in North America, Europe, Latin America, and Asia. Curtis specializes in global leadership development, managing conflict across cultures, coaching leaders, and helping organizations diagnose needs and design effective leadership development programs. Curtis has held leadership positions at Miami Dade College, the World Trade Center Miami, and Entrena Honduras/Nicaragua. He has an M.A. in international studies, an MBA, and is completing his dissertation for a Ph.D. in leadership at Barry University.

Curtis D. Curry
1050 Hollow Brook Lane
Malabar, FL 32950
(321) 724.1917
Email: curtis@leadershipqli.com
Website: leadershipqli.com
ASTD Chapter: Space Coast Florida

Chapter 2

Listening: The Second Half of Communication

Good communication is a two-way street. The most effective exchange of information happens when both a good sender and a good receiver are involved. Being a good receiver (or listener) leads to deeper understanding, shows respect, and helps ensure accurate perceptions. Besides, really listening is just plain courteous. But active listening is often more difficult for someone than being the speaker.

Why is excellent listening so difficult? The first reason is our perceptions. Generally, the person speaking believes his or her messages are more helpful, urgent, and interesting than the person listening thinks they are. A second reason is simply that effective listening is hard work, even though we believe listening is as natural as walking or any other basic human activity. But unfortunately, effort is necessary.

Part of the reason that listening is so hard is linked to how quickly the human brain can absorb information. Our brains are able to absorb information at a much faster rate than anyone can speak, so our brains take detours. A listener's thoughts may wander and focus on other more urgent things or he or she goes off on a mini "mind vacation" based on something the speaker says. Jargon-laced concepts as well as distractions in the environment are all common ways the listener becomes sidetracked.

But listening has its own rewards if you are willing to put in the necessary work. In addition to hearing critical information correctly and honoring the speaker, listening might even be good for you. When we listen—really listen—our heart beat increases, our pupils dilate, and our blood pressure raises just a bit. In effect, you are burning more calories when you work at listening.

This chapter on effective listening includes practical and creative activities. In "No Advice Please," communication and presentation expert Cyndi Maxey provides an activity that allows participants to experience good listening skills. Jeannette Grace shares a well-seasoned activity that helps participants understand what works best when listening and what does not. Luciana Rodrigues asks and answers the question, "Do You Know How to Listen?" Rachel Stromberg Wical introduces an activity used in improvisational theater to teach focus.

By the way, if you are not familiar with improv theater, visit a performance; you will leave with a number of ideas you will be able to use to rev up your training. Barbara Murray closes this chapter with an activity that I cannot wait to try, "Are You Smiling?" The activity confirms that people sound friendlier when they are smiling. This 15-minute activity is a great way to close out a session on listening, customer service, sales, or telephone skills. As a trainer, you will be happy to have these listening activities in your trunk.

No Advice Please

Submitted by Cyndi Maxey

Overview

Participants in this activity take turns practicing the art of listening following the strict guideline of "no advice" or feedback of any kind.

Objectives

- To listen actively without adding advice or "value"
- To effectively practice the verbal and nonverbal behaviors of listening

Audience

A minimum of two participants, no maximum

Time Estimate

10 to 15 minutes

Materials and Equipment

- A whiteboard, blackboard, or flip-chart and easel
- Markers

Area Setup

Appropriate for any room setup or configuration

Process

1. Review and give examples of the nonverbal and verbal behaviors of an active listener using the following examples:
   - *Nonverbal Behaviors:* nod, eye contact, non-word comments (uh-huh, umm), smile, eye expression, forward lean, open, uncrossed arms and legs
   - *Verbal Behaviors:* probing questions ("How did you arrive at that?" or "Why did your boss allow this?"), brief comments that support and encourage ("Oh?" "Tell me more." "I see." "Wow, no kidding?" "That's interesting." "Indeed!")
2. Draw a large "No Advice" sign on your blackboard, whiteboard, or flip chart in the format of the universally understood red circle with a line through it like

a no smoking sign. Remember to write only the word *Advice* and then circle it and draw a line through it, like this.

3. Allow the group to select partners and determine who will be the speaker and who will be the listener.
4. Tell those in the listener's role to ask their speaker partners just one question, "What's on your mind today?" Advise the listener that his or her job is to actively listen using the simple techniques provided at the beginning of this activity. Explain that the listener may provide absolutely no advice, or stories, or feedback of his or her own. For example, saying something like, "Yeah, that happened to me, too," is not allowed.
5. Allow 3 to 5 minutes for the conversation then call time and ask the partners to switch listener and speaker roles using the same question prompt.
6. Allow 3 to 5 minutes for the second interaction before beginning a debriefing.
7. Debrief by asking the participants to describe the experience from the perspective of both the listener and the speaker. You will likely find a mix of reactions. Some participants will say they enjoyed the experience of being paid attention to and understood. For others, the roles will be uncomfortable. Stress that listening skills are learned, developed, and perfected only with time and practice. Initiate a discussion of when this type of listening may not be appropriate and ask for suggestions on appropriate times to practice listening skills again.

InSider's Tips

- This is one of the simplest activities I conduct; no materials or setup are needed.
- Since participants all have something pressing on their minds, nearly everyone can benefit from concentrated, active listening practice.
- All job types and organizational levels have a good time with this activity. I've used it with fire fighters, physicians, and customer service representatives.

Cyndi Maxey is a twenty-eight-year ASTD member and frequent presenter at ASTD's International Conference. She is co-author of *Ten Steps to Successful Time Management, Training from the Heart: Developing Your Natural Abilities to Inspire the Learner and Drive Performance on the Job* with Barry Lyerly and Kevin E. O'Connor, *Speak UP: A Woman's Guide to Presenting Like a Pro*, a sequel to *Present Like a Pro: The Field Guide to Mastering the Art of Business, Professional, and Public Speaking.* She has her master's degree from Northwestern University.

Cyndi Maxey
Maxey Creative Inc.
5407 North Lakewood Avenue
Chicago, IL 60640
(773) 551.9599
Email: cmaxey@cyndimaxey.com
Website: www.cyndimaxey.com

I See You Listening

Submitted by Jeannette Grace

Overview

Participants use both their descriptive and artistic skills in this activity to explore and practice effective listening techniques.

Objective

- To practice listening skills for following directions
- To experience both the sender and receiver roles in a difficult communication series
- To demonstrate what happens when people are not fully engaged in the communication process

Audience

Ten to twenty participants

Time Estimate

30 minutes

Materials and Equipment

- One clipboard per participant
- Ten different clip art images, each on a separate piece of paper
- One blank sheet of paper for each participant
- One pencil/pen for each participant

Area Setup

Enough room for pairs of participants to sit back-to-back in chairs spaced comfortably around the room

Preparation

Before facilitating this activity, take time to select ten different clip art pictures from a copyright-free source of your choice (for example, the Microsoft Office website). Simple line drawings work best. Print each one full size on a sheet of paper.

Process

1. Ask participants to choose partners and select a set of the back-to-back chairs you have set up beforehand. Give participants each a clipboard and pen or pencil.
2. Assign activity roles. Explain that one person in each of the pairs is the art instructor charged with providing instructions. The other person is the artist who will draw what the instructor describes. Say that the roles in this activity will be determined alphabetically: "The initial letter of the participant's first name and its position in the alphabet will determine the role of the instructor." Give an example if necessary, for example, if the participants are named Allen and John, Allen would be the instructor.
3. Tell the pairs that the artist cannot ask questions, and neither the art instructor nor the artist may look at each other or see each other's papers during the activity.
4. Give each instructor a different image and tell the art instructors they have 5 minutes to describe what their artist partners must draw based solely on their powers of description.
5. Allow 5 minutes, then stop the activity and ask the instructors to look at what the artists drew, based on their instructions.
6. Ask the pairs to switch roles so that the instructor is the artist and the artist the instructor.
7. Next, collect the clip art images from all the participants and shuffle them. Redistribute the images ensuring each pair is working with a different image.
8. Begin the activity again with the new instructors giving directions to the new artists.
9. Allow another 5 minutes, then stop the activity. Ask the new instructors to look at what the new artists drew based on their instructions.
10. Allow a few minutes for the pairs to examine the results. Debrief the activity using questions such as these:
    - What happened? Why?
    - What does this tell us about communication?
    - What worked well?
    - What prevented you from communicating better?
    - What could you have done differently?
    - When does this happen back at our workplace?
    - What will you do differently as a result of this activity?

- Summarize by adding:
  - When the people involved in the communication are not fully engaged, a breakdown in communication is likely.
  - If you communicate by phone or email, this breakdown in communication is even more likely because the element of seeing what the other person is talking about is missing.
  - State that good communication requires work on both sides.

InSider's Tips

- Draw or select images from copyright-free clip art.
- This activity stresses the importance of tolerance when working with others as well as the importance of open and honest communication and clear channels of communication.
- Walking around the room during the activity will allow you to remind participants of their roles. They often forget they aren't supposed to be having a dialogue.
- When you hand out the blank paper and drawing diagrams, try to hand out one in the landscape direction and the other one in the portrait direction. Participants often miss the step of making sure they are both starting on the "same page"—that is, with both the diagram and the blank pages in the same direction.
- Frustrations and difficulties (pitfalls) occur for both the art instructor giving instructions and the artist receiving communication. Common complaints and comments include:
  - Not being able to ask questions, give feedback, or see what the art instructor was describing
  - The noise level makes it difficult to hear
  - Inability to explain the drawing
  - Difficulty understanding the explanation
- This is a variation of a classic activity that trainers have used for thirty years. I participated in a version of this activity more than fifteen years ago. I have modified and expanded it for my own purposes.

Jeannette Grace has always had a passion for helping others on their journey toward personal growth and helping other increase their confidence, celebrate who they are, and learn new skills. She is currently a consultant and partner at Integrated HR Solutions and co-founder of ShiFT the World, a happiness movement. She is living two of her greatest passions: helping companies and individuals capitalize on their talents and helping individuals become happier by working from the outside in. She has a BA from Metropolitan State University in professional communications and an MA from Bethel University in communication.

Jeannette Grace
4344 Madison Street NE
Columbia Heights, MN 55421
(763) 670.7465
Email: Jnntt_grace@yahoo.com
Website: www.integratedhrsolutions.com
ASTD Chapter: Twin Cities

Do You Know How to Listen?

Luciana Rodriques

Overview
Participants form pairs in this activity to explore the negative impact of poor listening skills. One of the two is asked to model inappropriate listening behavior as the other participant attempts to relate a story based on something he or she has read, heard, or experienced.

Objectives
- To raise awareness of and improve listening skills
- To provide an opportunity to practice communication skills

Audience
Appropriate for any number of participants

Time Estimate
30 minutes

Materials and Equipment
- Listening Cards with a poor listening behavior identified, one for each pair of participants (half the number of participants in the group)
- Do's and Don'ts of Active Listening for each participant

Area Setup
Arrange room so that participants can spread out and work together as pairs.

Preparation
Before the session create Listening Cards. Write each of the suggested poor listening behaviors below on an index card. Feel free to add poor listening behavior suggestions of your own.
- Don't look at your partner; let your eyes wander around the room.
- Interrupt constantly and ask for more details.
- Don't say a word and don't use any facial expressions. Just stare at your partner.

- Interrupt constantly.
- Criticize the way your partner is telling the story; say that he or she is not clear and you don't understand.
- Laugh ironically and make it clear you don't believe his or her story.
- Tell your partner, as he or she speaks, that the story is silly and boring, and that you are not really interested.
- Interrupt constantly to relate a similar story that happened to you or that you have heard. Don't let your partner tell the whole story.
- Pretend you are not completely paying attention and every 15 seconds or so ask your partner to repeat what he or she has just said.
- Interrupt and urge your partner to skip the details in order to jump to the conclusion.
- Use nonverbal cues that demonstrate you are not listening.

Process

1. Ask participants how many of them think they are excellent listeners. Acknowledge the few participants who raise their hands. Ask all participants to find partners and form a pair for the activity.
2. If the number of participants is odd, assign the extra person to be the observer.
3. Once everyone is settled, explain that one person in each pair must choose either number 1 or number 2 as an identifier. Ask the pairs to determine who will be identified as number 1 or number 2.
4. Find an area in the room large enough to gather all those participants identified as number 1 and ask this group to gather in the space you've selected. Make sure that the number 2 participants cannot hear the instructions you will give to the number 1 participants.
5. Once the number 1 participants have gathered, explain that their job during the activity is to tell their number 2 partners stories about something they have read, heard, or experienced. Emphasize that their storytelling must sound very confident and convincing, even though they will have no more than a couple of minutes to think of their stories while you are giving the activity instructions to their number 2 counterparts. *Note:* If you have an observer, that person observes while you give instructions to both groups.
6. Dismiss the number 1 participants to think of stories to tell and gather all the number 2 participants together in a place where the number 1 participants cannot hear you giving instructions.

7. Explain to the number 2's that the number 1's will tell them stories as part of the activity. Tell the number 2's that their job is to model a behavior that demonstrates poor listening skills. Give each number 2 participant a Listening Card that lists one of the poor listening behaviors from your list. Explain that their role during the activity is to model the behaviors written on their cards while their partners tell them stories.

8. Dismiss the number 2 participants and direct the two groups to find their partners to begin the activity. Once the pairs have reconnected, tell the participants they have 10 minutes to complete the activity following the instructions they were given. Start the activity.

9. While the participants tell stories, walk around the room. Observe their reactions and reinforce instructions individually if needed.

10. After 10 minutes, tell the participants to go back to their original seats for a large group discussion. Debrief the activity, noting what you observed while the participants worked. Use questions such as the following to review the learning:

    • Number 1's: What was your experience telling the story and how did you feel?

    • Number 2's: What role did you play, and how did you feel during the activity? How would you describe your partner's response to your behavior?

    • How many of you have been in a situation in which you wanted to communicate and you knew the other person was not listening to you? Explain how that felt.

    • How many of you have been accused of not listening before coming to this session? Who would be willing share an example?

    • How can you relate these simulations to real-life situations inside or outside your workplace?

    • How will you use this information in the future?

11. Close the activity by talking about the importance of active listening, using the Do's and Don'ts handout as a basis for discussion.

InSider's Tips

• Contracting with the participants is essential to obtain the expected outcomes, so make sure they are willing to participate and that it is clear what they are supposed to do.

- Debriefing is very important for the activity to be meaningful and provide a solid learning experience, so make sure you ask questions that help participants associate the activity to real-life work situations.
- To make the activity even more meaningful, you can explore specific interesting behaviors that you observed, commenting and asking those involved to explain to the group what they did and how that felt.
- Closing the activity is also critical. In the end, make sure the benefits of active listening are clear to the participants and that they understand how this contrasts with what they have just experienced.
- You may use the Dos and Don'ts of Active Listening to guide your discussion or as a handout for participants.
- I received this activity from a collection of learning activities a co-worker from Brazil sent me years ago and I have personalized it over the years. I have used it several times and I know of other HR colleagues who have successfully used this activity as well.

Luciana Rodrigues graduated from Mackenzie University in São Paulo, Brazil, with a B.S. in business administration. She has an M.S. in human resources management from the same university and is currently enrolled in the M.Ed. program in Penn State–Harrisburg. She has ten years of experience in human resources, mostly in organization development and learning. She works for Tyco Electronics as an organization development and learning manager in Harrisburg, Pennsylvania, responsible for projects such as performance management, employee engagement, leadership development, and training programs for the Americas.

Luciana Rodrigues
6633 Terrace Way, Apt. B
Harrisburg, PA 17111
(717) 805.1231
Email: lprodrigues@tycoelectronics.com
ASTD Chapter: Central Pennsylvania

Dos and Don'ts of Active Listening

Active listening shows that you are listening with both your ears and your mind. You will demonstrate that you are listening by what you say and what you do. Speakers want to be reassured that you understand their message. Practice these active listening behaviors to be a good active listener and to show you understand.

Do
- Pay attention, show interest, and display curiosity.
- Listen for tone of voice and inflection.
- Show that you are listening through your posture and by nodding your head.
- Provide supportive feedback.
- Defer judgment.
- Respond appropriately.
- Allow the speaker time to find the right words.
- Summarize to ensure the speaker that you understand.
- Ask clarifying questions to help you understand.
- Paraphrase to ensure you understand correctly.
- Concentrate and find relationships within the message.
- Connect with the speaker by making good eye contact.
- Respond verbally with positive responses such as "yes," "I see," or "I understand."
- Acknowledge the speaker's feelings.

Do Not
- Interrupt.
- Say "yes, but."
- Complete the speaker's sentences.
- Assume you know what the speaker is going to say.
- Show your impatience.
- Be judgmental.
- Be critical of the delivery.
- Provide evaluative feedback.

Which of these is easiest for you to do?

Which are most difficult?

For additional information go to http://www.mindtools.com/CommSkll/ActiveListening.htm.

Ball

ed by Rachel Stromberg Wical

Overview

This theater-based activity requires participants to form a circle and toss imaginary "balls" and other items to each other in order to practice focus and listening in a confusing and multiple-message environment.

Objectives

- To improve communication skills by practicing active listening, focus, being present, concentration, and giving feedback
- To bring awareness of the larger picture instead of just a few of the details

Audience

Six to twenty participants

Time Estimate

20 to 35 minutes

Materials and Equipment

None

Area Setup

A room with a medium to large open area is needed. Participants need enough room to stand in a circle about an arm's width apart so that they are able to move freely. In some situations, participants may need to help you move tables and chairs to accommodate the setup.

Process

1. Invite the participants to form a circle. You are a part of the circle and will lead the activity from that position.
2. Hold up an imaginary ball and mimic its size (about the size of a tennis ball) using your thumb and index finger. Introduce the imaginary ball to the group as the "Yellow Ball."

3. Explain that as part of the activity you will toss the "Yellow Ball" to someone else in the circle and that the person you select to catch the "Yellow Ball" must say "Yellow Ball. Thank you." Further explain that the person who receives the "Yellow Ball" must then throw the ball to someone else in the circle and call out "Yellow Ball" when he or she tosses it to the next person.

4. Demonstrate throwing the "Yellow Ball" to someone in the circle. Call out "Yellow Ball" as you mimic tossing it.

5. Tell the participants that there is no pattern to the tossing of the ball and give the group a couple of minutes to practice tossing the ball around the circle.

6. After the imaginary "Yellow Ball" has been tossed for a while, shout, "Freeze." Ask the person who has the "Yellow Ball" to hold onto it.

7. Introduce another imaginary "Red Ball" and explain that it is a little bit bigger in size. Toss the "Red Ball" to someone in the circle and call out, "Red Ball." The person catching the "Red Ball" should respond "Red Ball. Thank you." before throwing it to someone else in the circle who follows the tossing pattern established for the "Yellow Ball."

8. Signal to the person who was last holding the yellow ball to toss it to another person in the circle. Now there are two balls in motion, both being identified as they are tossed to participants in the large circle.

9. After 2 minutes of activity shout, "Freeze." Ask the people who currently have the "Yellow Ball" and "Red Ball" to hold them up.

10. Introduce another imaginary object that will be tossed around in the same manner. Chose something of a different size, shape, and weight. The object may be anything—typewriter, glass of water, Samurai sword, baby, greased pig, anvil, or even an octopus. The point is to make it fun and to give the participants a visual cue to focus on. *Note:* Make sure whatever items you choose are big enough to be "seen" (visualized) by the group.

11. Pause and introduce new items to the game periodically. Depending on the size of the group, a total of five to seven imaginary items might be flying through the air during the activity.

12. If the group is having difficulty keeping track of who is supposed to be catching or tossing the imaginary items, pause and ask, "What would make this activity easier?" Possible answers might include:

   • Eye contact (important for active listening)
   • Saying the person's name before throwing (Is your audience ready for your message?)
   • Looking for someone who was open (Is this a good time to deliver your message?)

Listening: The Second Half of Communication   **39**

- Acknowledgement/feedback of the message by saying what item you received and "thank you" (Repeating or paraphrasing the message; checking for understanding)

13. Restart the activity once you have addressed the group's concerns and allow the activity to continue before calling out "freeze" again.

14. Debrief the activity using questions such as these:
    - What made the activity easier for you?
    - How were you able to accomplish the task?
    - What made the activity challenging?
    - How was catching or holding more than one item at a time like communicating (multi-tasking prevents active listening)?
    - How was finding someone open like communicating (getting your message heard and timing your message)?
    - How can confusion affect communication (not focused on the big picture)?
    - How was the introduction of more items like communication in the workplace (difficult to be an active listener with a lot of distractions)?

15. Summarize by asking: Do you feel like this activity mirrors your job (or life), having to juggle so many messages and activities? How do you deal with this in your workday so you can remain effective? Possible responses include:
    - Make sure the timing is right when delivering important information.
    - Maintain eye contact.
    - Focus on the message.
    - Give feedback to show I am listening.
    - Handle one thing at a time.
    - Prioritize.

InSider's Tips

- Participants usually discover the association of the items being tossed with a "message" and how easy it is to drop something important in their busy day of "juggling" messages and activities.
- Learners become very creative with the ideas during the debriefing section and the learning that occurs from the activity.

- Typically, the concepts below are identified by the participants during the debriefing. If not, you may pose additional questions such as the ones below to help participants discover the key points on their own:
    - What did you have to do to make sure you could focus on all the activity happening at once? (Leads to discussion on concentration, being present, actively listening, being aware of the larger picture instead of just a few of the details.)
    - What steps did you take to make sure you were actively listening to the others in the group? (Leads to discussion on being present, giving feedback to identify that you understood the message.)
    - What worked better for you: focusing on everything that was happening at once, or on only a few things? (Leads to discussion on the limitations of just focusing on the details instead of the big picture.)
  - This can be a team-building activity as well, as participants work together to keep the items in the air.
  - This activity is typically used in improvisational theater to teach performers to focus on listening to their scene partners and not on what is happening in the scene around them. Like many theater-based activities, this one has been used for years, and I'm not sure about its widespread use in a corporate environment.

Rachel Stromberg Wical is the vice president of training and development for Mad Cowford Improv, an organization that specializes in entertainment and corporate training. During her career Rachel has launched a corporate university for front-line managers, directors, and vice-presidents and has managed and developed workplace learning professionals, employees, and volunteers in non-profit and commercial business. Rachel has served on the board of directors for the Northeast Florida chapter of ASTD since 2002, including as chapter president.

Rachel Stromberg Wical
2421 Provost Road E
Jacksonville, FL 32216
(904) 608.1148
Email: Rachel@madcowford.com
Website: www.madcowford.com
ASTD Chapter: Northeast Florida

Are You Smiling?

Submitted by Barbara Murray

Overview
Participants learn that it is nearly impossible to hide your mood or attitude, even without obvious visual cues as a guide.

Objectives
- To improve listening skills
- To confirm that people *sound* friendlier with smiles on their faces
- To prove that people do not *sound* as happy with frowns on their faces

Audience
Two or more participants

Time Estimate
10 to 15 minutes

Materials and Equipment
- One sheet of paper for each participant with the phrase "If you are happy and you know it, your voice will surely show it" printed on it

Area Setup
Any arrangement will work. It will be less noisy and the other participants will be able to hear better if the partners formed for this activity have some space between them.

Process
1. Ask participants how many can tell what mood someone is in just by talking to him or her on the phone? Ask how soon they can make this determination? After a few responses, state that this activity will allow them to conduct their own smile experiment. Ask them to stand up and find partners for the activity.
2. Explain that one person in each pair will be Participant A and the other Participant B. Say that Participant A is the person with the first letter of his or her first name closest to the letter Z. The other person is Participant B.

3. Hand out the sheets of paper you have prepared to every participant.
4. Tell the pairs to stand back-to-back.
5. Tell all the A participants that they will have three opportunities to read the sentence you passed out with either a smile or a frown on their faces. Tell the A participants that their job is to trick the B participants into guessing incorrectly as to which expression they wore while reading the printed sentence. Remind the B participants to listen carefully and to track the number of correct guesses.
6. Once the participants are properly spaced in back-to-back position, begin the experiment.
7. After a few minutes, stop the action and ask A and B partners to switch roles. Start the experiment again. Remind the A participants to listen carefully and to track the number of correct guesses.
8. When everyone has completed the activity, summarize with a couple of questions such as the ones below:
   - How many times were you correct? Why were you able to guess correctly?
   - What does this tell us about communication?
   - What role did listening play in your ability to determine whether your partner was smiling or frowning?
   - Why is this important to you in the workplace?

InSider's Tips

- The participants will likely find that it is extremely difficult to sound happy with a frown on their faces.
- It is amazing how clearly you can "hear" whether others are smiling without any facial visual cues.
- Most participants "get it" when they realize how difficult it is to coordinate opposite emotions and why tricking the listener is not easy.

Barbara Murray is currently president of the ASTD Great Plains chapter. She has been a dual member of ASTD for nine years, actively serving on the Great Plains ASTD board for six years. Barbara has worked in training and development for more than eleven years. She is responsible for PREMIER Bankcard Management Development, serving over three hundred managers and key personnel. Barbara prides herself in being a servant leader. She has developed and delivered numerous management development courses to serve the needs of the PREMIER team. She provides the tools and training necessary to assist the managers in becoming great PREMIER leaders.

Barbara Murray
4902 South Oxbow Avenue
Sioux Falls, SD 57106
(605) 357.3401
Email: bmurray@premierbankcard.com
ASTD Chapter: Great Plains

Chapter 3

Customer Service and Sales: Imperative for Organizations

A 2010 IBM report based on insights from IBM's Global Chief Executive Officer Study entitled *Capitalizing on Complexity* offered organizations a clear wakeup call concerning the importance of customer loyalty and offering great customer service.

The report reaffirms what *every* trainer (and *every* savvy CEO) already knows about the importance of customer service, but it takes the need for customer information to new levels of detail. The IBM report emphasizes this by using the word "intimacy" when describing the critical need to get close to customers. Moreover, the report states that 88 percent of all CEOs in the study selected "getting closer to the customer" as the most important dimension of their organizational strategy in the next five years.

Why this strong emphasis? The key motivation is that customer loyalty is more unpredictable than *ever*. Well-informed and smart customers have a never-ending variety of product and service choices, so their loyalty must be earned over and over again or you risk losing even the most loyal customers to your competitors. This fact of life requires that all organizations understand and even predict what their customers want by using *every* tool available, including social networking platforms. When the very lifeblood of your business is dependent on what your loyal customers decide to text, tweet, blog, or post on Facebook, everything that your business does matters. In the modern world, your customers' satisfaction, approval, contentment, and allegiance to your organization and the products it offers can rise and fall in a digital minute.

With that reality as a backdrop, a chapter on customer service and sales is highly appropriate for this book.

Andrew Cook starts the chapter with an experiential activity that encourages participants to create their own definitions of great customer service. Participants in this activity learn that they have 100 percent control over most of the factors that define customer service.

Steffi Paskow uses newspapers, journal articles, and other pertinent newsworthy resources to help participants in sales acknowledge the relevance and impact current events have on their success. One of the greatest roadblocks in sales is to overcome objections. Lori Spangler provides an easy-to-implement activity that will help your salespeople deal with resistance.

Select one of these activities to help ensure excellent customer service and sales success in your organization.

Defining a Great Customer Experience

Submitted by Andrew S. Cook

Overview
Participants learn they have more control over creating positive customer interactions than they imagined through the creative use of lists and lively discussion.

Objectives
- To create a list of tangible, observable components of a great customer service experience
- To link the definition of great customer service to the real world

Audience
Groups of five to one hundred people

Time Estimate
15 to 30 minutes

Materials and Equipment
- Three flip-chart pages prepared before the activity with three different headers written at the top: LOOK, FEEL, SOUND
- Markers
- Paper and pens for each participant

Area Setup
Tables with space for writing

Process
1. Tell the group that they will be creating a definition of "great customer service" and note that no prerequisites or expertise is required, as everyone has had both positive and negative customer service experiences. State that, to make it easier, you've broken the concept into three categories:
   - What does great customer service LOOK like?

- What does great customer service FEEL like?
- What does great customer service SOUND like?

2. Provide additional definitions for the three categories. You might differentiate them like this:
   - *Look* requires observable factors such as the nonverbal actions a customer service person might do.
   - *Feel* refers to what emotions are evoked by a service person's behavior.
   - *Sound* is what you hear a service person say that might define great service.
3. Ask participants to think about a recent service experience and decide whether it was a good experience or a negative experience.
4. Ask everyone to stand. Tell all the participants who thought about a positive experience to move to one side of the room and the participants who recalled a negative customer service experience to move to the other side of the room.
5. Once the participants are in place, give them take 3 minutes to discuss among themselves what made the experience either positive or negative. *Note:* If the group is very large, tell them to work in small groups of three to four participants.
6. After 3 minutes, ask all the participants to shout out quick statements that describe what they "saw" during their experience (the LOOK of great customer service). Next, ask the participants to shout out what they "felt" during their experience (the FEEL of great customer service). Finally, ask the participants to shout out what they heard during their experience (the SOUND of great customer service).
7. Ask the participants to return to their tables and assign each table a category of LOOK, FEEL, or SOUND.
8. Tell the participants they have 2 minutes to create a list of descriptors and characteristics that define their assigned aspect of excellent customer service.
9. Look at your watch, and say, "Time starts now!"
10. After 1 minute, tell the group, "1 minute left!"
11. Announce when the time is up after the final minute has elapsed.
12. Move to a position in front of the flip charts and announce that you (or a designated recorder) will document their answers under the correct category on the flip charts. *Note:* You can also offer to create an aggregate definition based on the discussion if you wish.
13. Go through each category (LOOK, FEEL, and SOUND) one at a time. Ask each group of participants for one answer per category as you go around the room. After each table group has provided its feedback, open the discussion

for other ideas from the entire group. Ask whether anything is missing from the lists on the flip chart.

14. Summarize by asking these questions:
    - Is there anything on the list that is not necessary? Why?
    - What percentage of these items do you agree with? Ask for a show of hands as you say: 50 percent, 60 percent, 75 percent, 90 percent, 100 percent.
    - What percentage of control does each of us have over what's on this list? Ask for show of hands as you say, 50 percent, 60 percent, 75 percent, 90 percent, 100 percent. (*Note:* The correct answer is actually 100 percent; we have control over everything on the lists.)
    - What will you do differently as a result of what we have listed?

15. Ask each person to write down one thing he or she will do differently or improve back in the workplace as a result of this activity.

InSider's Tips

- People usually come up with responses to the categories such as the following:
    1. LOOK: smile, eye contact, body language, professional, grooming
    2. FEEL: valued, important, comfortable, respected
    3. SOUND: friendly, polite, engaged, focused, attentive
- It's interesting that not everyone immediately recognizes that he or she has 100 percent control over all these factors.
- Since the group creates the definition, there's no push-back later.
- I keep the definition (flip charts) up for the remainder of the workshop and mention that, when all these factors exist, you're doing well; the absence of some or any of the factors indicates there's some work to do.
- For a very large group, use three flip-chart stands and three recorders to keep things moving quickly.
- I'm sure the generic idea of creating a definition has been used before. This activity is one I created specifically for a workshop I do with my medical practice clients that focuses on enhancing the patients' experience. You can easily broaden the activity to fit any customer service arena.

Andrew S. Cook works for Lehigh Valley Health Network in Allentown, Pennsylvania. He is the manager of operations support for the Lehigh Valley Physician Group. In that role, he supports and delivers organization development and service culture initiatives for more than ninety medical practices throughout the network. He also leads a team of service culture ambassadors who assist with implementation efforts. Andrew holds two bachelor's degrees from Penn State University and a master's degree in organization development and leadership from Saint Joseph's University. He is also the vice president of communications for the ASTD Eastern Pennsylvania chapter and has been on the board since 2005.

Andrew S. Cook
1793 Center Street
Bethlehem, PA 18017
(484) 221.6042
Email: asc63@yahoo.com
Website: easternpa.astd.org
ASTD Chapter: Eastern Pennsylvania

What's in the News?

Submitted by Steffi Paskow

Overview

Participants read and discuss recent business, market or economic news, and trends based on facilitator-provided materials and discover the importance of keeping abreast of developments that impact their particular industry as well as any important news in the world at large.

Objectives

- To discuss the relevance of current news and how it impacts a business, its customers, and its sales
- To identify ways to stay on top of current events that may impact a salesperson's success

Audience

Up to thirty participants from the sales professions

Time Estimate

About 45 minutes

Materials and Equipment

- Newspapers, magazine articles, newsletters, and other pertinent newsworthy information, including domestic and international news, news about the industry of your audience, current news about the stock market, local business newspaper, recent news about your audience's competition, or any news relative to your audience's business
- Paper and pencils for each group
- Flip chart
- Markers

Area Setup

Tables set up for groups of three participants

Process

1. Introduce the activity by stating that the best salesperson is well informed. State that this activity will provide your participants with the opportunity to work with recent information and events that may impact their industry, company, and their ability to sell. Ask participants to divide into groups of three and choose group leaders who will speak for their groups.

2. Hand out the newspapers, recent journals, or other news materials you gathered prior to the activity.

3. Assign the groups of three the task of reading the news and then identifying how what they learn might impact their company and/or any of their customers or prospects. Allow about 15 minutes for the groups to complete their reading and analysis.

4. During the activity, observe each group and assist them as needed.

5. At the end of the designated time, ask each group to share the information, event, or intelligence they gathered during the activity and to explain how they think what they learned might impact their company, customers, and/or their ability to sell.

6. After each group has reported out, spend a few minutes discussing all of the information with the entire group. Debrief the activity using questions such as the following:
   - Who stays current by reading the news daily? What do you read?
   - What is the relevance of reading the news?
   - How could keeping up with the latest news affect your sales?
   - What ideas do you have for keeping the entire group abreast of what is happening in the world that could impact your company, customers, and your ability to sell?
   - What will you do differently as a result of this discussion?

InSider's Tips

- During the discussion make a list of the resources the group shared and solicit additional ideas for other resources the group should be reading in order to stay current.
- Make it easy for participants to subscribe to the resources you have used in the session. For example, have subscription postcards or website addresses available for them to take when they leave.

- Ask the group how they could share strategic or market information with their entire sales group. Suggest an internal blog and/or intranet "news file folder."

Steffi Paskow is a sales performance consultant with over twelve years coaching and training sales people of all skill levels. She has worked for Fortune 500 companies, including Xerox and ADP, in the capacity of sales and management and earning number one recognition in each position. Steffi is able to transfer cutting-edge sales strategies, obtaining quick results.

Steffi Paskow
P.O. Box 8103
Gaithersburg, MD 20898
(240) 329.4446
Email: spaskow@smartperformance.biz
Website: www.smartperformance.biz
ASTD Chapter: Maryland

Objection Resolution

Submitted by Lori Spangler

Overview

Confronting sales objections and how to overcome them are discussed in this simple but highly effective activity.

Objectives

- To explore the sales objections that sales professionals experience
- To prepare the learner to overcome objections

Audience

Four or more participants

Time Estimate

15 to 30 minutes

Materials and Equipment

- Index cards
- Pens or pencils

Area Setup

Writing surfaces for learners

Process

1. Ask how many participants have ever received an objection on a sales call. Acknowledge that everyone receives objections and that this activity will help them to identify effective responses to objections.
2. Give each participant an index card and a pen or pencil and ask them to write one objection they commonly encounter when selling a specific product. The objection might be that the "price is too high," for example.
3. Give the participants a minute or so to write down an objection and then collect the index cards.
4. Shuffle the stack of index cards and hand one of the cards to each participant.
5. Ask participants to read the objections on the cards they received and to write a solution or way to overcome the objection on the flip side of the index card.

6. After the participants have recorded their solutions (give the group a few minutes to do this), ask participants to share the sales objections they received and the responses they wrote to overcome the objections.
7. Lead a discussion about other possible ways to overcome the objections noted on the index cards.
8. Once the objections have been discussed by the group, end the activity. If you wish, offer to return the index cards to the original authors.

 InSider's Tips

- This activity is simple to explain and implement. Participants like to learn from others.
- Learners like real-life objections and real-life solutions.
- You can use this process during supervisory skills training, communication training, or other types of training. During a supervisory session, for example, you might ask participants to identify one dilemma or situation faced by supervisors.
- *Option:* For larger groups arranged in a U-shape or circle seating, try asking the participants to pass their index cards six people to the right, then two people to the left, then four to the right (or any other shuffling method based on passing cards) instead of collecting the cards. This adds movement and interactivity to the activity.

Lori Spangler is a lead performance consultant at Deluxe Corporation, where she works with a remote sales force, consulting, assessing, and implementing sales training strategies. Lori loves to facilitate training when she can adjust "on the fly" to meet the needs of her learners, either in person or online. In addition to being certified in SPIN Selling, Strategic Selling, and IMPAX Strategic Account Sales, she holds master's degrees in adult education and communication.

Lori Spangler
205 Primrose Court
Vadnais Heights, MN 55127
(651) 483.1172
Email: Lori.Spangler@Deluxe.com
ASTD Chapter: Twin Cities

Chapter 4

Creativity and Innovation: Most Important in a Complex World

If you asked most people for a general definition of creativity, they would likely say that it is the ability to create something new or view something differently. If you followed up with a question on the importance of creativity in business, you would no doubt be told that creativity was extremely important, if not vital, to an organization's long-term success and competitiveness.

Interestingly, the fifteen hundred CEOs interviewed for IBM's 2010 Global Chief Executive Officer Study (mentioned in the introduction to Chapter 3 of this book) also identified creativity as the most important leadership quality and predictor of success in the marketplace. The CEOs in the study noted that creativity is the basis for what they called the "disruptive innovation and continuous re-invention" required of every organization. Moreover, the CEOs said that this breakthrough thinking is required not only at the top, but must be present throughout an organization.

In short, this study supports the idea that creative leaders need creative employees in their organizations to help fuel needed changes and solve problems as organizations reinvent and redefine themselves.

Unfortunately, most people do not believe they are (or can be) creative. Your job as a trainer is to help change this belief. As Henry Ford once said, "If you think you can do a thing or think you can't do a thing, you're right." As a trainer your role is to influence attitudes so that learners can be "right" about being creative so that their organizations (or yours) can move beyond the status quo.

The activities in this chapter are designed to start your participants' creative juices flowing and to engage their right brains to think of innovative ideas they never thought possible. All learners have the capacity to be more creative; they need to first believe that they can be that way. The four activities in this chapter will help learners believe in their own creativity and acquire the skills to put this knowledge to work.

The first activity, contributed by Rodger Adair, helps build that needed confidence in participants and broadens their understanding of the topic.

Karen Sieczka's activity was inspired by the book *Outliers* by Malcolm Gladwell. Her activity encourages participants to think up new uses for common items. I will just say that the participants will never look at a brick in the same way again!

Sandi Ruther combines a number of techniques, including brainstorming, mind mapping, and teamwork, to enable participants to learn a technique that encourages interaction and creativity. I guarantee you will love this activity and that you will find many other instances to use it as a training tool.

Paul Signorelli rounds out this chapter with a technique he learned from a writing instructor that will help your participants create short, pithy statements for almost any use.

Each of the four activities in this chapter will enhance creative approaches in organizations and support new, innovative approaches and strategies.

The Penny Story

Submitted by Rodger Adair

Overview

Participants in this activity imagine the life story of a penny and use the stories they are asked to write as an endorsement of the creative potential in everyone.

Objective

- To stimulate creativity in the workplace and to move beyond what we see to what we can imagine accomplishing

Audience

Any size audience from a single participant to an audience large enough to fill an auditorium

Time Estimate

At least 30 minutes (or more if you have time)

Materials and Equipment

- A blank sheet of paper for each participant
- Pens or pencils for each participant
- One penny per participant

Area Setup

Space enough for participants to write

Process

1. Introduce the activity by telling the participants the following: "For this activity, each of you will receive a penny. Look at this penny carefully; turn it over in your palm and notice the penny's age, how worn or new it is, or perhaps where it was minted. Using this information, I'd like you to write a story about your penny. Be as creative as you can. I'll give you 5 minutes before we move forward."
2. Pass out pennies, paper, and pens or pencils to all participants.
3. Allow 5 minutes for the creative writing activity.

4. Call time after 5 minutes and ask several people to read the stories they've written.
5. Initiate a discussion about creativity. Use questions such as the following:
   - How did feel about doing the activity?
   - What made the task difficult?
   - What made the task easy?
   - How did you feel when I said that you should "be as creative as you can"?
   - How is creativity an important part of work?
   - Do you believe you are creative? Why or why not?
   - What prevents you from being more creative?
6. Summarize the discussion by saying that everyone has the capacity to be more creative. Make the point that the first step toward being more creative is a belief that creativity is within our grasp.

InSider's Tips

- After the activity, I select participants to share their stories. If you form small groups, all participants can share their stories within their groups. In larger groups, time constraints and audience attention prevent a wider sharing of the stories.
- Some participants may have a difficult time creating a story, so a few prompts may help these participants begin. I often ask, "How old were you when you found your first penny. Imagine this is it. What do you think has happened to that penny since that time?"
- This activity not only helps stimulate creativity, but also reveals a lot about the person telling the story. The penny's story is often a proxy for the storyteller's own life experiences.

For the last twenty years **Rodger Adair** has focused on organization development, industrial psychology, and corporate training, twelve of those years mainly in the Arizona market. He has a B.S. in adult/workforce education from Southern Illinois University. He has a master's of organizational management and MBA from the University of Phoenix. He is in a Ph.D. program in I/O psychology with Northcentral University. He serves as a director of continuous quality improvement with the University of Phoenix. He is a former member of the board of directors for the local Valley of the Sun ASTD chapter. He is also a former scholarship member interest group chair for the International Leadership Association (ILA). Rodger recently contributed a chapter on this topic to the book, *The Art of Followership: How Great Followers Create Great Leaders and Organizations*. He presented at ILA and the VOS chapter's ASTD Arizona annual convention. He consults with several non-profits.

Rodger Adair
4605 E. Elwood Street
Phoenix, AZ 85040
(602) 557.7035
Email: rodger.adair@apollogrp.edu
ASTD Chapter: Valley of the Sun

It's Not What You Think

Submitted by Karen S. Sieczka

Overview

An exploration of the many uses of familiar objects is the touchstone in this activity that spurs participants to think "outside the box" and explore creative approaches and solutions.

Objectives

- To seek new uses for an ordinary object
- To learn a creativity technique that sparks extraordinary associations
- To warm up for creativity, innovation, and brainstorming sessions

Audience

Groups of eight to one hundred

Time Estimate

15 to 30 minutes (depending on number of participants and the number of items used)

Materials and Equipment

- One copy of either of the It's Not What You Think handouts for each team
- Pens
- Timer
- Whiteboard or flip chart

Area Setup

Tables separated by enough space to allow participants to work in small groups

Preparation

Decide what common, everyday items you would like to use. The examples given are a brick and a pen, but you may use other ordinary items to create several rounds of the activity. For example, you might bring an empty jar, a spatula, a newspaper, a coffee mug, a stapler, a rock, a paperclip, or anything else you can think of that might be fun. If you wish, find some clip art or other illustration of your chosen item and replace the one provided in the handout to create a new handout.

Process

1. Ask the participants, "How many of you wish you were more creative?" Explain that this activity is easy and that it will help to get everyone's creative juices flowing. Give one handout to each table group.

2. Request one volunteer from each group to serve as the recorder and spokesperson.

3. Briefly explain the purpose of the handout, using the examples given. State that the goal is for each team to list as many uses for the selected item as possible in a short period of time.

4. Explain that they have 3 minutes to complete the activity. *Note:* Allow 2 to 5 minutes, but less time is preferable because it makes the session more lively and fun.

5. Start the timer.

6. At the end of 3 minutes, ask the spokesperson for each group to share some of their ideas for the alternate use of your chosen object. To ensure that everyone has a chance to share ideas, limit the number of alternate use ideas from each group in the first round. You might say, "Report on three of your ideas for the first round." If time is still available, you can ask for additional ideas at the end of the round. An alternate way to save time is to ask each team to offer its most creative, most unusual, or most practical idea in the first round.

7. You can pose the question again using more everyday items or, if appropriate, substitute current products, processes, or services that the participants' (or your) organization offers.

8. Summarize the activity by asking:
   - How did it feel to be free to think of crazy ideas?
   - Why aren't we that creative at work?
   - Are there times when it would be appropriate to be more creative at work? When would that be?
   - What might you do in the future based on what happened here today?

InSider's Tips

- Emphasize that there are no wrong answers and that no answer is too "silly." In fact, the sillier, the better.
- The discussion can be expanded to organizational products, services, processes, challenges, and opportunities.

- Encourage participants to freely associate uses by combining two common items for a new use; this really gets participants to use out-of-the-box thinking.
- This activity was inspired by Malcolm Gladwell's book *Outliers*. He writes about divergence tests to measure creativity and asks the reader to write down as many different uses as he or she can think of for a brick and blanket.

Karen S. Sieczka is a people developer, trainer, Creativity@Work expert, author, and founder of Growing Great Ideas.com, a training resources website. She has facilitated over 250 workshops and trained over 3,000 participants in a variety of programs including creativity, technology, supervisory skills, and customized training workshops. In 2008, Karen authored the book *Growing Great Ideas: Unleashing Creativity at Work (1)*, a guide to the creative process in the workplace. She also has a Creativity@Work training program available to help participants understand the creative process. Karen is an active member of the ASTD Greater Atlanta chapter and serves as the communications manager for the chapter's Community Involvement Group. The activity will be included in the second edition of my own training book *Growing Great Ideas: Unleashing More Creativity at Work.*

Karen S. Sieczka
4020 Ridgeland Drive
Douglasville, GA 30135
(404) 219.8246
Email: growinggr8ideas@gmail.com
Website: www.growinggreatideas.com
ASTD Chapter: Greater Atlanta

References
Gladwell, M. (2008). *Outlier: The story of success*. New York. Little, Brown.
Sieczka, K. (2008). *Growing great ideas: Unleashing creativity at work*. Raleigh, NC: Lulu.

It's Not What You Think: When Is a Brick Not a Brick?

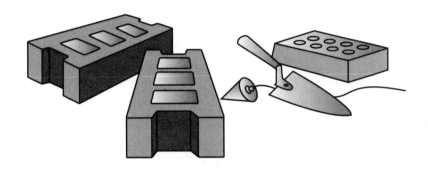

We all know you can build things with bricks, but what else can you do with a brick? You would be surprised at the many uses for this simple and versatile construction item! The point is to move from ordinary thinking to extraordinary thinking.

How many unusual uses can you think of for a brick? List them below after the sample.

1. Doorstop

2. _____

3. _____

4. _____

5. _____

6. _____

7. _____

8. _____

9. _____

10. _____

11. _____

12. _____

13. _____

14. _____

15. _____

It's Not What You Think: When Is a Pen Not a Pen?

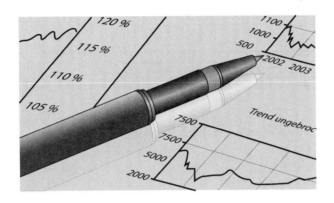

We all know you can write with a pen but what else can you do with it? You would be surprised at the ways this simple item can be used! The point is to move from ordinary thinking to extraordinary thinking.

How many unusual uses can you think of for a pen? List them below.

1. Hole punch

2. _____

3. _____

4. _____

5. _____

6. _____

7. _____

8. _____

9. _____

10. _____

11. _____

12. _____

13. _____

14. _____

15. _____

Creative Storming

Submitted by Sandi Ruther

Overview
Combining the concepts of brainstorming and mind-map techniques is the twist that makes this creativity-boosting exercise unique.

Objectives
- To introduce a technique for encouraging interaction and creativity
- To give everyone a voice when generating ideas

Audience
Twenty to forty participants, in groups of three to five

Time Estimate
15 to 30 minutes (depending on the topic being "creative-stormed")

Materials and Equipment
- Flip charts (each group needs one or two pages)
- One marker (various colors) for each person
- (Optional) Small prizes

Area Setup
Any type of room setup with sufficient wall space for each group to gather around posted flip-chart pages

Preparation
Depending on the number of participants and group sizes, post two flip-chart pages for each subgroup of three to five participants along the wall. Groups will gather in front of these posted pages to do the mind-map activity. See Sidebar 4.1 for an overview of mind-mapping techniques and/or do an Internet search for more information on mind mapping and related techniques.

Process

1. Explain and provide an example of how mind maps work. Explain that a key word or concept initiates the "creative storming" and that this word is written in the middle of the page and circled. Topics or categories related to the key word in the center are written around it, circled, and connected to the concept in the center by drawing lines. Each of the additional topics or categories associated with the central idea becomes the focal point for the creation of additional subcategories.

2. Ask the participants to divide into groups of three to five and stand at the blank flip-chart pages you have previously posted on the wall. Note that every participant should have a marker for the activity.

3. Present a problem or provide participants with a concept to place in the middle of one flip-chart page. Tell the participants to select someone from the group to write the concept in the middle of the posted flip-chart page.

4. Provide further explanation of "creative storming" if necessary, but note that this is a methodology much like brainstorming.

5. Give the participants 5 minutes to list as many words and ideas as they can that relate to the key word or concept that you provided earlier in the process. Note that the protocol for the activity allows for multiple entries on the mind map at the same time—meaning that it is OK for two or three participants to add their ideas to the mind map at the same time.

6. Start the activity and end it after 5 minutes. You may wish to give a prize to the team with the most ideas. If you tell the participants about the prize before beginning the activity, the teams will have incentive to avoid editing their ideas during the process. The key is for everyone to participate and for each group to fill the flip-chart page with connected words and ideas.

7. Next, ask participants to group their words and ideas on a second flip-chart sheet or by circling related ideas with a same color marker on the original sheet.

8. As a final step, give each group an opportunity to present three to five of their most creative ideas.

InSider's Tips

- If you are unfamiliar with mind mapping, visit an online source such as Wikipedia or use your favorite search engine to find more information or an example.

- As an alternate to markers, you can have participants record their words and ideas on Post-it Notes and stick these on the flip-chart paper.
- Encourage the participants to write as many words and ideas as possible.
- Playing upbeat classical music (100 to 120 beats per minute) during this activity helps the creative process.
- This is a variation on brainstorming activities that are pretty typical in the training world. I am not sure who originally came up with dividing into teams and placing the ideas on a flip-chart page. My twist is having a team combine creativity and a mind map captured on a team flip chart.

Sandi Ruther is the founder and principal of ProGold Consulting, LLC, a successful documentation, training, and consulting firm, whose mission is to help businesses improve employee morale, operational efficiency, and business profitability by aligning people, processes, and systems. Bringing more than eighteen years of experience in business process optimization, internal auditing, technical writing, technical and business skills training, facilitating, and consulting, ProGold Consulting, LLC, helps clients eliminate organizational roadblocks and implement cost-effective solutions. Sandi is also an expert communicator delivering dynamic and persuasive keynotes and seminars on the topic "Polished, Not Perfect! A New Definition of Success."

Sandi Ruther
P.O. Box 632156
Highlands Ranch, CO 80163–2156
(303) 593.0025
Email: sandiruther@comcast.net
Website: www.progoldconsulting.com
ASTD Chapter: Rocky Mountain

Sidebar 4.1. Mind Maps

A *mind map* is a diagram used to represent ideas, tasks, or other items linked to and arranged around a central key word. Mind maps are used to generate and order ideas. They have been successfully used to assist studying, organizing information, solving problems, or making decisions.

The elements of a mind map are arranged in sequential order, like an outline, using groupings and branches instead of Roman numerals and letters. Ideas are presented in a radial, non-linear way. According to Tony Buzan, the self-identified creator of the mind mapping process, mind maps encourage more creative thought. This process encourages users to identify and connect concepts without a pre-conceived framework. Most generally agree that there is no rigorous right or wrong way to create a mind map. Proponents believe that, because it is more concise than outlines or paragraphs of prose, it is easier to scan for ideas, is more memorable, and leads to more creative outcomes.

Mind maps begin with a word in the center of a page. Words, symbols, or graphics are placed around the central word to represent categories. Branches (connecting lines) are drawn from the center word to the categories; additional branches, like a tree, continue to move away from the categories to identify subcategories. For example, if we were to start with a central word "mind map," branches might reach out to category topics such as "how to develop," "uses," "advantages," "style," and others.

Creative Word Toss

Submitted by Paul Signorelli

Overview
Participants use a time-limited window to access creative ideas and concepts sometimes blocked by "self-editing" and then refine these ideas toward creating final complete statements and ideas.

Objective
- To stimulate ideas that lead to effective mission statements, elevator speeches, business marketing tag lines, or other concise, snappy phrases to catch an audience's attention

Audience
Appropriate for one-on-one coaching or training with groups gathered together with a common interest or goal in mind

Time Estimate
20 to 40 minutes (The initial exercise is completed in 2 minutes, and repeated as many times as needed. A concluding conversation refines the lines to be created.)

Materials and Equipment
- Paper and pencils/pens if working one-on-one
- Flip charts or an erasable board if working with a group
- Markers

Area Setup
If working one-on-one, the facilitator and the participant should sit across from each other; if working with groups, participants should, as much as possible, be able to see and interact with each other. The flip chart or erasable board(s) should be clearly visible to everyone.

Process
1. Begin by clearly defining the topic to be addressed and the time limit of 2 minutes. Encourage the participant(s) to avoid editing anything during

the activity. Note that the point is to identify as many words related to the topic you are addressing as possible and that thinking too much stifles the flow of words. This dynamic plays out if two ways:

- For groups, if the reason for the activity is to craft a mission statement, ask the participants to call out loud ("toss out") as many words or phrases that positively describe the organization or describe what might attract someone to the organization. You should record what the group calls out before the 2-minute time limit.
- For one-on-one situations, sit quietly for the 2 minutes while the participant addresses the topic at hand on a piece of paper.

2. When the 2-minute period ends, ask the participant(s) to attempt to string the words together into a cohesive statement. Tell participant(s) to look for the links between the words and to identify the words that speak to them the strongest. It is OK to fine-tune some of the words or concepts during this part of the activity. *Note:* If you are working with a group, this part of the activity is a collaborative process.

3. If this initial work offers further opportunities for exploration, then you may repeat the activity using these key words or phrases as the starting point for another 2-minute round. The refinement process works the same for both group and individual sessions.

4. Continue this refining process until the group (or an individual participant) has created a short, catchy phrase or statement or other statement outcome that meets the original goal and purpose.

InSider's Tips

- Do everything possible to encourage rather than discourage suggestions during the 2-minute word toss in a group situation.
- Encourage participants in group situations to build off of each other's ideas.
- Producing a successful statement in a group setting helps all participants identify what they have in common and explore ways to overcome any differences identified.
- Margo Perin, a San Francisco–based writer, writing instructor, and editor, introduced me to this technique during a writing workshop she led.

Paul Signorelli is a writer, trainer, and consultant who has served as president-elect and president for the ASTD Mt. Diablo chapter and joined ASTD's National Advisors for Chapters for a three-year term effective January 2011. He explores, uses, writes about, and helps others become familiar with new technology to creatively facilitate positive change within organizations. He also develops and manages workplace learning and performance programs; helps clients improve their face-to-face and online presentation skills; writes for a variety of print and online publications, and develops and delivers innovative online learning opportunities.

Paul Signorelli
1558 16th Avenue
San Francisco, CA 94122
(415) 681.5224
Email: paul@paulsignorelli.com
Website: http://paulsignorelli.com
http://buildingcreativebridges.wordpress.com
ASTD Chapter: Mt. Diablo

Chapter 5

Diversity and Inclusion: Valuing Differences

Trainers work with everyone in organizations; in fact, you might say trainers operate at the center of today's diverse workforce, charged with developing individuals and with shaping organizational culture.

Diversity and our approach to the topic have evolved subtly over the past twenty years toward the concept of inclusion and away from policies based on meeting legal requirements. The most successful organizations recognize and celebrate their diverse workforce and actively seek out new perspectives and unique thinking these groups offer. Yet, with this recognition comes the responsibility for organizations to make these individuals and groups of employees feel welcome and included. What is your organization doing to answer the challenge?

Organizations that are serious about this challenge need to identify the barriers to inclusion in their policies, culture, work assignments, development, or other practices and actively work to make changes that eliminate barriers and ensure equitable access and benefits to all employees.

Trainers should consider what their organization is doing, in large or small ways, to move to a culture of inclusion. The activities in this chapter will help you bring awareness about valuing differences and practicing inclusion to your entire workforce.

"We Are All Different," contributed by Kathy Shurte, is a lively activity that takes learners from an attitude of "me" to one of "we" in under 30 minutes. Be sure to customize the handout to meet your needs. Rob Denton introduces us to the "Diversity Quilt," along with some amazing and powerful discussion suggestions. Marilyn Marles uses action and movement to address difficult issues.

She provides several variations so that you can use this activity as an icebreaker or as energizers throughout the day.

"Cultural Networking" by Kenny Sturgeon and Randall LaBranche is a 30-minute, high-impact activity focused on learning outcomes. The activity itself is fun (even funny), but the true value is in the ease with which it can segue into a variety of diverse topics and the learning that occurs during the debriefing session. Finally, Jeanne Baer offers ten mini scenarios that address generational questions in the workplace.

As your organization's "hub" for developing its diverse workforce, you will welcome these tried-and-true diversity activities.

We Are All Different

Submitted by Kathy Shurte

Overview

Participants explore their differences and similarities through the words they choose to describe themselves and by doing so discover new insights and connections to others.

Objectives

- To learn what's important to the people by the words they choose to describe themselves
- To define diversity beyond culture or ethnicity

Audience

Any size group

Time Estimate

20 to 30 minutes

Materials and Equipment

- One copy of the We Are All Different handout for each participant
- One pen or pencil for each participant

Area Setup

A room large enough for the participants to move around comfortably

Process

1. Introduce the activity. State that each of us is different in hundreds of ways. Give each participant a copy of the We Are All Different handout and a pen or pencil.
2. Ask the participants to circle all the words on the sheet that they would use to describe themselves. (Emphasize that the words chosen should reflect their current state, not as they would like to be.) Tell them to take 2 or 3 minutes to complete the task.

Diversity and Inclusion: Valuing Differences

3. When the participants have finished, ask them to stand up (taking their sheets with them). Explain that their task is to find someone else in the room who circled the same words as they circled. Give the participants 4 minutes to complete this activity.

4. After 4 minutes, call time and ask, "How many of you found someone who circled the exact same words—no more or no less—as you did?" It is rare that this would occur, so don't expect any matches. Ask the group:
   • Why did this happen?
   • What does it tell us?

5. Explain that, in the next part of the activity, the participants' job is to find someone who has circled *none* of the same words. Give them 4 minutes to complete the activity.

6. After 4 minutes, call time. Ask, "How many of you found someone who circled none of the same words as you?" Ask the group:
   • Why did this happen?
   • What does it tell us?

7. Tell participants to sit down. Summarize learning from the activity with questions such as these:
   • Who circled the most words? How many?
   • Who circled the fewest words? How many?

8. Have the two people who circled the most and the least stand and ask the group to identify ways in which they are the same. Ask, "What can we surmise from this comparison?"

9. Have the two participants sit and resume with these questions:
   • What did you learn about yourself and others?
   • How do the words people chose reflect what is important to them?
   • How do you define diversity? Is it just culture and ethnicity? What else is it?
   • Why is it important to have a broad definition of diversity?
   • How can you implement something you learned today in the workplace?
   • How does what you learned carry over to your personal life?

InSider's Tips

• If you use this as an opening activity, you can ask participants to introduce themselves by reading the words they circled.

- You may use the grid in a time management session to discuss the different roles we play in life, for example, parent, choir member, student, mentor, boss, coach. Ask how they prioritize those roles. Which ones get most of the attention? Why?
- When creating the handout, make a table with five or six columns and between seven and fifteen rows. Use words that will be meaningful to the group. For example, if the lesson is on Equal Employment Opportunities issues, use words from the protected classes, such as, race, color, religion, sex, national origin, age, political affiliation, marital status, sexual orientation, and ability. You do not have to put a word in every cell, and it's OK to throw in some off-topic words just for fun, such as left-handed, blonde, vertically challenged. Sometimes I insert graphics showing diverse people such as a child, a musician, a person in ethnic dress, someone wearing eyeglasses. When I print the handout, I do not display the lines of the table.

Kathy Shurte, CPLP, plays many roles in life, including wife of Kevin; a singing cowboy and seventh grade language arts teacher; manager and internal consultant for the Florida Department of Transportation; board member for ASTD's Fort Lauderdale chapter; Elf Queen Supreme, wrapping gifts during the holidays to raise money for the Florida Breast Cancer Resource Network; avid reader and book club member; and Alpine Village Polka Queen during the Oktoberfest.

Kathy Shurte, CPLP
P.O. Box 24782
Fort Lauderdale, FL 33307
(954) 777.4414
Email: rubyslippers@atlantic.net OR kathy.shurte@dot.state.fl.us
ASTD Chapter: Fort Lauderdale

We Are All Different

Circle any words you would use to describe yourself.
Count your circles, and write the total here: _____

Pregnant	Nervous	Hairy	Ex-Military	Bald	Muscular
Fair	Divorced	Wrinkled	Generous	Helpful	Hearing Impaired
Vegetarian	Overweight	Young	Mexican	Well-Traveled	Single
Male	Swedish	Tone-Deaf	American	Jewish	Athletic
Lesbian	Intelligent	Single Parent	Good Dancer	Loud	Aggressive
Shy	Happy	Patient	Canadian	Catholic	Student
Rich	Married	Creative	European	Disabled	African-American
Parent	College Graduate	Female	Elderly	Thin	Asian
Friendly	Native American	Gay	Physically Challenged	Southerner	Hispanic
Sight-Impaired	Tall	Muslim	Republican	Cancer Survivor	Defensive
Bilingual	Intern	Colorblind	Pacifist	Democrat	Blonde
Immigrant	Independent	Respectful	Bad Driver	Honest	Vertically Challenged
Caucasian	Columbian	Spiritual	Open	Hermit	Life of the Party

Diversity Quilt

Submitted by Rob Denton

Overview
Participants produce their own multi-colored paper quilt and discover that their differences create an interesting mosaic that only makes sense when all the individual quilts are joined.

Objectives
- To explore levels of personal diversity among groups of learners
- To learn how individuals affect diversity within a group
- To experience how including or excluding individuals can affect the diversity of a group

Audience
Sixteen to thirty people from the same organization

Time Estimate
60 minutes

Materials and Equipment
- One sheet of colored paper, 8.5 × 11, for each participant
- Sheets of white paper
- Colored markers for all participants
- Masking tape
- Flip chart (optional)

Area Setup
Tables large enough for participants to use for writing and drawing

Process
1. Introduce the activity. Explain the idea that a quilt is made up of multiple squares and that sometimes the squares are similar and sometimes each square is very different. Tell the participants that they will be making their own quilt. Say that the activity they are about to do involves drawing a picture or shapes or writing words that best express who they are as people.

2. Encourage the participants to explore possibilities by asking themselves questions such as: What is important to you? What is unique about you? What is your personal brand? Lead a brief discussion about the values, beliefs, culture, heritage, and traditions of the participants. Suggest that the pictures they create might reflect certain knowledge, hobbies, or special interests. (You may wish to share your own example with the group before beginning the activity.)

3. Distribute one colored piece of paper and colored markers to each participant. Tell everyone to turn the paper in a landscape orientation before beginning work.

4. Allow 10 or 15 minutes for everyone to complete their drawings. Provide a time warning at about 4 minutes.

5. Call time and ask the participants to display their patches on the wall using the masking tape you brought. Invite them to make a pattern on the wall by placing their patches in a pattern to mimic a patchwork quilt. Give them 10 or 15 minutes for this activity.

6. Allow the participants to view and walk around the quilt. Ask them what some of the obvious similarities and differences are among the patches.

7. Ask, "What happens if we change a few of the patches? For example, what if new people join the company or someone leaves?" Illustrate your point by swapping patches with blank white sheets, illustrating the unknowns that others bring to the group. Lead the participants in a discussion around the fact that, initially, these white sheets stick out and don't conform.

8. To illustrate the impact of change, swap out more quilt pieces with sheets of white paper. Lead the discussion around how the "blanks" impact the rest of the culture. Ask what they might do to get to know others and embrace the diversity.

9. Debrief the activity by asking questions such as:
   • How is a quilt like a company?
   • What "aha" did you have during this activity?
   • What is the relationship between organizational change and diversity? How does one affect the other?
   • What will you do more of based on this activity?
   • What will you do less of based on this activity?

10. Summarize by adding some of the following observations, if not already made in the previous discussion:
    • By upholding corporate values and personally embracing integrity and respect, we make all individuals feel valued. This is fundamental to a culture that embraces diversity.

- The quilt is best when it conforms to a pattern and when all the squares are in place. (You can make a point about the importance of respecting difference, but at the same time developing a rich pattern or culture that is joined together by a common purpose.) Note that this is all a part of "life's rich pattern or tapestry."
- No two squares are alike in terms of color or content, but the sum of the parts is greater than the whole. You may think one square is not as artistic as others, but without all the squares the quilt is not complete. If we lose one square or add one square, the quilt changes.
- Some quilt squares are similar, creating bonding points; others are different, creating celebration points.
- Note that there is always room for more patches.

InSider's Tips

- If it is a nice day, this is a great outdoor activity.
- If wall space is not available, you may wish to use the floor to construct your quilt.

Rob Denton is a learning and development specialist at CenterPoint Energy. He has more than fifteen years of diverse experience in organization development and corporate training for a variety of industries. Rob holds a master's degree in adult education and training from Seattle University.

Rob Denton
CenterPoint Energy
1111 Louisiana Street
Houston, TX 77251
(832) 494.7670
Email: rob.denton@centerpointenergy.com
Website: www.centerpointenergy.com
ASTD Chapter: Houston

Are You This or That?

Submitted by Marilyn Marles

Overview

Commonalities and differences are explored in this fast-paced activity that encourages participants to vote for their likes, dislikes, agreements, and disagreements using their feet.

Objectives

- To demonstrate similarities and differences within the group
- To increase energy by getting people out of their seats to engage in quick physical movement
- To progressively increase tension between the choices to surface value, ethical, or other differences within the group as foundation for discussion

Audience

Ideal size is eight to sixteen, but works with larger groups if you have room

Time Estimate

30 to 45 minutes including debriefing; 15 minutes when used as an icebreaker or 3 to 5 minutes when spread throughout a workshop as an energizer

Materials and Equipment

- List of paired words and phrases customized for your organization or group that represent opposites or differing values, choices, experiences, labeled Option A and Option B. For example, you like chocolate or you like vanilla.
- (Optional) Large signs designating area "A" and area "B"

Area Setup

Open space that allows participants safe, easy movement between two defined areas, A and B, with a distance of 20 to 30 feet between the two areas

Process

1. Explain that you will read two options from your list of opposite phrases and words. The first phrase or word is Option A and the second word or phrase

is Option B. Tell the participants that they must select between the options to determine which is most suitable for them.

2. Ask the participants to stand.
3. Explain that when the first pair of options is read, each person should move quickly to the corresponding area (A or B) based on how closely they identify with it or believe in the option stated.
4. Read the first pair of options as examples before beginning the activity. Use these two examples:
   - "Go to A if you have traveled out of the country; go to B if you have never left the country."
   - "If you prefer chocolate, move to A; if you prefer vanilla, move to B."
5. Step up the pace of the activity by offering some innocuous examples, such as
   - "If you would rather vacation in the mountains, move to A; if you prefer the ocean, move to B."
   - "If you would rather read fiction, move to A; if you prefer nonfiction, move to B."
6. Ask the participants to notice who else is in their group and then to scan the other group and take note of those who made a different choice.
7. Increase the tension by asking questions about current events or ethics or another topic that may interest the participants. Begin to relate the choices to the reasons you are doing this activity. Have you ever had a speeding ticket or not? Are you in favor of the recent legislation that was passed or not? Do you support decision A or decision B made by our team? Remember to have participants take note of who else is in their group and to scan the other group and notice who made a different choice.
8. Encourage participants to silently note their own thoughts and feelings during the activity.
9. Continue the activity and announce the pairs as many times as you believe are required to make the point.
10. Debrief while the participants remain in the last groups they chose. Debrief around your specific goals:
    - What did you observe during this activity?
    - What did you learn about this group and its members?
    - As we increased the level of self-disclosure, how did you feel as the options became increasingly personal?
    - If anyone stood between options, allow that person to explain his or her inability to commit fully to either A or B. If some ultimately refused to select, ask why.

- We were only making a selection between two options. What caused the increased tension?
- Where do our intense feelings and opinions come from?
- What might you consider in order to understand someone else's choices?
- What does this activity say about all of us?
- What might you do differently as a result of what happened here today?

InSider's Tips

- For simple icebreakers or energizers, keep the options benign and fun, even silly: food likes and dislikes, travel or hobbies, low-risk work-related (A, less than five years of service; B, more than five).
- For use as an energizer, spread the activity out across the session, using one or two before a break or one or two if you see energy lagging.
- This is a variation of the "Four Corners" activity that delves more heavily into values and involves paper-and-pencil answers.

Marilyn Marles is founder a of the Marles Group, an organization consulting firm focused on leveraging organizational and individual strengths to improve performance and productivity. She holds a master's degree from American University/NTL and is a facilitator with strong practical and theoretical background in group dynamics, group process, organization behavior, and MBTI, as well as results-based performance measurement. Her work has extended through more than thirty states and internationally. A recent success involved team development and training in results-based measures for the entire staff of a federal agency, contributing to a 400 percent increase in department productivity.

Marilyn Marles
1935 Mill Creek Road
Macungie, PA 18062
(610) 398.0125
Email: marilyn@marlesgroup.com
Website: www.marlesgroup.com
ASTD Chapter: Eastern Pennsylvania

Cultural Networking

Submitted by Kenny Sturgeon and Randall LaBranche

Overview
In this activity, participants deal with different and sometimes annoying cultural norms and use the experience to take away new insights about acceptance of cultural differences.

Objectives
- To experience cultural differences first-hand
- To prepare to discuss cultural tolerance in the workplace

Audience
A minimum of sixteen participants divided equally into six to eight subgroups

Time Estimate
30 minutes

Materials and Equipment
None

Area Setup
Space for individuals to move around and "network"

Process
1. Ask the participants to stand and form eight equal subgroups and to move away from each of the other subgroups.
2. Make this statement: "In a few moments, you will have the opportunity to participate in a networking exercise with your colleagues. When I say, 'go' you will circulate around the room and meet as many people as you would like. While you are meeting them, you will behave appropriately for your culture. I am going to move to each of your groups and tell you about your group's cultural norms."

3. Circulate to each group and quietly assign one of the listed cultural characteristics to each group. Examples of interesting cultural characteristics you could use include:
   - No eye contact
   - Touchy feely/huggy
   - Wait 7 seconds before speaking
   - Cannot show a full "frontal" stance when meeting people (side stance only)
   - Repeat their own or the person's name five or six times
   - Speak very softly (or slowly, or loudly)
   - Squat or sit each time they meet someone
   - Repeat everything the other person says before saying something else
4. After all of the groups have been assigned their cultural norms, begin the networking activity. Allow participants to circulate and network until you feel the room begin to "lose energy" (3 to 5 minutes).
5. Stop the activity.
6. Ask groups to stand in one large combined circle, near their original cultural subgroup teammates.
7. Explain that the point of the activity is not to guess the assigned behavior of the other teams. Instead tell the participants to use "feeling words" that describe how they felt about those they met. After a few comments are made (the comments may at first be guarded or not completely honest), ask about anything that they are leaving out. *Note:* Reinforce that each team behaved appropriately for its assigned culture.
8. Continue taking comments from each of the participants in the circle. You will likely hear a number of negative, loaded words such as "creepy," "molesters," "slow," "dumb," "sneaky," and so forth.
9. Once these negative feelings have surfaced, ask each subgroup to state its assigned cultural behavior characteristic. Ask whether the participants have ever experienced any of these cultural norms before (some will admit they have). Ask what the positive aspect of each of these norms might be. For example, someone repeating names again and again might be using a technique for remembering the other person's name.
10. Use this discussion to segue into your topic.

InSider's Tips

- This activity provides trainers with a great "soft" lead-in to tougher, more sensitive conversations for workshops on sexual harassment, conflict resolution, or cultural diversity. The "fun factor" of the activity is substantial, and with the addition of a thoughtful and bold debriefing, this can be a high-impact learning activity without a great investment of time.
- You can also use this activity in a team setting or segue into departmental, gender, or regional differences. You might say, for example, "Let's talk in stereotypes for a minute. Let's discuss the differences between New Yorkers and Californians" or "Tell us about the folks in HR."
- If you have fewer than sixteen participants, you may wish to eliminate several of the cultural characteristics. This activity has been adopted, adapted, evolved, and developed from a wide variety of sources; verbal descriptions, various Internet resources, books, and years of trial and error. Specific similarities to other activities are coincidental and unintentional.

Kenny Sturgeon and **Randall LaBranche** are co-founders of Team Training Unlimited, a learning and development firm that partners with clients to create and deliver high-value, interactive, and immediately applicable training, team building, and coaching experiences. They have been traveling the world over the past several years, designing and using activities, games, simulations, exercises, and experiences to enhance learning. Both have led unique sessions, ranging from translating a leadership program entirely into Japanese to creating experiential social media workshops. Kenny and Randall have experience with a wide variety of teams and individuals, including corporate groups, public-sector organizations, colleges, and schools.

Kenny Sturgeon and Randall LaBranche
Team Training Unlimited
5036 Dr. Phillips Boulevard, Suite 195
Orlando, FL 32819
(863) 214.6626, (407) 230.1001
Email: ksturgeon@teamtrainingunlimited.com, rlabranche@teamtrainingunlimited.com
Website: www.teamtrainingunlimited.com/blog.teamtrainingunlimited.com
ASTD Chapter: Central Florida

Generation Genius

Submitted by Jeanne Baer

Overview
In competition with other teams, participants test their knowledge about generational differences.

Objectives
- To prompt insights about generational differences in the workplace
- To provide thirty ways to handle potentially difficult workplace situations

Audience
Ten to thirty-five in small groups of four to seven, ideally with three to five teams

Time Estimate
30 to 50 minutes

Materials and Equipment
- One copy of the Dear Generation Genius handout for each participant
- One set of four Voting Cards for each team; each team will have different colored cards with one letter, A, B, C, or D on each
- Flip chart or whiteboard
- Markers

Area Setup
A space large enough for learners to sit in small discussion groups without being overheard by others

Preparation
Create a set of Voting Cards for each team from colored cardstock (4¼" × 5½" works well). Make enough cards to give each team four cards in a color you have assigned to that team; one card with a giant A printed on it, another with a B, a third with a C, and the last with a D on it.

Process

1. Explain that this is an activity that allows participants an opportunity to be advice columnists.

2. Form three to five small groups of learners and distribute the Dear Generation Genius handout to each person. Then distribute a set of A, B, C, and D cards to each team, remembering that each team should have its own color set. To increase *esprit de corps,* you can ask the participants to take 4 or 5 minutes to choose a team name based on the color of their cards. Offer some examples, such as the Green Hornets, the Red Raiders, the Blazing Blues.

3. Post the team names on a flip chart and leave enough room so that you can record scores for correct responses in the activity to follow.

4. Introduce the activity by asking something like, "Have you ever wanted to be an advice columnist or thought you'd make a good one? Now is your chance to try out your skills." Explain that, after you read each question aloud, the teams will have 2 minutes to discuss the four answers that appear on the handout you gave them. The team's job is to decide which answer is the *incorrect* one.

5. After you read the question from the handout, allow about 2 minutes for discussion and then announce the end of the allowed time.

6. Explain that each team will provide its responses using their response cards. Say something like, "When I count to three, hold up the letter that represents your team's answer, A, B, C, or D.'"

7. If all teams agree on an answer, record one point for each, and move on to the next question. However, if there is disagreement, call on members from different teams and ask them to share their team's thinking about the choices they made. Manage the discussion, gently guiding everyone to the correct response. Once the discussion has come to a conclusion, record points for the teams that chose the correct answer. Occasionally, a discussion may ensue about real-life issues brought up by the question. You may wish to take a short detour to facilitate.

8. The correct responses are listed here. Remember, learners should choose the action that should *not* be taken.
   - 1. d
   - 2. a
   - 3. c
   - 4. d

- 5. c
- 6. a
- 7. d
- 8. c
- 9. d
- 10. a

9. After all ten questions have been answered and discussed, count up the points and award prizes to the team(s) who won or to everyone "for working so hard."

10. End the activity by stating that in each case they identified the *wrong* answer, that is, the action that should *not* be taken. State that the good news is that if they ever face any of the situations discussed, they will know three successful actions to take.

InSider's Tips

- Creating a team name really increases the team spirit and allows you to act as an occasional cheerleader, "Come on, Lemons, you can still catch up!" or "Way to go, Green Hornets!"

- To make this activity less like a multiple-choice quiz and more game-like and exciting, introduce the element of chance. Set a timer to go off randomly about three times during the game and let a representative of each team draw a card from a deck of playing cards. If the participant happens to draw a face card, the team earns an extra point; if another card is drawn, nothing happens.

- This is an engaging activity because *everyone* is involved in discussing the situations and deciding on answers. The game format is a great change of pace, providing a way to increase learners' knowledge without having to lecture. Participants explaining their answers will make the same points you would have made.

- If you have fewer than four people, you can treat the ten situations as small case studies. The group can discuss and decide on an answer, and then you can reveal the answer and discuss it further.

Chapter 6

Teamwork: Get to Know Your Team

Teams are important to every organization, and the number of submissions received for this topic (more than twenty) is proof enough for that statement. Because there were so many submissions, we decided to organize the ones we used into two groups and two chapters. The group of activities in this chapter addresses ways to help team members get to know each. The second set of team activities (to help participants address the challenges they face) is in the next chapter.

Clarifying backgrounds, exploring the likes and dislikes of team members—while at the same time improving team member skills—helps teams be more effective and efficient. Knowing who to depend on for what tasks or who has the knowledge, experience, or expertise to complete a project is often helpful information.

In many ways, teams are like cars. Teams need a tune-up now and then in order to run efficiently and reduce waste. The eight activities in this chapter will ensure your teams take advantage of the best tools available to run efficiently—while at the same time, laughing, thinking, competing, and praising their teammates. Use these activities as a team is forming or as part of regularly scheduled maintenance along the way. But don't limit your team-building focus to the activities in this chapter. The truth is, almost any activity in this book can be used to help team members solve problems and/or get to know each other better.

Joni Goodman offers us an activity that uses the given names of individuals' to describe themselves, while Cynthia Solomon shows you how to use the concept of speed dating as a team-building tool. Jennifer Fetterhoff presents an activity that expands the definition of art on the wall to build teams and Tera Denton uses the format of a commercial as a way to quickly reveal a great deal of information about team members. Luciana Rodrigues uses the power of storytelling to reveal new information about each team member.

Lisa Downs, Bob Zimel, and Laura Mendelvow round out the team-building activities offered in this chapter. Lisa gets team members all tied up as they express appreciation for each other's support and Bob shows us how to energize a team with a game he invented called "Favorites Poker." Finally, Laura's activity uses the Myers-Briggs Personality Types as a basis to explore and strengthen teams.

The activities in this chapter (and the next) offer some great ways to build your teams in some surprising and powerful ways.

Conceptualization of You

Submitted by Joni Goodman

Overview

Participants use the letters in their first names to gain a better understanding of their teammates and of themselves.

Objectives

- To bond a new group into a team
- To gain better self-knowledge, ultimately resulting in a better understanding of others

Audience

Twelve to fifteen participants from an intact work group

Time Estimate

20 minutes

Materials and Equipment

- Markers with water-soluble ink
- One flip-chart sheet for each participant
- Masking tape

Area Setup

U-shape

Process

1. State that the purpose of this activity is to gain a better understanding of each member through the use of their first names. Give each participant a sheet of flip-chart paper as well as a marker.
2. Ask each participant to post his or her flip-chart page on a wall somewhere in the room.
3. Tell the participants to write their first names vertically down the left side of the flip-chart paper. Write your name down the left side on a demonstration flip-chart sheet.

4. Explain that they have 5 minutes to come up with one word (noun or adjective) that begins with each letter of their first names. Provide a couple of examples using your name and write them on your flip chart. Emphasize that their descriptors should reflect who they are or some aspect about them.
5. Start the timing period.
6. At the end of 5 minutes, ask each participant, in turn, to share his or her descriptors and explain why he or she chose the words.
7. Summarize the activity. Note that the activity was valuable because team members gained a better understanding of each other and of themselves. Make the point that this new level of understanding will translate to a greater connection within the entire team.
8. Ask for a few examples of what participants learned about their teammates. Ask what the benefit might be and how this benefit might be realized back on the job.

InSider's Tip

- Leave the flip charts posted throughout the remainder of the training event if over multiple days. The participants will continue to reference the flip-chart pages throughout the session and continue finding new insights into each other.

Joni Goodman, CPLP, been a member of the national ASTD organization since 2006 and recently joined her local CIASTD chapter. She received her Certified Professional in Learning and Performance (CPLP) certification in 2007. Joni is currently employed as a sales training consultant and has been involved in a training role for the past twelve years.

Joni Goodman, CPLP
12730 Bristow Lane
Fishers, IN 46037
(317) 443.1580
Email: jonidgoodman@gmail.com
ASTD Chapter: Central Indiana

Team Speed-Dating

Submitted by Cynthia Solomon

Overview

One-on-one interviews between all team members highlight the need for getting to know other team members in this "speed-dating" inspired activity.

Objectives

- To engage new team members to know one another on a personal level
- To initiate conversations among team members about how they might work best as a team

Audience

Eight to twenty members of an intact learning team

Time Estimate

35 to 80 minutes, depending on the number of participants

Materials and Equipment

- One copy of the Speed-Dating Questions for each participant

Area Setup

Tables and chairs in a horseshoe fashion around a room with equal numbers of chairs on the outside of the horseshoe and chairs across the inside of the horseshoe

Process

1. State that the purpose of this activity is to allow participants an opportunity to get to know all the others in the group as part of the team development process. Distribute a copy of the Speed-Dating Questions to each participant.
2. Review the list of questions. Explain that participants directly facing each other on the inside and outside of the horseshoe arrangement are considered a pair. State that each pair of participants will interview each other and that they are to listen carefully to each other's answers. Note that they have the option of recording responses on paper, but it's not required.

3. Tell them that they will have 3 or 4 minutes to complete the interviews. Announce that they may begin the activity.
4. At the end of the time period, call, "Stop." Ask the participants to switch roles so that their partners have an opportunity to be interviewed.
5. Start the timing period again.
6. At the end of 3 to 4 minutes, call "Stop." This time ask the participants in the inner horseshoe to rotate clockwise to the next position. Tell the participants in the outer horseshoe position to remain in place.
7. Begin another interviewing session, as described previously with participants sitting inside the horseshoe shifting clockwise at the end of each round.
8. Repeat the process until each participant has interviewed all the other participants.
9. Conclude the "speed-dating" activity by asking participants to predict how the group will work together better as a result of the interviews.

InSider's Tips

- Use or adapt the suggested list of questions to suit the needs of the group.
- Keep it as fast-moving as possible. When 1 minute is left in each session, announce "1 minute left" to help participants gauge the use of their remaining time. Part of the fun is that there is no time to stray off from the interview questions.
- If helpful, you may record on a flip chart any conclusions and observations the team suggests.

The Book of Road-Tested Activities

Cynthia Solomon, Ph.D., is an associate professor of education and coordinator of the graduate program in human resource development at Tusculum College, Greeneville, Tennessee. In addition to her primary academic responsibilities, Cynthia manages her own consultant service CSolomon and Associates, specializing in leadership and team development skills, organizational performance management, organizational culture studies and change, all functions of the instructional systems design model, and train-the-trainer workshops. Her work has been published in two ASTD *Info-lines* and in the *Pfeiffer Team and Organization Development Annual*.

Cynthia Solomon, Ph.D.
Associate Professor of Education
Tusculum College
114 Walosi Way
Loudon, TN 37774
(865) 408.1520
Email: kcsolomon@att.net
ASTD Chapter: Smoky Mountain

Speed-Dating Questions

Select or adapt the questions as appropriate for the unique nature of the team.

1. What is your name and what type of work do you do?
2. How do you usually like to contribute to a team activity or work assignment?
3. What four words best describe your personality? (If the participants have been assessed using Myers-Briggs, DiSC, or other types of assessments, they may refer to these behavior and style dimensions.)
4. What particular professional skills do you rely on to make yourself and our team successful?
5. What are you not very good at doing that you would rely on others to perform for the benefit of the team?
6. What "ground rules" are important to you to enjoy working with us and helping us be successful?
7. What experiences have you had in the past that interfere with a team working successfully? How can we avoid this happening to us?

The Book of Road-Tested Activities

Acquainted Antics

Submitted by Jennifer Fetterhoff

Overview

During this activity each team member is allowed to select four bits of information he or she would like to know about the rest of the team and place those items on a flip-chart page to be completed by the rest of the team.

Objectives

- To improve the dynamics of a group
- To appreciate differences of individual members of a team, committee, or group

Audience

Six to ten members of a single group such as new employees, a new committee, or a team

Time Estimate

30 to 45 minutes, depending on the size of the group

Materials and Equipment

- One flip-chart page for each person
- Art supplies such as markers, scissors, colored paper, glue sticks, stickers
- Old magazines
- Masking tape

Area Setup

A room large enough for one flip-chart pages for all participants to be posted on the wall and space enough for a table of art supplies and magazines to be placed in the center of the other tables in the room

Process

1. Post one flip-chart page for each person on the wall. Place markers around the room.

2. Ask participants to each select a flip-chart page. Tell them to use the markers to divide the pages into four quarters by drawing a line down the middle both vertically and horizontally, as shown below.

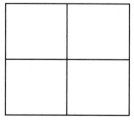

3. Ask the participants to write their team names (department, committee, or project) through the middle where the two lines intersect.
4. Tell the participants to think of four things they would like to know about the other members of the team, such as favorite sport or activity, favorite season, favorite pet, family members' names, best vacation, or other personal information. They should write these categories, one per quarter on the flip-chart page, as shown.

Favorite Work Assignment	Family Members
Safety | Team	
Pets	Favorite Book

5. Tell the participants to begin filling in the information under the categories they have written on their own sheets. The responses may be communicated in the form of words or drawings, or by using the stickers and/or magazines you have provided. Allow 10 minutes for this step.

6. Once participants complete their own information, ask them move around the room and respond to all the other flip charts in the room. Allow about 20 minutes for this step.
7. Once everyone has responding to all of the charts, select a few interesting items and ask participants to guess who wrote or drew each item.
8. Ask the participant responsible for the item or drawing to explain why he or she chose to highlight a particular item or the meaning of the drawing.
9. Take some time to summarize the activity. Ask participants to find commonalities among team members. Allow at least 10 minutes for this step.
10. Utilize the examples to demonstrate how they may not have known about each other's families, hobbies, likes, or dislikes previously, but they were able to work together as a team to find similarities and "common ground." Note that we are each different and unique in our own way, but if we work together for the good of the organization (customers, team, department, or whatever is appropriate) and learn, we grow together and with each other. The more we know about each other, the better we can work together to overcome obstacles.

InSider's Tips

- Be sure to use markers that do not bleed through the paper.
- Utilizing the participants' specific examples and playing off of their conversations helps drive the "debriefing" portion of this session.
- This is a great activity to use for new employee orientation, especially when no one knows much about any of the other participants in the room.

Jennifer Fetterhoff is the training coordinator with Belco Community Credit Union. She is responsible for ongoing strategic employee development, including leadership, service, and technical skills. She is currently working on her associate's degree in business. She is passionate about learning and educating others and about spending time with her daughter, Kerri Anne, and her two dogs, Buttons and Kevin. She is also active within her church and community and is the 2010 co-editor of the Central Pennsylvania ASTD chapter newsletter, "Hello Central."

Jennifer Fetterhoff
Training Coordinator
Belco Community Credit Union
449 Eisenhower Boulevard
Harrisburg, PA 17111
(717) 720.6232
Email: fetterhoffj@belco.org
Website: www.belco.org
ASTD Chapter: Central Pennsylvania

Team Commercial*

Submitted by Tara Denton

Overview

Participants form groups tasked with creating commercials that tout the "greatness" of their group to highlight talents and expertise resident in a team.

Objectives

- To encourage a team to examine the strengths within the team
- To explore experience, expertise, and skills within a team

Audience

Ten to twenty-five participants who work together

Time Estimate

20 to 30 minutes

Materials and Equipment

None

Area Setup

A space large enough for groups of two to five to work without disturbing other groups

Process

1. Explain that this activity will give the group an opportunity to get to know their teammates better. Tell the participants to form subgroups of from three to five people.
2. State that the task of each group is to create a 30-second commercial that will inform the others in the room about the experience and abilities

---

* Originally inspired by Bob Pike's "Write a Commercial" activity. Published in Bob Pike and Lynn Solem, *50 Creative Training Openers and Energizers*. San Francisco: Pfeiffer, 2000.

of their team. Encourage the groups to tout the greatness of their teams. Tell them that the commercial should include the following information:

- Name of the team
- Team "tag line"
- Special skills or talents of each individual on the team (preferably non-work related)
- Statement of why the team should be qualified as "great"

3. Start the activity with a 10-minute time limit.
4. At the end of the 10 minutes, ask each team to present its commercial, in turn.
5. Praise the diversity and richness of the experience. Laugh and have fun with the participants. Take notes on the styles and experience levels you see emerge. Use these notes to help group people for future assignments, pick team leaders, or facilitate contributions.
6. Summarize with a general discussion based on questions such as these:
   - What did you learn about your fellow team members?
   - What expertise do we have in the room?
   - How can we exploit the expertise and experience of this group?

InSider's Tips

- Encourage the team to be creative and add other elements to their commercial, for example, music, a logo or mascot, nicknames for individuals, and anything else they care to incorporate.
- This activity is a good "opener" to kick off a training session.

Tara Denton has designed and delivered learning solutions since 2001. She specializes in building learning products that meet business objectives, facilitating training programs, and coaching others to deliver participant-centered experiences. Tara's learning products have been named a finalist in training product competitions, and her jovial style has made her a repeated speaker and presenter. Tara's flexibility allows her to work on a range of projects, from consulting to a Fortune 500 company on an internal certification program to designing and delivering live online courses.

Tara Denton
Life Cycle Engineering
4360 Corporate Road
Charleston, SC 29405
(843) 744.7110
Email: tdenton@LCE.com
Website: www.lce.com/institute
ASTD Chapter: South Carolina Midlands

Three Truths and a Lie

Submitted by Luciana Rodriques

Overview

Each participant in this trust-building activity presents four separate personal stories to the entire participant group. Three of the stories must be true, but one story must be entirely fabricated. The participants decide among themselves which of the four stories is a lie.

Objectives

- To provide a forum for team members to get to know each other better and to strengthen the team
- To build trust in a team

Audience

Four to fourteen members of a work team

Time Estimate

45 to 120 minutes, depending on the number of participants

Materials and Equipment

- Pen and paper for each participant

Area Setup

A room arrangement that allows participants to see each other, such as a circle or U-shape

Process

1. Tell the participants that getting to know the other members of the team is the key to building understanding and trust. Explain that this activity offers team members such a learning opportunity. Hand out pens and paper to the participants.
2. Explain the activity. Tell the participants that they will each present four short stories about themselves. Note that the stories can be about anything: childhood, pets, sports, hobbies, funny situations, travels, unusual

experiences, or other personal stories. Explain that three of the stories must be true, but one of the four stories must be entirely fabricated. Tell the participants to use the pen and paper you handed out to make some quick notes about the stories they will tell. Emphasize that writing out the entire story is not necessary. Encourage them to be creative. Allow 10 minutes for the preparation of the stories.

3. When everyone has finished, ask for a volunteer to begin. Tell the first volunteer to take a couple of minutes to briefly tell his or her four short stories. Remind the presenter to be as convincing as possible when telling the stories. Also encourage the volunteer and the rest of the participants to avoid telling the fabricated story in the same order as the other presenters do, that is, first, second, third, or fourth in the line up. *Note:* Participants often tell the fabricated story last.

4. When the volunteer completes the storytelling task, ask the group to work together to identify which story is not true. Remind the participants of the ground rule that all questions to the presenter must be closed-ended (yes/no) questions.

5. Tell the group they must reach agreement before the presenter can reveal which story is a lie.

6. Follow the same procedures for the rest of the participants until all participants have presented their stories and the group has rendered a decision about which story is fabricated.

7. Discuss the activity using questions such as the following:
   - What new information did you learn about your team members?
   - What information surprised you the most?
   - What skills do members of your team possess that were not evident before the storytelling?
   - How is your team strengthened by what you learned?
   - How will you use the information you learned about your team today?

InSider's Tips

- Encourage the participants to create believable stories that others might reasonably think are true based on interests that are not apparent at work.
- This is a good activity for new leader assimilation sessions.

- Keep the activity moving. Don't let the guessing go on too long.
- This activity is a classic that has been around for at least thirty years. Its source is long ago lost. However, Bob Pike contributed a version in *90 World-Class Activities by 90 World-Class Trainers* (Biech, 2007).

Luciana Rodrigues graduated from Mackenzie University in São Paulo, Brazil, with a B.S. in business administration. She has a master's in human resources management from the same university and is currently enrolled in the M.Ed. training and development program at Penn State–Harrisburg. She has ten years of experience in human resources, mostly in organization development and learning. She works for Tyco Electronics as an organization development and learning manager in Harrisburg, Pennsylvania, where she is responsible for projects such as performance management, employee engagement, leadership development, and training programs for the Americas.

Luciana Rodrigues
6633 Terrace Way, Apt. B
Harrisburg, PA 17111
(717) 805.1231
Email: lprodrigues@tycoelectronics.com
ASTD Chapter: Central Pennsylvania

Ties That Bind

Submitted by Lisa Downs

Overview
Team members toss a ball of yarn or string as they name other team members on whom they depend or appreciate.

Objectives
- To identify how each person contributes to a team or organization
- To show appreciation for others' support

Audience
Ten or fifteen people within the same work group or department

Time Estimate
10 to 15 minutes, depending on the number of participants

Materials and Equipment
- A large ball of string or yarn

Area Setup
Space enough for all participants to stand in a circle

Process
1. Introduce this activity to the participants by saying that team members must depend on each other to reach their goals. Ask the participants to stand in a circle and to think about someone in the group they depend on or something they appreciate about another team member.
2. Give one person in the circle the ball of string and begin the activity. Hold onto the loose end and ask the person holding the string to cite one source of support, data, counsel/help, or resource they received from someone else in the group.
3. Once the person has been named, ask the person to throw the ball of string to that person.
4. When the second person catches the ball of string, that individual names someone he or she depends on and that person tosses the ball of string to

the team member just named. Continue the process until everyone in the group has exhausted their lists of team members they depend on. By this time, each person should be holding a section of string to form a web.

5. Ask one person in the circle to release his or her section of the string. Point out to the group what happens to the web when one person is removed (there should be some collapse of the string web).

6. Ask the participants what conclusions can be drawn from this activity and what it implies about teamwork.

 InSider's Tips

- Ensure that all participants have a chance to say something appreciative about at least one other team member and has had something appreciative said about them so that no one is left out of the web.
- This is a good activity to use if conflict or tension has occurred among team members because it enables them to take a step back and appreciate each other.
- I've seen many variations this activity in Pfeiffer publications, but I'm not sure where. The words used here are mine and the instructions are my version.

Lisa Downs is a learning consultant with Intrepid Learning Solutions in Seattle, Washington. Previously, she was a leadership development manager with T-Mobile USA, where she conducted and developed manager, leader, and personal effectiveness training and coaching. Before working at T-Mobile, she worked in the accounting industry as a training manager and consultant. In addition to serving as the 2008 president and 2006–2007 vice president of membership for the ASTD Puget Sound chapter, she is the 2010 chair of the ASTD Chapter Recognition Committee and a member of the National Advisors for Chapters committee. Lisa is the author of three books in the ASTD Trainer's Workshop series: *Listening Skills Training, Time Management Training*, and *Negotiation Skills Training*.

Lisa Downs
16207 NE 90th Court
Redmond, WA 98052
(425) 216.3015
Email: lisa@developmentwise.com
Website: www.lisadowns.net
ASTD Chapter: Puget Sound

Favorites Poker

Submitted by Bob Zimel

Overview
Participants use the competition and challenge of a card game to match "favorite things" cards and discover new things about team members and the advantages of collaboration.

Objectives
- To help team members get to know each other so that collaboration happens more freely
- To energize a team by interlacing competition and cooperation
- To explore the compete/collaborate conundrum

Audience
Ideally, ten to twenty-five (With smaller groups, some of the competitive and cooperative aspects diminish. With larger groups, the dynamics of the activities can become overwhelming, and the preparation increases.)

Time Estimate
15 to 30 minutes, depending on number of participants

Materials and Equipment
- Memo to Participants for the trainer
- Five Favorites Cards per participant (see the Sample Categories, Sample Template, and Sample Completed Cards)
- (Optional) Instruction Sheet on a PowerPoint slide or as a handout
- (Optional) Sample Handout

Area Setup
Any room with space enough for all participants to meet and mingle in pairs and small groups. This activity works well in a hotel or office lobby or outside; since there will be a lot of talking, choose a location where participants will not disturb others.

Preparation

Before the session, ask each participant to provide his or her favorite things via email or in person using the Memo to Participants. Allow plenty of lead time for participants to respond and for you to create the Favorites Cards (see the samples). All submitters must participate in the session so that all the Favorite Cards are accounted for. If participants will be unavailable during the activity, do not include their information on cards.

Copy (either electronically or by hand) each of the five answers from each participant onto a 4-by-6-inch card. When you are finished you will have five cards for each participant. For example, with fifteen participants, you will create seventy-five cards. See the sample template for the 4-by-6-inch cards.

When you have finished, shuffle the cards so they are in random order. Place five random cards on a stack, creating a "hand" of five cards for each participant. If desired, complete a handout with all the favorites of all the participants, as shown in the sample. Participants like to see all the answers once the activity is completed.

(*Optional:* Add a code to the bottom right of each card to help you identify whose card it is. This will make it easier for you to recognize whether a person has "five of a kind" without having to ask the group. Participants should not know why that code is on the card, so it is important to create a code that is not recognizable. When asked, you might joke that the cards will be more valuable on eBay with the special codes on them. The code on the sample cards contains ten characters. The person's initials are the first two letters when reading the code backwards. For example, if Dale Johnson's favorite movie is *Star Wars*, the code on the *Star Wars* card would be something like 7H5FG9J8D7.)

Get excited, because your participants are going to have great fun!

Process

1. Explain the setup and rules of the game by explaining to participants how many cards are in the set (for example, one hundred cards for twenty participants). Tell them that each card shows one favorite item from one person, but does not indicate whose card it is since the name is blank (see the sample cards). State that everyone will begin the game with a hand of five random cards.

2. Tell them that the objective of the game is to get all five cards that belong to one person (not your own cards).

3. Explain the process and how the game is played. Tell them that that they will first pair up with someone to learn whether they have any cards that are

the favorite things of the other person. If they do, they write the name of the person in the space provided.

4. Give additional rules by stating, "You can make a 1-for-1 trade with someone at any time, that is, you trade one card for another." Tell the participants that they should continue to pair up and look for favorites. Remind them that they need to find five cards that belong to the same person.

5. Be sure they understand that the winner is the first person who collects five favorite things from the same person. You may find it helpful to model the first steps. For example, walk up to a participant and ask, "What is your favorite movie?" When the person answers, you respond "Oh, I don't have that. How about your favorite book?" When the person answers, you respond. "Oh, I have that, so I'll write your name on that card." Remind them to continue until they both have shared all five favorite things. Move to another person to continue the demonstration.

6. Begin the game once you have completed the demonstration.

7. Hand out five cards to each participant and tell everyone to begin. Remind them to announce when they have five of a kind.

8. As the group completes the activity, offer help to anyone struggling with any part of the process. Other participants usually coach people, so there is usually little for you to do.

9. When someone has "five of a kind," announce it to the group. Ensure that all five cards belong to the same person. If you do not use the codes on the bottom of the cards, you can ask that person whether the five favorites are truly his or hers.

10. The activity ends if someone has "five of a kind." Continue the game if you discover the first "five of a kind" was announced incorrectly.

11. If you want to take this activity to another level, debrief with questions like these:
    - What happened?
    - Did people compete, collaborate, or both? Why?
    - How does the compete/collaborate conundrum play itself out in the workplace? In this team? Why?
    - What does this tell you about your team?
    - How might what happened here help you in the future?

InSider's Tips

- Participants will compete and collaborate at the same time. Watch the unique interpersonal and team dynamics unfold each time as participants learn about each other and become energized by the process.
- Although participants may wrestle with the instructions early on, participants "get it" quickly and start to gain momentum. Resist the urge to over-explain the activity; some ambiguity is expected until they begin.
- Move around the room to see progress and ask whether anyone needs help (which they rarely do).
- Don't over-administer the activity. For example, some participants think that it might be beneficial to create small groups rather than pairs. Sometimes this expedites the activity, and for others it is not beneficial. These dynamics are all OK.
- The activity consists of two separate processes: (a) identifying the name that belongs on each card and writing that name on the card and (b) trading cards to collect five of a kind. Sometimes participants start trading cards before they have written names on all five of their cards. That is OK as well.
- Participants will find it enjoyable to have a list of everyone's favorite things (see the Sample Handout). If you completed that matrix, you may wish to hand it out once the activity has ended.
- If guests will be joining the group, such as executives, clients, or others, feel free to request information from them and include them in on the activity.

Bob Zimel has experienced learning from both sides. With The Children's Place and Benjamin Moore and Co., he has focused on identifying, designing, developing, facilitating, and managing organization development, learning, and talent management solutions. With AchieveGlobal and The Forum Corporation, Bob developed and managed client relationships and designed learning solutions for clients. Bob treasures his involvement with ASTD, both nationally and locally. After serving on the Mid-New Jersey ASTD chapter board for seven years, including two years as chapter president, he was appointed to the volunteer role of ASTD's National Advisors for Chapters (NAC) for 2009–2011.

Bob Zimel
84 Washington Street
Rumson, NJ 07760
(973) 769.9443
Email: bobzimel@msn.com
ASTD Chapter: Mid-New Jersey

Memo to Participants

Hi _____:

As part of an upcoming activity for your work group, please tell me (just me) the following five things about you:

Please reply only to me—DO NOT "REPLY ALL." Do not discuss this with members of your work group prior to the meeting.

Favorite Movie: _____

Favorite Book: _____

Favorite Band/Singer: _____

Favorite Vacation Spot (be specific): _____

Favorite Food: _____

Thank you!!

Instruction Sheet

Setup

For seventeen participants, there are eighty-five cards; for twenty there are one hundred.

Each card shows one person's favorite, but does not indicate who that person is.

Process

Everyone starts with a hand of five random cards.

The object is to have five of a kind (five cards from the same person, not yourself).

Action: Pair up and find out whether you have any cards that represent the other person's favorites by asking each other the five questions. If you do have a card that matches the person's favorite for that category, write the person's name on your card.

You may make a 1-for-1 trade if you desire at any time. But remember that you always must have five cards in your possession.

Continue to pair up and ask questions of one another until someone has five of a kind and is declared the winner.

Sample Template

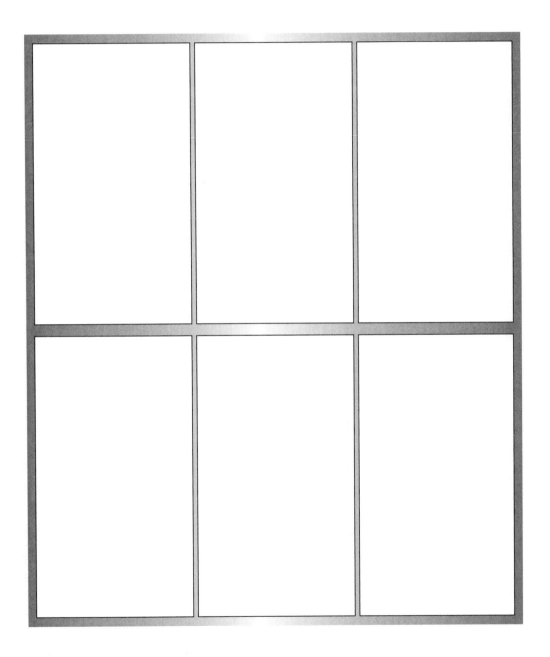

Sample Categories

Movie: XXXXXXXXXXXX Name: - - - - - - - - - - - - - - - XXXXXXX	Book: XXXXXXXXXXXXXX Name: - - - - - - - - - - - - - - - XXXXXXX	Band/Singer: XXXXXXXXXXX Name: - - - - - - - - - - - - - - - XXXXXXX
Vacation Spot (be specific) XXXXXXXXXX Name: - - - - - - - - - - - - - - - XXXXXXX	Food: XXXXXXXXXX Name: - - - - - - - - - - - - - - - XXXXXXX	

Sample Completed Cards

Movie: **Dead Poets Society** Name: - - - - - - - - - - - - - - - - L2FDB43HC4	Book: **Redeeming Love** by Francine Rivers Name: - - - - - - - - - - - - - - - - 4G4FH23CB	Band/Singer: **Van Halen** Name: - - - - - - - - - - - - - - - - 3GWPBCOH48
Vacation Spot (be specific): **Venice** Name: - - - - - - - - - - - - - - - - 3BVBC39HB2	Food: **Asparagus** Name: - - - - - - - - - - - - - - - - 2H1HWVMBD5	

Sample Handout

Person	Favorite				
	Movie	Book	Band/Singer	Vacation Spot	Food
Bob	Princess Bride	Crime and Punishment	Eric Clapton	Venice	Oysters
Christie	Freedom Writers	The Leadership Challenge	Rascal Flatts	New York City	Chicken Parmagiana
Dave	Fried Green Tomatoes	A Voice in the Wind by Francine Rivers	Celine Dion	Walt Disney World	Carrot Cake
Evelyn	Dead Poets Society	Redeeming Love by Francine Rivers	Chris Tomlin	Hawaii	Organic Vanilla Ice Cream
Harry	Sideways	Memoirs of a Geisha	BB King	Paris	Asparagus
John	Back to School	"I Love Being the Enemy" by Reggie Miller	The Clancy Brothers	Thailand	Romanian Strip Steak
Kristin	Sound of Music	Horses Make the Landscape More Beautiful by Alice Walker	Diana Krall	Yosemite National Park	Pizza
Mary	Saturday Night Fever	Beyond Bureaucracy by Warren Bennis	Rolling Stones	Florida Keys	Gyros

Personality Polaroid

Submitted by Laura Mendelow

Overview
In this activity, participants form groups based on personality types and use differences to find new connection points.

Objectives
- To identify personality differences on a team
- To begin to establish a common language of type differences as a team
- To provide a snapshot of Myers-Briggs categories and temperament in a short period of time

Audience
Ten to twenty-five team members who have a basic working knowledge of the Myers-Briggs Type Indicator (MBTI)

Time Estimate
45 to 60 minutes

Materials and Equipment
- One copy of the Personality Polaroid handout for each participant
- Flip-chart paper
- Markers

Area Setup
Any room that allows participants to walk and gather in the four corners of the room under signs posted in each corner identifying temperaments

Process
1. Introduce this activity by explaining that it allows for a quick snapshot of different types of personalities. Remind the participants that attending a Myers-Briggs Type Indicator (MBTI) session is a good idea to fully understand the model and theory.

2. Distribute the Personality Profile handout and briefly discuss each type highlighted and key information. Ask the group to share examples. Take about 10 minutes for this step.
3. Point out that each type of temperament is posted in one corner of the room. Ask participants to identify with one of the four temperaments and to move to that corner of the room.
4. Once the participants have taken their places in the four corners of the room, ask the four small groups to discuss what they bring to the team, under what conditions they produce the best work, and what upsets them when working within any team. You may wish to post these three items on a flip chart as a reminder.
5. Tell the four groups they should spend 15 minutes discussing these three topics—about 5 minutes on each.
6. Bring the entire group back together and ask for a brief review from each of the four groups.
7. Present a real work scenario such as "Imagine that you have been tasked to (you fill in the blank)."
8. Ask each small group to describe how they would respond from their perspective. Tell them to form their small groups again and discuss the question. Allow about 5 minutes for discussion. At the end of 5 minutes, ask each group to share their response and explain why they felt this way.
9. Lead the group in a discussion of the different approaches. Focus on what each group has to offer and how they can leverage each other's differences.
10. Remind the group to imagine that what they have done is a snapshot of the team and what everyone brings to the team. Summarize the activity with questions such as:
    • What did you learn about your team?
    • What are your team's strengths?
    • How can you leverage the various strengths of each temperament type in your team?
    • What can we all do as a team to be more successful in the future based on what we discussed today?

InSider's Tips

- The most important thing to remember is to keep the activity positive and discuss how to leverage each other (rather than what's so annoying or frustrating about other types).
- It's sometimes hard to manage a large group when some are familiar with MBTI and others are not. Try to use the temperament words rather than say "J" or "P" because some of your audience may not be fluent with the MBTI letter codes.
- You should be qualified to administer MBTI or conduct workshops on temperament to be successful with this activity.
- This activity is new, and the content is based on the book *Please Understand Me* by David Keirsey and Marilyn Bates. We often recommend this book or provide it as a take-away for participants.

Laura Mendelow has a master's degree in organization development, certificate in instructional systems design, and has extensive experience with experiential education techniques. She has been active in the learning industry since 1994 and joined Booz Allen Hamilton in 2002, where she now oversees the OD and coaching programs within learning and development. Outside of Booz Allen, Laura leads the American Society for Training and Development OD special interest group for the Metro Washington, D.C., chapter and also provides "Time Out" group coaching sessions for parents dealing with spirited children to help them reframe and reconnect with their children.

Laura Mendelow
16200 Kimberly Grove Road
Gaithersburg, MD 20878
(301) 325.5123
Email: mendelow_laura@bah.com
ASTD Chapter: Metro Washington, D.C.

Personality Polaroid

A useful way to group preferences is by temperament based on the book *Please Understand Me* by David Keirsey and Marilyn Bates. Based primarily on observable clusters of behavior or "activity patterns," there are four variations instead of the sixteen you may be familiar with from the Myers-Briggs Type Indicator (MBTI). Behavioral themes are easier for people to identify and remember.

The four temperaments are based on six of the MBTI dimensions: N (intuitive), S (sensing), J (judging), P (perceiving), T (thinking), and F (feeling)

- SJ—Guardians
- SP—Artisans
- NF—Idealists
- NT—Rationals

People with the SJ temperament are sometimes called the Guardians. Descriptive words include:

- Duty
- Utility
- Service
- Security
- Stability
- Membership
- Preservation
- Responsibility

Guardians:

- View logistics (how and when things are done) as important
- Value maintenance of the organization
- Regard efficiency as important
- Have a high need for membership and belonging
- Need to provide service
- Want to follow the rules
- Believe responsibility is important

People with the SP temperament are sometimes called the Artisans. Descriptive words include:

- Impulse
- Aesthetics
- Variation

- Action
- Impact
- Skillful performance
- Troubleshoot
- Tactics

Artisans:
- Want to make an impact
- Need freedom to act on impulse
- Are motivated to do things that are exciting (right now)
- Regard resolving a crisis as important
- Respond to what is currently happening
- Are risk-takers
- Focus on the present

People with the NF temperament are sometimes called the Idealists. Descriptive words include:
- Growth
- Integrity
- Imagine
- Ethics
- Unity
- Becoming one's true self
- Meaning and significance
- Catalyst
- Authenticity

Idealists:
- Value personal relationships highly
- Strive to maintain individuality
- Believe in their own ideals
- Have ability to involve others
- Do things for the greater good of society

People with the NT temperament are sometimes called the Rationals. Descriptive words include:
- Knowledge
- Understanding
- Insight
- Competence
- Concepts
- Ideas

- Strategy
- Logic
- Design

Rationals:
- Value knowledge and competency
- Enjoy creating models
- Engage in logical reasoning
- Need to understand the underlying principles
- Are visionary
- Are skeptical, analytical, and self-criticizing

Reference

Kiersey, D., & Bates, M. (1984). *Please understand me: Character and temperament types*. New York: Prometheus.

Chapter 7

Teamwork: Working Together

A high-performing team working together can accomplish more than all the individuals on the team working alone. To achieve this, however, a team needs to be hitting on all cylinders. The members need to work together to value the different strengths that each member brings to the team. High-performing teams also must build an environment of trust and cooperation; set and achieve goals; and appreciate the process and the results of planning. It takes hard work to build a good team and to be a contributing team member.

Teams don't start off great, they learn to be great. As a trainer you provide the opportunity for teams to acquire the skills and knowledge that they require to become great. Dedicating yourself to building high-performance teams requires you to encourage team members to do many things differently, and unfortunately it's not that easy to accomplish. The activities presented in this chapter range from easy to difficult; each one presents an opportunity for teams to grow and learn more about themselves.

The contributors in this chapter share many examples of ways to help good teams become great teams. Meri Villane starts the action with quick proof that teams can be more resourceful than individuals. Darrell Uselton shares an activity that takes a little longer to do but proves the value of teams as well. Lisa Hughes provides an activity you can use to explore the ideal characteristics of teams and, as a bonus, the team identifies a development plan that will help them reach that "ideal" state. Gale Mote continues the exploration of team characteristics and focuses on the reluctance of leadership.

I can't wait to try the next two activities. Rob Denton's "Pipe Dream" activity explores the frustrations teams must work through when facing a challenge. Carolyn Nilson's activity will help you move teams down the road to accomplishing tasks more productively.

Activities that involve building have long been a way to explore team dynamics. This chapter offers three building activities submitted by Rob Denton, Patti Ulwelling, and Deborah Covin Wilson. Using straws, marshmallows, spaghetti, or paper cups, each takes about an hour. The time is well worth it because the rich, bold debriefing opportunities made possible by these activities can lead to essential learning for teams. To be most successful, don't wimp out on your debriefing questions.

If your participants are willing to risk being blindfolded, Joe Sanchez and Jeanne Baer offer you two activities guaranteed to lead to interesting discussions. The preparation for "Think on Your Feet" contributed by Sharon Dera, may be challenging, but the options for learning are broad, varied, and easily tied to your team's daily work life.

This chapter is one you will return to again and again to tap into its collection of tools you can use to help teams learn to be high-performing teams.

A Cat and a Fridge

Submitted by Meri Villane

Overview

Making a list of the similarities between two very different objects is the fun and energizing entry point into a discussion about collaboration and the benefits of teams.

Objectives

- To explore ways teams can be more resourceful than individuals
- To energize the group

Audience

Six to fifty participants

Time Estimate

10 to 15 minutes

Materials and Equipment

- A flip chart or whiteboard
- Markers
- Paper and pen or pencil for each participant
- (Optional) Small prizes

Area Setup

No special arrangement

Process

1. Draw a cat head and a refrigerator on the flip chart or whiteboard. Give everyone paper and pens or pencils.
2. Tell the participants they each have 30 seconds to come up with a list of ways that a cat and a refrigerator are similar. State that they cannot speak to each other as they make their lists.
3. At the end of the 30 seconds, divide the group into teams of three to five individuals.

4. Tell them they now have 1 minute to collaborate as a team on the lists they just created.
5. After 1 minute, ask teams to report out on some of their ideas. (If using prizes, award them to the team with the longest list.)
6. Debrief the activity by asking:
   - What did you learn from this activity?
   - How can it make a difference in your typical work life?
   - How does what you learned make a difference in your expectations of your team?
   - What will you implement back on the job as a result of using this activity?

InSider's Tips

- Give prizes to the team with the longest list to increase participation.
- A debriefing is important to ensure the group makes the connection to the benefits of a team approach (team versus individual).
- This is a pleasant way for individuals to discover how teamwork can be effective. Besides, similarities between the cat and the fridge can be extremely creative, energizing, and fun for your learners.

Meri Villane is president of CEDS/Creative Employee Development Solutions. Her clients include Fountain Utilities, Colorado Springs Utilities, Goodrich, FedEx, OPM, Air Academy Federal Credit Union, Premiere Technologies, and Pikes Peak Library District. Meri is the creator of TheBizBookBuzz™, a business book club program that serves as a turnkey learning solution to national markets. She has been involved in the local learning and development community for more than fifteen years, serving on the board of ASTD and as president in 2001. Meri is also actively involved in Leadership Pikes Peak and the BBB of Southern Colorado's Excellence in Customer Service Program.

Meri Villane
CEDS
1317 E. Dale Street
Colorado Springs, CO 80909
(719) 473.6735
Email: ceds@mvillane.com
Website: www.mvillane.com
ASTD Chapter: Pikes Peak

Capital Team Building

Submitted by Darrell B. Uselton

Overview

Participants explore the advantages of a team approach as they race the clock to name all the U.S. capital cities.

Objectives

- To recognize the importance of communicating and working with others to meet important goals and organizational objectives
- To appreciate the diversity of skills of other team members
- To articulate that many factors measure success

Audience

Between twenty and thirty (smaller groups also can be successful)

Time Estimate

30 to 60 minutes

Materials and Equipment

- A copy of the Individual Answer Sheet for each participant
- One copy of the Team Answer Sheet for each team
- A pen or pencil for each participant

Area Setup

Round tables are preferable so that team members can easily communicate. Conduct the exercise in a relatively controlled environment so you can hear and observe each team.

Process

1. Divide the group into separate teams of six to ten participants each. Team members can be assigned at random or you may assign individuals to a particular group.
2. Tell the participants that their task is to identify as many state capitals as possible within 20 minutes. Give one Individual Answer Sheet to each person and one Group Answer Sheet to each team.

3. Advise the participants that they may not use any electronic handheld devices to find the answers. Remind the team members that this is a competitive activity and that they should speak softly to avoid their answers being shared with nearby teams.
4. Tell the participants that they have a choice to work individually or as a group.
5. Once the team has decided on a strategy, observe the actions of each team. Note the strategies and actions taken by each group.
6. Keep the teams informed of the remaining time (5 minutes remaining, 2 minutes remaining, and so forth) so they may alter their strategy as needed.
7. At the expiration of the designated time, ask the participants to stop writing and turn over their Answer Sheets.
8. Bring the group back together and debrief what happened, using the following questions:
   - Did your team develop a strategy? Why did your team decide on that strategy?
   - How successful was your team in meeting the objective?
   - Describe the process of working with others to achieve the goal. What skills sets were required to work through this activity?
   - What factors determined success for your team?
   - Did a "leader" or "leaders" emerge within your team?
   - Did everyone have the opportunity to be heard?
   - Did all members participate? Did anyone feel left out or refuse to participate?
   - Did anyone notice others' body language throughout the activity? What did you notice?
   - In retrospect, would you have used the same method or strategy again?
   - How can you transfer what you experienced today to your workplace team?
9. You may wish to note the reactions of the team members before, during, and after the activity and share your observations and comments with the larger group, using specific names with care.

InSider's Tips

- Traditionally, groups work feverishly to list as many capitals as possible and will miss the point of how the objective is achieved. The main objective is not the number of correct answers but to examine the dynamics of effective teamwork through group interactions.

- Small teams should be able to communicate more effectively. Larger teams tend to have members who feel left out or are not heard.
- Participants will often raise their voices during the exercise so the tables should be 10 to 15 feet apart.
- Because most people can recognize at least a few U.S. state capitals, this activity can be used for participants from age nine to ninety or more. Educational background or socio-economic status of the participants is not a prerequisite.
- Groups that use the Group Answer Sheet often find it is the key to their success. Working together collectively as a group and allowing only one person to list the answers saves time and usually ensures greater number of correct answers.
- One option is to declare that there are "No Rules" in this exercise. This added dimension often allows members begin to think creatively, whereby they may include the use of hand-held electronic devices to "look up" their answers. Since there are "No Rules," this is a perfectly acceptable, but sometimes controversial strategy.

Darrell B. Uselton serves as corporate training manager for Memphis-based Barnhart Crane. Prior to 2009, he was president of LEAD Training Systems, a management consulting and training firm started in 2005. He is a recognized expert in the field of leadership training and has developed creative programs that provide honest self-appraisals while encouraging people to "be all they can be." His workshops deliver strategies that can be applied immediately to help individuals and organizations meet their goals. With more than twenty-five years of corporate administrative, management, and college classroom instructional experience, Darrell has helped many organizations create a more positive corporate culture, while improving overall working relationships. Darrell received his bachelor's degree and master of arts from the University of Memphis and has received both national and state teaching awards.

Darrell B. Uselton
6321 Staffordshire
Memphis, TN 38134
(901) 619.8499
Email: duselton1@gmail.com
ASTD Chapter: Memphis

Individual Answer Sheet

List the capitals of the fifty United States on the sheet below.

1. Alabama _____

2. Alaska _____

3. Arizona _____

4. Arkansas _____

5. California _____

6. Colorado _____

7. Connecticut _____

8. Delaware _____

9. Florida _____

10. Georgia _____

11. Hawaii _____

12. Idaho _____

13. Illinois _____

14. Indiana _____

15. Iowa _____

16. Kansas _____

17. Kentucky _____

18. Louisiana _____

19. Maine _____

20. Maryland _____

21. Massachusetts _____

22. Michigan _____

23. Minnesota _____

24. Mississippi _____

25. Missouri _____

26. Montana _____

27. Nebraska _____

28. Nevada _____

29. New Hampshire _____

30. New Jersey _____

31. New Mexico _____

32. New York _____

33. North Carolina _____

34. North Dakota _____

35. Ohio _____

36. Oklahoma _____

37. Oregon _____

38. Pennsylvania _____

39. Rhode Island _____

40. South Carolina   _____

41. South Dakota   _____

42. Tennessee   _____

43. Texas   _____

44. Utah   _____

45. Vermont   _____

46. Virginia   _____

47. Washington   _____

48. West Virginia   _____

49. Wisconsin   _____

50. Wyoming   _____

Team Answer Sheet

List the capitals of the fifty United States on the sheet below.

1. Alabama _____

2. Alaska _____

3. Arizona _____

4. Arkansas _____

5. California _____

6. Colorado _____

7. Connecticut _____

8. Delaware _____

9. Florida _____

10. Georgia _____

11. Hawaii _____

12. Idaho _____

13. Illinois _____

14. Indiana _____

15. Iowa _____

16. Kansas _____

17. Kentucky _____

18. Louisiana _____

19. Maine   _____

20. Maryland   _____

21. Massachusetts   _____

22. Michigan   _____

23. Minnesota   _____

24. Mississippi   _____

25. Missouri   _____

26. Montana   _____

27. Nebraska   _____

28. Nevada   _____

29. New Hampshire   _____

30. New Jersey   _____

31. New Mexico   _____

32. New York   _____

33. North Carolina   _____

34. North Dakota   _____

35. Ohio   _____

36. Oklahoma   _____

37. Oregon   _____

38. Pennsylvania   _____

39. Rhode Island   _____

40. South Carolina   _____

41. South Dakota   _____

42. Tennessee   _____

43. Texas   _____

44. Utah   _____

45. Vermont   _____

46. Virginia   _____

47. Washington   _____

48. West Virginia   _____

49. Wisconsin   _____

50. Wyoming   _____

Picture Your Ideal Team

Submitted by Lisa Hughes

Overview
Teams tap into their creative talents as well as their logical traits to identify the characteristics of an ideal team and what developmental opportunities it will take to reach the ideal.

Objectives
- To develop a list of characteristics of an ideal team
- To identify ways to strengthen the characteristics of a team

Audience
Five to twenty members of a new or existing team

Time Estimate
1.5 to 2 hours

Materials and Equipment
- One copy of the Picture Your Ideal Team Development Plan handout for each participant
- One flip chart and paper for each subgroup
- Markers
- Pens or pencils for participants
- Masking tape

Area Setup
A room large enough for subgroups to work together

Process
1. Ask participants to form subgroups of five to seven people. If you have a team of fewer than ten, you may wish to keep them all in one group. Give each group a flip chart and markers.

2. Tell the participants that their subgroups will have 7 to 10 minutes to respond to the following questions (post them on a flip chart if you wish):
    - What is your team trying to accomplish, to what purpose, and for what results?
    - Does your team have the resources and ability to accomplish your purpose and results?
3. Start the timed period.
4. Once time is up, ask the groups to report out on the two questions. Facilitate the discussion, but don't necessarily come to any conclusions. Allow no more than 10 minutes.
5. Tell participants that next they are to describe and draw their ideal teams on the flip charts. Explain that the time limit is 20 minutes and that the use of pictures, words, or metaphors is permitted—or anything else they wish to use. Remind them to include what makes their team ideal given what they must accomplish. Tell them to think about this from their own perspective as well as the perspectives of their managers, organization, and customers.
6. At the end of 20 minutes, ask the participants to post their completed pictures on the wall or the flip-chart easel where everyone can see them. Ask each team to take no more than 5 minutes to present their ideal team to the other subgroups. Applaud each team after its presentation.
7. Ask them to identify the similarities and the differences between lists. Ask how these ideal team descriptors express characteristics of a team. Makes sure you allow discussion.
8. Instruct participants to go back to their small groups. Hand out the Picture Your Ideal Team Development Plan worksheets. Ask participants to review the pictures and consider the similarities to identify seven characteristics that make their team ideal. Allow about 10 minutes for this and then have them write the seven characteristics on their flip charts.
9. Bring all the participants together as a large group and use the posted flip-chart pages to look for similarities among all the groups. Based on the discussion, ask the participants to reach consensus on the six, seven, or eight characteristics that best describe the entire team.
10. Once the final list of characteristics of this ideal team is agreed on and recorded, ask the participants to return to their small groups to work on the second part of the handout, Development Opportunities for Our Entire Team. Ask the groups to identify and list the steps needed to move their team even closer to their ideal.

11. Allow about 10 minutes for this part of the activity and then ask the participants to gather as a group again.
12. In the large group, solicit comments and questions about the development opportunities. Agree on at least five things the team can do.
13. Ask, "How and when will you check progress?" Ensure that they select a review date prior to leaving the discussion.

InSider's Tips

- Do this activity only with healthy teams who want to strengthen teamwork and communication, not conflicted teams or teams with "issues."
- Set a positive tone: moving from good to better, better to best, and best to the next level.

Lisa Hughes designs and guides retreats, meetings, and workshops where people connect, build relationships, remove barriers, respect difference, and appreciate conflict. She works with teams to develop effective communication, trust, and productive cooperation. With over twenty years of experience helping people work together for individual and corporate achievement, Lisa enjoyed fourteen years at AT&T in management positions in sales and training. In 1994 she started her facilitation practice to improve the quality of communication and relationships in a changing workplace. Lisa holds a B.A. in American studies, an M.A. in organizational management, plus certificates in EQ, MBTI, DiSC®, and mediation.

Lisa Hughes
9190 Windsor Court
Loveland, OH 45140
(513) 677.9448
Email: lrhughes@fuse.net
Website: www.wiseheartswillingspirits.com
www.worklifeassoc.com
ASTD Chapter: Greater Cincinnati

Picture Your Ideal Team Development Plan

Characteristics of Our Ideal Team

Of all the characteristics discussed in this session, list those that best fit your team based on your purpose and desired results.

1. _____
2. _____
3. _____
4. _____
5. _____
6. _____
7. _____

Place a plus beside each characteristic that represents your team strengths.

Development Opportunities for Our Ideal Team

What steps would you take, if any, to get your team closer to your ideal? List them below.

1. _____
2. _____
3. _____
4. _____
5. _____

How and when will you check progress? Agree on a date and process.

People to People

Submitted by Gale Mote

Overview
Participants take turns leading the other group members in this lively, highly physical activity to learn real lessons in team leadership and reasons that prevent members from stepping into a leadership role.

Objectives
- To explore and discuss the deeper, personal elements of teamwork
- To explore the reluctance of leadership

Audience
No limit

Time Estimate
20 minutes

Materials and Equipment
- None

Area Setup
An open area large enough for participant to physically move around

Process
1. Ask all participants to stand and find partners. If you have an odd number of participants you may partner with one of the participants to begin the activity. If there are tables and chairs, ask participants to push their chairs in and move anything else that is on the floor to minimize tripping hazards.
2. Ask pairs to face one another, extend their arms, and place their hands palms to palms. Tell them that this position is called "home base" for this activity.
3. To make sure they understand the concept, tell the pairs to stand back-to-back. Say, "Home base." They should all turn to face their partners, extend their arms, and place their hands palm to palm.

4. Tell them that whenever you say "people to people," they need to change partners. Encourage them to avoid using the same person for consecutive commands if possible.
5. Tell them that you will give commands of various kinds in addition to the "home base" and "people to people" commands. State that when you give the commands they should follow them as much as possible and do so while being respectful and courteous.
6. Begin the activity by giving the first commands. Say: "Right foot to right foot, left knee to left knee, back to back, right elbow to right elbow, and people to people." Watch the flurry as people work to find new partners and not be left alone.
7. Begin a second set of commands by saying; "Back to back, right index finger to right index finger, left hip to left hip, home base, and people to people."
8. After this series of commands, announce that there will be a change. *Note:* If you began the activity with an odd number of participants, stop playing the facilitator. If you had an even number of participants at the beginning, you will still play the facilitator at this point. The goal of this part of the activity is to force a situation in which one participant will be left stranded without a partner. Inform the participants that the person who is left stranded after the next set of commands will be the new leader and that he or she will give the commands.
9. Begin a new set of commands. Say: "Left hand to left hand, back to back, and people to people." Tell the person who is isolated that she or he is now the leader and must give the commands. Remind the new leader that she or he can give the command "people to people" whenever she or he chooses and until that point she or he will continue to be the leader.
10. Ask the new leader to provide the new set of commands.
11. After three or four people have become the leader following this process, stop the activity.
12. Debrief using questions such as:
    * What did you notice when someone said "people to people"? What does this tell us about how people view teamwork? (People need each other; don't want to be ostracized or separated from the group; are generally happy for each other's success and appreciate the shared leadership; have enthusiasm and passion for one another and the team.)
    * People seemed frantic to find partners and avoid a leadership position. What do you think is the reason for this? (Some don't want to be the center of attention, some prefer to follow, some are unsure of what is expected, some take too much control.)

- What lessons can we apply from this activity to our own teams? (Be committed to one another's success, be there for each other, be inclusive, look for what's right, help each other be successful, don't be afraid to take the lead when your expertise is needed.)

InSider's Tips

- Keep it fun and demonstrate high energy.
- It is important not to let this activity go too long because people tire of it quickly.
- Remind people to be courteous and respectful when giving instructions.
- Be sure to allow people to opt out for any physical disabilities.

Gale Mote has been designing and delivering motivational workshops and training classes for all types of industry and organizations for more than twenty years. When people come to Gale's presentations and workshops, they usually leave with one key question, "Where does she get that energy?" Her firm, Gale Mote Associates, specializes in high-performance work cultures, core interpersonal skills training, and organization development consulting. Her sessions are creative, energizing, participant-centered, and obtain results. She is also a lecturer for the University of Iowa, Tippie College of Business, in the MBA program for professionals and managers.

Gale Mote, MBA
1435 31st Street NE, Suite D
Cedar Rapids, IA 52402–4056
(319) 364.2739
Email: gale.mote@galemoteassociates.com
Website: www.galemoteassociates.com
ASTD Chapter: Hawkeye

Pipe Dream

Submitted by Rob Denton

Overview

Participants try to keep a plastic pipe from "floating away" in this activity, which stresses the skills needed to operate as a team and new ways to meet challenges and obstacles.

Objectives

- To explore team responses to a frustrating challenge
- To explore behaviors that define the concept of teamwork

Audience

Ten to thirty participants

Time Estimate

20 to 40 minutes, depending on group size and discussion

Materials and Equipment

- Stick made of PVC pipe long enough for all team members to touch it at the same time

Area Setup

A space large enough for the participants to stand in two rows facing each other with about 2 feet of space between them

Preparation

Purchase several 3-foot lengths of 1-inch diameter plastic PVC pipe used for plumbing. Buy several couplings to connect the lengths of pipe and some end caps to cover the two ends. Add lengths of pipe as needed, depending on the number of participants, to form a pipe that reaches the full length of a line created by one-half the number of participants in the group.

Process

1. Tell the participants the activity is a team challenge.
2. Ask the participants to form two lines facing directly across from each other. Ask them to bend their arms at a 90-degree angle so that their elbows are at their sides and their fingers are pointing at the person across from them. The participants' fingers should alternate in the line so that every other finger belongs to a different person.
3. Place the PVC pipe on the participants' fingers down the line and rest your hand on one end of the stick while you explain the directions. Tell them that the objective is to lower the stick evenly to the ground as a team. If it rises up they must start over. The rule is that they must all be touching the stick and lower it as a team.
4. Remove your hand from the stick and say, "Go." Allow the participants to try several times. Ensure that they have time for making suggestions and solving problems.
5. Once you sense frustration, stop the action and have them return to their seats. Debrief using these questions:
   - What was your initial reaction to the problems you experienced?
   - How well did the team cope with this challenge?
   - What skills did it take to be successful as a team?
   - What creative solutions were suggested? How were they received?
   - What would an outside observer have seen as the strengths and weaknesses of the team?
   - What roles did people play?
   - What did each of you learn about yourself as a team member?
   - Who emerged as a leader? Did leadership change? Why?
   - When did the group begin to act as a team? What were the signs?
   - What situations at work are like this activity?
   - What can you do about them when you go back to the workplace?

InSider's Tips

- The stick seems to defy gravity. The reason (keep it to yourself) is that the collective upward pressure created by everyone's fingers tends to be greater than the weight of the stick. As a result, the more a group tries, the more the stick tends to "float" upward.
- If you have too many people for the line you can ask some to be observers.
- The Wilderdom Store allowed me to describe and publish this activity. This activity and others may be accessed through this link: http://wilderdom.com/games/descriptions

---

Rob Denton is a learning and development specialist at CenterPoint Energy. He has more than fifteen years of diverse experience in organization development and corporate training for a variety of industries. Rob holds a master's degree in adult education and training from Seattle University.

Rob Denton
CenterPoint Energy
1111 Louisiana Street
Houston, TX 77251
(832) 494.7670
Email: rob.denton@centerpointenergy.com
Website: centerpointenergy.com
ASTD Chapter: Houston

Team Think-ING

Submitted by Carolyn Nilson

Overview
Participants discover the value of actively pursuing goals and accomplishing team and organizational initiative through this simple but powerful list-making activity.

Objectives
- To encourage team members to think in terms of doing, not just understanding
- To guide participants in creating "ing" words

Audience
Any size group just beginning to work as a team

Time Estimate
20 to 30 minutes, depending on the size of the group

Materials and Equipment
- Pencil and paper for each participant
- Flip chart and markers

Area Setup
Seat participants around a conference table so that they have a place to write and so that they can see each other. Position the flip chart so that everyone can see it.

Process
1. Begin the session by writing the word "Think-ING" on the flip chart.
2. Ask the group, "What's the difference between the words 'think' and 'think-ing'?" Focus on the idea of continuous processing when using a verb ending with "ing."
3. Collect participants' ideas of processes at this company/organization that need fixing; encourage "ing" word responses. Facilitate group discussion.
4. Ask a volunteer team member to be in charge of recording more intense discussion on the flip chart; guide participant interaction around ideas such

as managing time, solving problems, using resources, or making decisions. Encourage participants to take notes and make their own lists.

InSider's Tips

- This is an exercise in helping new teams and team members to think and plan in terms of doing, to be active and not passive, as they learn and work together.
- Encourage participants to make their own lists of "ing" words of special importance to them personally on the job and as they contribute to the team.
- Keep the activity going until you're sure participants see the value of think-ing.
- ASTD published a list in 2002 of similar "ing" words in the book *How to Start a Training Program* by Carolyn Nilson. This is the first time this activity has been published as a training activity.

Carolyn Nilson, Ed.D., is author of thirty training books, with editions in hard cover, paperback, self-study, and e-learning. Her books have been translated into Spanish, Chinese, and Arabic and are selling in thirty countries worldwide. Four of her books are among amazon.com's "50 Best-Selling Training Books." Carolyn was a member of the technical staff at Bell Laboratories in the advanced programs, standards, audits, and inspections group; she was also manager of simulation training at Combustion Engineering. Her consulting work included service at The World Bank, USAID (Egypt), and National Institute of Education. She serves on the *Harvard Business Review* Advisory Committee.

Carolyn Nilson, Ed.D.
13415 Shaker Boulevard, 9E3
Cleveland, OH 44120
(216) 283.0542
Email: carolyn_nilson@yahoo.com
ASTD Chapter: National

Build a Bridge

Submitted by Rob Denton

Overview

Team members take home lessons in cooperation, resourcefulness, and working under pressure in this creative and exciting activity that requires participants to plan and build a working bridge.

Objectives

- To discuss how teams welcome new members and the impact on the team and on the new member
- To explore better ways to work as a team with limited resources, changing team members, and time pressure

Audience

Any number of participants from the same organization in teams of six to eight members

Time Estimate

Approximately 60 minutes, depending on the number of teams

Materials and Equipment

- Four paper cups for each team
- Four paper plates for each team
- One pair of scissors for each team
- One roll of masking tape for each team
- Six sheets of flip-chart paper for each team
- A lightweight ball to roll across the completed bridges
- (Optional) Small prizes

Area Setup

A room large enough to accommodate a separate table for each team

Process

1. Introduce the activity saying that they will explore many of the same issues that their teams face in the workplace. Divide the participants into teams of six to eight people.

2. Tell teams that their job is to build a bridge that spans the table and that it must be at least 1 foot above the surface of the table. In addition, the bridge must be strong enough to support the weight of a lightweight ball rolling across it. Put the materials on the tables.

3. Tell the participants that they have 10 minutes to plan their construction and 10 minutes to build their bridges, for a total of 20 minutes. During the planning time they may not touch the materials. Begin the planning phase timing.

4. After the 10-minute planning process, tell the teams they will have 10 minutes to build the bridge based on the plans they discussed.

5. Give the signal to start the building phase.

6. After 2 minutes, halt progress and move one participant from each team to a new team.

7. Begin a timing countdown again, calling out the amount of time left every 2 or 3 minutes.

8. Call time after a total of 10 minutes and begin the bridge test phase.

9. Test each team's bridge construction by rolling your ball across each one. Encourage support from everyone by applauding each bridge.

10. Debrief using questions such as:
    - How did you feel when I moved team members to a different team?
    - How did the interjection of a new team member affect production of your bridge?
    - How did group members respond to the new team members? Were they welcomed?
    - Team members, how did you feel being moving to a different team?
    - What did the teams do to bring the new members up to speed and to encourage them to participate?
    - How many teams asked the new team member for ideas? Did anyone recognize that they were building a bridge in a previous team and brought skills with them?
    - How does this project compare to your work?
      - Limited resources?
      - Unclear directives?
      - New team members?

- Loss of team members?
- Time pressure?
- How can you apply what we have learned back on the job?

InSider's Tips

- If you wish, make prizes available for the successful teams or those completed first, or any other criteria you wish to use.
- Interactive Associates Facilitative Leadership Program allowed me to publish this activity. More Interactive Associates resources and information may be found at this link: www.interactionassociates.com/services/facilitative-leadership.

Rob Denton is a learning and development specialist at CenterPoint Energy. He has more than fifteen years of diverse experience in organization development and corporate training for a variety of industries. Rob holds a master's degree in adult education and training from Seattle University.

Rob Denton
CenterPoint Energy
1111 Louisiana Street
Houston, TX 77251
(832) 494.7670
Email: rob.denton@centerpointenergy.com
www.centerpointenergy.com
ASTD Chapter: Houston

Planning with Spaghetti and Marshmallows

Submitted by Patti Ulwelling

Overview
This construction-based activity requires creative thinking to succeed and teaches important lessons about team dynamics and leadership.

Objective
- To experience various elements of team dynamics
- To discuss the importance and relationship of strategic planning to final results

Audience
Up to twenty-five participants divided into at least two teams of four to seven who work together or need to explore aspects of team dynamics

Time Estimate
30 to 45 minutes

Materials and Equipment
- One bag of regular size marshmallows per team
- One or two extra bags of marshmallows
- One pound of uncooked spaghetti per team
- One or two extra pounds of spaghetti
- One plate to hold supplies for each team
- One pad of Post-it® Notes per team
- A set of markers for each team
- Tape measure
- 100 Grand® candy bars for prizes

Area Setup
A table for each team with a flat, washable work surface and plenty of space to move around it. One large table is needed for a final product judging. Ideally, the larger table should be centrally located or at the front of the room.

Preparation

Prepare a "construction plate" for each team by placing a plate with an equal amount of marshmallows and dried spaghetti, a Post-it Note pad, and set of markers on the plates.

Process

1. Introduce the activity by saying, "We are all members of many different teams. This activity explores the dynamics that contribute to the creation of a great team." *Note:* If this activity occurs in the middle of a longer workshop, ask participants to clear off their tables.

2. Set up the activity and explain that the teams will be completing a project for a client with the potential of a great monetary reward. Explain the setup by saying, "A large client has invited us to design their new headquarters building. Each team will create a model of a building design. The specifications are that you can only use the materials at your workspace, the completed model must be at least 20 inches tall, and you must be able to move the model to the display table for judging. The winning model will be judged on two aspects: strength, as evidenced by being able to make it to the display table in one piece, and beauty and creativity, as judged by me. Each person on the winning team will win a hundred grand."

3. Pass out the construction plates, one per table group.

4. Tell the teams they have 25 minutes to complete their building design. State that they may create a team name with the markers and Post-its to enhance team camaraderie if they wish and they may borrow the tape measure from you if they need to check height. In addition, they may ask for additional spaghetti and marshmallows.

5. Tell them to begin and start the timing. Provide 10-minute, 5-minute, and 1-minute warnings.

6. Call time and ask the teams to bring their models to the display table.

7. Judge the best models by measuring the final product and awarding points for beauty and creativity, such as colorful marshmallows, Post-it flags, or other designs you see. Give the winning team 100 Grand candy bars or find other ways to reward all the teams' designs by giving prizes for categories such as, "worked the hardest," "the most original," or "the team that had the most fun."

8. Ask everyone to sit with their teams. Debrief the activity using some of these questions.

Group Dynamic Focused Questions

- What group roles did individuals take on? Who was the initiator, the cheerleader, the expert? Were any roles missing?
- Are those roles you typically take on? Why or why not? How do certain roles help or hinder the group results?
- What creates a successful group dynamic? Did you finish the task and also work together well?

Planning Focused Questions

- What happened? What was your process?
- Were you satisfied with the results? What would have led to better results?
- How much time did you spend identifying who had strengths that might help you? How much time did you spend discussing strategies?
- What is the relationship of planning to results?
- What assumptions did you make about the task?

Final Summary Questions

- What would you have done differently?
- What did you learn from this experience?
- How can you apply what you learned in this activity to your workplace?

InSider's Tips

- Be sure to remind the participants that they can use the items at their workspace without giving away that some teams are more creative and use the Post-its as flags to add height or use the markers to color the marshmallows to add beauty or use the plate to add stability. This leads to great discussion about creativity at the end of the activity.
- The height requirement must be just longer than two times the spaghetti you provide. They need more than two "floors," which makes the models a little wobbly.
- Most groups jump right in but then pause later to try to "fix" their earlier decisions, which can also lead to rich discussion.
- Most groups will look at the spaghetti and marshmallow materials and start building a structure like the old Tinkertoys®, using the spaghetti as the sticks and the marshmallows as the connectors. This is a great opportunity for

discussion about how sometimes our previous experiences get in the way of success (doing things the way they have always been done). The problem is that the spaghetti breaks easily and the marshmallows are pliable. The participants recognize those issues early so they put several spaghetti sticks together, which makes the "floors" heavy, so they start adding support stakes on the outside or risk having their second floors collapse.

- The best solution is to put the spaghetti in a big bundle and telescope it up to over 20 inches tall, using the marshmallows at the base like a rubber band— a solid structure rather than an external framework.
- Some groups borrow ideas and materials from other groups. This leads to a discussion about the benefits of learning from external groups and collaboration.
- Some groups have people with building or engineering expertise. They often steer the group astray because they don't think outside of the box.
- Some teams have people who don't speak up when they have a better idea, or they have someone who dominates the process. This leads to discussion about the benefits and drawbacks of having a naysayer or a gatekeeper in the group.
- Some groups get messy with mashing the marshmallows. Have hand wipes, a large trash can, and table-cleaning products available.
- I originally found a similar activity in a teacher's guide for a communications textbook, but I can't remember which one. I've since adapted it as a team-building and group dynamic activity, making up scenarios and changing the rules as needed to make a point.

Patti Ulwelling is an organization development specialist for a mid-size insurance company in Milwaukee, Wisconsin, where she is focused on management and leadership development. She was previously a training manager at an investment company, director of a continuing education program, facilitator for a community leadership program, and adjunct professor at a private university. Patti is a past president of the Southeast Wisconsin ASTD chapter. She has acquired an M.A. in communication, MBA, SPHR, and certificate in organization development.

Patti Ulwelling
7514 W. Dakota Street
West Allis, WI 53219
(414) 321.4727 or (414) 347.6970
Email: patti.ulwelling@mgic.com
ASTD Chapter: Southeast Wisconsin

Straw Towers

Submitted by Deborah Covin Wilson

Overview
Plastic straws are used in this activity to build tall towers that illustrate why building a strong foundation is central to successful careers and strong teams.

Objectives
- To demonstrate the importance of having a strong foundation for career growth, leadership, or other aspects of development
- To illustrate the importance of planning prior to undertaking a task, especially a group task

Audience
Any number in teams of three (For large numbers of participants, such as seventy-five, you could have groups of five to seven.)

Time Estimate
45 minutes, 15 for the activity and 30 to debrief

Materials and Equipment
- Forty to fifty plastic drinking straws for each team
- Tape measure

Area Setup
Individual groups need a surface to build a straw tower; the floor may be used

Process
1. Divide the group into teams of three to five participants.
2. Give each team forty to fifty plastic straws. Each team should have exactly the same number of straws.
3. Tell the participants that their task is to build the tallest free-standing tower that they can in 15 minutes. Tell them that "free-standing" means that the tower does not have to be supported by leaning against a table or any other object.

4. Explain that they are allowed to use *only* the plastic straws to construct the tower. They can manipulate the straws in any fashion, but must not use a scissors, tape, glue, or other tool. State that the team with the tallest free-standing tower will be declared the winner.

5. Start the activity. After 15 minutes, call time and measure the tallest free-standing tower. The team with the tallest free-standing tower wins.

6. Debrief the exercise. This is the key in the learning. Use questions such as these:
   - How do you feel about your tower?
   - Why didn't you build a tower as tall as you wanted to build it?
   - How much time did you spend planning? How did this affect your results?
   - What did you do that helped contribute to your success?
   - What did you learn about yourself?
   - What could you do to improve your contribution next time?
   - How solid is the foundation for your tower?
   - What do you think are the key lessons for your team?
   - What could your team do better next time?
   - In what situations will you be able to use what you learned today?

6. Summarize by stating that the key learning is that, without a firm foundation and supplemental support, you cannot have a successful structure. The same is true with a career, a successful team, or a successful leader (depending upon your topic). The second key learning is recognizing the importance of planning first. Most teams dive right in and begin to build without any planning.

InSider's Tips

- Many teams rush to start building the tallest tower and fail to plan how to accomplish the task.
- Many teams fail to build a strong foundation and supplemental supports to maintain the structure's height.
- Many teams fail to use the strengths of all the team members.

170

Deborah Covin Wilson, CPLP, is a seasoned workplace learning and performance professional with more than twenty-five years of experience. She is the principal of Wilson Associates, an organization development and training firm that specializes in organizational effectiveness, coaching, mentoring, and training. Deborah has served as the director of career development at a major research university. She served ASTD at the national level as a member of the National Advisors for Chapter, a member of the 2011 ICE Program Advisory Committee, CPLP reviewer, and volunteer coordinator for the 2010 ICE conference. Locally, Deborah has served as the board chair and the president of the Greater Atlanta chapter.

Deborah Covin Wilson, CPLP
3640 Masters Road
Ellenwood, GA 30294
(404) 667.4277
Email: wilsonassociates@mindspring.com
Website: www.waconsulting.net
ASTD Chapter: Greater Atlanta

Hula Hoop Challenge

Submitted by Joseph Sanchez

Overview

Trust and leadership are explored in this activity that requires blindfolded team members to navigate to the center of a Hula Hoop® placed on the floor and pick it up with minimal direction or assistance from the other team members.

Objectives

- To build teams and enhance trust
- To create an opportunity to discuss the relationship between trust and leadership

Audience

Any number of participants divided into teams of four to six

Time Estimate

40 to 60 minutes

Materials and Equipment

- One Hula Hoop® for each team
- Two scarves that can act as blindfolds for each team
- (Optional) Small prizes for the team members who were willing to be blindfolded

Process

1. Introduce this activity by stating that building trust is important in a team and that communication is an important element of building trust. Explain that this activity provides an opportunity to discuss both of these topics.
2. Create teams of four to six participants and ask for two volunteers from each team who are willing to be blindfolded. Ask these volunteers to leave the room for a few minutes.
3. Once the volunteers have left the room, give two blindfolds to the remaining members of each team. Explain that when the volunteer team members return they will first be blindfolded (ask some to assist the volunteers in this task).

Explain that once all the volunteers are blindfolded you will place one Hula Hoop on the floor for each team. Ask for volunteers or assign someone on each team as the object spotter.

4. Now explain that the task is to move the two volunteers from each team into the center of the Hula Hoop without telling them there is a Hula Hoop on the ground. The team members providing direction cannot touch or allow the blindfolded team members to hold onto to them as a way to guide them to the Hula Hoop. Remind the participants that they may not say the words "Hula Hoop" out loud. Instead, the team members may only use the following words when giving instructions to their blindfolded teammates: Left, Right, Turn, Up, Down, and Stop. Also remind them that they may not touch the Hula Hoop. However, note that the two blindfolded teammates may touch each other during the activity.

5. Finally, explain to the participants that once they get the blindfolded teammates to the Hula Hoop and in the center, they must have them stand in the center back-to-back. Once the two people are in the back-to-back position, the team may use additional words to guide them; however they still may not say the words "Hula Hoop." Despite this prohibition, the team must instruct the blindfolded members to lift the Hula Hoop at their feet without bending over. When the volunteers have completed this task, the activity is complete. *Safety Note:* Non-blindfolded teammates must serve as safety monitors to prevent blindfolded team members from tripping or walking into objects. They can use the word STOP!

6. After all instructions are given and clarified if necessary, retrieve the volunteers who have been waiting outside. Ask them to return to their teams to begin the activity. When all the volunteers are blindfolded, tell them that their team members will ask them to move to a specific spot to pick up an item, but that they must accomplish this task by following the directions of Left, Right, Turn, Up, Down, and Stop.

7. Assure all volunteers that their safety is the top priority and if they hear the word "STOP" to freeze all movement.

8. Begin the activity after you have the attention of the spotters and placed the Hula Hoops on the floor about 10 feet away from each team. Assign each Hula Hoop by pointing to the team and the Hula Hoop.

9. When all the Hula Hoops are in place, tell the participants to begin the activity by calling out instructions to their blindfolded members. Remind them one more time to be safe.

10. When both blindfolded teammates from all teams are standing in the Hula Hoop with the Hula Hoop in their hands, cheer and applaud the success. Invite the volunteers to remove their blindfolds.

11. Discuss what was learned and experienced. Suggested debriefing questions include:
    - If you had your eyes open during the activity, what were you thinking?
    - If you had your eyes blindfolded, what were you thinking as your team was giving instructions? (Relate their response to learning a new job, following a new leader, or working on a new team.)
    - What were the challenges of giving instructions? (Relate responses to working with new supervisors, policies, or top-down directions or leadership/ team styles.)
    - How much trust was required to be successful?
    - What is the relationship between trust and leadership?
    - How do you build trust? How do leaders build trust?
    - How do some of the aspects of this activity relate to your job?
    - How can you apply the lessons learning to the workplace?

12. Give another round of applause to the volunteers and give them prizes for helping to make the learning a rich experience.

InSider's Tips

- Remember that the Hula Hoop must remain unnamed to those who are blindfolded. Therefore, do not list the name of this activity as "Hula Hoop" on your agenda and be sure the Hula Hoops are not visible to participants as they enter the room.
- Once the two people are inside a Hula Hoop, they can balance and support each other.
- To grab the Hula Hoop, they each can slip one foot under it and lift their legs (keeping them straight) so that the Hula Hoop can be raised to a position to be grabbed. Another way the Hula Hoop can be lifted is by having one teammate stand on the Hula Hoop, gently putting forward pressure on it. This motion will cause the Hula Hoop to lift off the ground high enough for the other person to grab it with his or her foot.

Joseph Sanchez has been with LifeShare Blood Centers in Shreveport, Louisiana, since January 2005 as the education and training director. Prior to joining LifeShare, Joseph served in the U.S. Air Force for thirty years. He has been involved with employee development for more than twenty-five years. Joseph is the current past-president of the local ASTD chapter in Shreveport and stays involved in local community and business events. He has two graduate degrees from Louisiana Tech University, one in industrial and organizational psychology and the other in counseling and guidance.

Joseph Sanchez
Director, Education and Training
LifeShare Blood Centers
8910 Linwood Avenue
Shreveport, LA 71106–6508
(318) 222.7770 or (318) 673.1543
Email: jsanchez@lifeshare.org
ASTD Chapter: North Louisiana

From Seeing to Achieving

Submitted by Jeanne Baer

Overview

Participants connected by a rope and blindfolded must figure out how to create a square shape by practicing the cooperative and collaborative skills essential to highly successful teams.

Objectives

- To verbalize that achievement starts with a clear vision
- To internalize lessons about aspects of successful teamwork

Audience

Fourteen to forty participants, in two competing teams if more than twenty-six

Time Estimate

30 to 40 minutes, including 20 minutes to debrief

Materials and Equipment

- One blindfold for each participant
- A rope long enough for each participant to carry about 3 feet of it, for example, if there are fourteen participants, the rope should be 42 to 45 feet long (If the group is large, you will need one rope for each team.)
- One Debriefing Questions handout for each participant
- Pencils or pens for all participants

Area Setup

Because you may be working with a long piece of rope, this activity requires a large amount of space if you have a large group. You must have enough space for each rope to be laid in a line across the room so the group can line up on one side of the rope and enough space in two directions to form a square. If you will have two groups, they must be far enough apart so that the blindfolded members do not run into each other during the activity.

If you have good weather and level ground, you may wish to conduct the activity outdoors.

Process

1. Before the activity, arrange the rope in a straight line on the floor.

2. Invite participants to line up on one side of the rope. Then give each participant a blindfold, and instruct them to put on their blindfolds. Once everyone is blindfolded, instruct them to carefully bend down and pick up the rope.

3. Explain that their goal, as teammates connected to each other by the rope, is to form a square shape. Remind them that the first step for a team to achieve a goal is to agree on and envision the final result, and, "Since everyone can picture a square, this should be easy!" Of course, working without the benefit of eyesight adds to the challenge. Say, "When you have consensus as a team that you have, in fact, formed a square shape, then very carefully bend over, place the rope on the floor, and remove your blindfolds to see how square your shape actually is." Allow about 10 to 15 minutes for them to complete the activity.

4. As the group is working, refrain from making any comments or giving hints. Take care to ensure participants' safety; be sure people aren't running into objects. Once the group has finished the activity, lead them in applause for a job well done.

5. Ask them to take their seats again, and debrief the activity. Give each person a copy of the Debriefing Questions and a pen or pencil. Suggest that the group individually think about what happened during the activity and jot down a few notes in response to the questions. Allow about 5 minutes, and then lead a group discussion using the questions to guide discussion.
   - What happened and why?
   - How was this activity like "real life" as you try to achieve a goal with the people you work with?
   - What helped you succeed?
   - What did you or others do that got in the way of success?
   - What are some of the "ahas!" you experienced from this activity?
   - Based on your insights from participating in this activity, what do you want to take back to the workplace?
   - What do you want to start doing, stop doing, or continue doing?

InSider's Tips

- Participants experience and realize several aspects of teamwork as a result of this activity:
  - They must adjust their communication to fit the situation. For example, it's not enough to call out, "I'm over here!" when no one can see where the voice is coming from.
  - To accomplish great results, *everyone* must commit and participate fully. When some "opt out" and simply stand in one spot, the group is unable to form the required square.
  - To accomplish goals, it's wise to be open to new, creative ideas and not everyone can be talking (or listening) at once!
  - Great leadership can spring from anywhere, when they allow it. Being blindfolded is a great way to level the playing field, and it is often *not* the positional leader who suddenly suggests, "Hey, I know—let's count off and divide by four. That's the number of people who should be on each side!"
  - In every team endeavor, there will be conflict between members who simply want to "get it done" and those who want to "get it right." Some members are always ready to "call it good" and put the rope on the floor, while perfectionists want to continue working on the task. Team members must be willing to compromise or negotiate these differences.
- There are two situations whereby having a participant join you in observing the activity, rather than participating in it, might be appropriate:
  - If a participant is very anxious about being blindfolded.
  - If the number of participants is too easily dividable by four. If there are sixteen or twenty participants, for example, the task is not enough of a challenge to provoke insights. However, if you ask one participant to "Help keep people safe," fifteen or nineteen people will be challenged by the activity.
- This activity carries with it some lessons about listening, communicating in new ways, negotiating, arriving at shared understanding and consensus, being open to others' ideas, being an active participant in achieving a goal, and more.
- If you have more than twenty-six participants, form two teams, and invite them to "compete to see who can form the squarest square." After the first group has finished and participants have removed their blindfolds to look at the shape they have created, invite them to very quietly join you in observing the second

178

group. Their observations will prompt additional insights during the debriefing discussion.

- If a group seems to be finishing too quickly, make this a challenging activity. Approach the group and announce, "I'm so sorry, but 'Tina,' here has been assigned to another project. You'll have to complete the square without her." This life-like event will give the group more of a challenge and more to talk about during the debriefing step. You can also (or instead) *add* a new member to the team, in the middle of the task. This will reveal how team members welcome and accommodate a new member when they were already functioning quite well without him or her.

- Use this activity with larger groups. Fewer than thirteen make the activity too easy to provoke insights.

- I heard about the activity in 1992 and have been using it ever since. It may be one of those "classics" that has been around forever. The option of adding or taking away participants in the middle of the activity was my idea, but then again, maybe others have had the same idea. I wish I knew whom to thank for creating it in the first place.

Jeanne Baer is president of Creative Training Solutions, a cutting-edge company that helps teams and individuals improve vital interpersonal skills, addressing leadership, customer service, selling, persuasive speaking, team building, and more. A well-known author, Jeanne has had management advice and training designs published in eighteen books by McGraw-Hill, Harvard Business School Press, ASTD, Pfeiffer, and others. She's been quoted by *Investor's Business Daily,* and has written more than two hundred "Managing Smart" articles for *Strictly Business* and other magazines. Jeanne has been active in ASTD since 1987 and has been honored with local and national awards for her leadership in the profession.

Jeanne Baer
1649 South 21st Street
Lincoln, NE 68502
(402) 475.1127
Email: jbaer@ cts-online.net
Website: www.cts-online.net
ASTD Chapter: Lincoln

Debriefing Questions

Think about what just happened and jot down a few thoughts in answer to the following questions.

- What happened and why?

- How was this activity like "real life" as you try to achieve a goal with the people you work with?

- What helped you succeed?

- What did you or others do that got in the way of success?

- What are some of the "ahas!" you experienced from this activity?

- Based on your insights from participating in this activity, what do you want to take back to the workplace?

- What do you want to start doing?

- What do you want to stop doing?

- What will you continue doing?

Think on Your Feet

Submitted by Sharon Dera

Overview

Participants must use all their "resources" and strategic thinking skills to win a race that is a real balancing act.

Objectives

- To understand the importance of critical thinking and its role in problem solving
- To understand how to build a cohesive, results-oriented team from a group of diverse individuals

Audience

Fifteen to sixty participants, in two to four teams with a maximum of fifteen on any team

Time Estimate

60 to 90 minutes

Materials and Equipment

- Cut 2-by-4 boards into 12-inch lengths, fifteen per team; one per team member
- Stop watch
- Four plastic cones (two cones indicate the start line and two cones indicate the finish line)
- (Optional) Three bandanas per team

Area Setup

This activity works inside or outside. Allow for a 40-foot by 50-foot open area, or larger. Set the starting cones far enough apart for individuals to line up behind them. The ending cones may be anywhere from 10 to 50 feet from the starting point, based on the team size, team performance, and capacity of the area. For example, for a small team containing five to ten people you might place the ending cones 20 to 30 feet away. For a large team of ten to fifteen people, put the cones 30 to 50 feet away. The "finish line" cone can be placed anywhere by the facilitator, depending on team size (sufficient space for team), team performance (cone can be moved closer if team is struggling or farther away if team is speedy), and capacity of area (may be limited if restricted by obstacles).

The cone for the "finish line" can be put in place before or during the activity. If before the activity, the facilitator places the cone at chosen location. If during the activity, the facilitator explains the "finish line" is undetermined at this time, then later places the cone at a chosen location.

Note: Regardless of whether you are conducting the activity inside or outside, the area needs to be open and free of obstacles.

Process

1. Stack the wooden planks in a pile at the starting line for each team. There should be one plank for each team member. Divide the participants equally into two to four teams, depending on how many participants you have.
2. Explain that the objective is to successfully cross the finish line as a team, without committing any fouls or losing any team members.
3. Explain the activity rules and then answer any questions:
   - This is a timed event. Teams will have 45 minutes to complete the activity: 5 minutes to strategize, and 40 minutes to execute their plans. To be successful, all team members must cross the finish line within the 40-minute time limit.
   - Individuals must work as a team to cross the finish line using their "resource" (wood) to traverse the open area. Tell team members, "The plank of wood represents your 'resource.' You must always protect your 'resource.' Otherwise you may lose it."
   - Once past the start line, individuals cannot step off their planks until they cross over the finish line. If a person steps off or falls off a plank and his or her foot touches the ground, that person has fouled, and the person (along with that plank) returns to the start line.
   - Safety is paramount. Feet stay on the plank. No climbing or "piggybacking" allowed. Tell them that unsafe behavior can lead to participants being disqualified.
   - You will be judge, determine fouls, and call disqualifications as necessary. Tell them that you might also interject obstacles that will ensure that this activity more accurately represents what happens at work.
4. Ask the teams to distribute planks of wood, one for each team member.
5. Announced that you are starting your stop watch for their strategy sessions.

6. Allow teams 5 minutes to strategize. Call time when appropriate.
7. State that the participants may now begin to traverse the course. Start your stop watch again.
8. Allow 40 minutes for completion of task. Call time when appropriate.
9. Conduct a large-group debriefing using questions such as these:
   - What did you think of the activity?
   - Did your team have a strategy? If so, what type of strategy was planned? If not, why not?
   - Did the strategy work? If so, why? If not, why not?
   - How did you differentiate between creative and critical thinking?
   - How are both creative and critical thinking important to problem solving?
   - What observations did you make during the strategizing session?
   - What observations did you make during the execution of the activity?
   - How was this activity similar to completing a project on the job?
   - What aspects helped to build your team?
   - What was most significant in achieving your results?
   - What could you have done differently to strengthen your team?
   - What did you learn from participating in the activity that you will take back to work with you?

InSider's Tips

- It is not necessary to specify the exact finish line at the beginning of the activity. Point out that many organizations begin projects without the "end in mind," having to adjust as they go. If asked, just state, "The finish line is out there somewhere," pointing away from the start line. Once the activity begins, you can place the plastic cones where you want the finish line to be.
- You can also move the finish line at any time during the activity. State that, "In organizations project timelines often change. Here is your new timeline/goal/finish line." Moving the finish line gives you the flexibility of monitoring the pace of the activity. For example, if a team is moving fast, without committing fouls or having disqualifications, the finish line can be moved farther away. If a team is struggling with fouls and disqualifications, the finish line can be moved closer.

- You may create and add obstacles to the activity to change the dynamics of the team and enhance the learning. The reason for obstacles can be related to any industry's process or procedure. Examples of obstacles include:
  - Blindfold a person(s) for a few minutes (using the bandanas) to represent a lack of management, lack of communication, unavailability, out of office, at lunch/break, attending a meeting, removed from the project, employee injured on the job, a cut in personnel, or others.
  - Mute a person for a few minutes to represent a lack of communication, employee excluded from project, employee out sick, or missed deadline.
  - Confiscate/remove any abandoned/unattended planks to represent loss of resources, budget cuts, or a cut in hours. Note that an unattended plank means that no one is standing on or touching the plank. One of the rules states, "The plank of wood represents your resource. You must always protect your resource, otherwise you may lose it." That's how they lose it. Watch for opportunities to confiscate and remove any planks.
  - Disqualify any team member acting in an unsafe manner. The person(s) along with his or her resource leaves the team.
- This activity engages all participants in teamwork and communication, demonstrating critical thinking skills for adapting to any obstacles, defines leadership roles and how leaders engage members in power plays for authority and control.

Sharon Dera, CPLP, has more than seventeen years of experience in needs assessment, human performance, process improvement, and organization development. Her broad experience was acquired by working in the retail, finance, healthcare, government, manufacturing, hospitality, and travel industries in operations, business management, customer service, sales, communications, marketing, succession planning, leadership, coaching, and training. Sharon is owner and CEO of The Proficience Group, Inc., working in partnership with organizations to identify the root cause of performance deficiencies and determine the best solutions/interventions that close a performance gap. The company lends a "fresh set of eyes," exposing possible blind spots. Sharon is currently serving on the National ASTD Chapter Recognition Committee. She earned an MBA from the University of Dallas.

Sharon Dera, CPLP
8948 Random Road
Fort Worth, TX 76179
(817) 236.7594
Email: sdera@charter.net
Website: www.proficiencegroup.com
ASTD Chapter: Fort Worth Mid-Cities

Chapter 8

Leadership: What It Takes to Make a Leader

More organizations have committed to spending more money on leadership development in the past couple of years than on any other topic. Is it any wonder? The most valuable investment any organization can make is the development of its future leaders. This vital task ensures that leaders possess competencies to achieve the organization's strategy, continue to mature the organizational culture, and inspire the workforce.

Due to the upcoming Baby Boomer exodus from the workforce, many organizations face losing 30 to 50 percent of their key leaders in the next half-dozen years. Unfortunately, many organizations have been lax in developing new leaders to replace the current generation of leaders. At the same time, the essential leadership skills expected of new leaders continues to climb. Senior leaders' positions are more challenging than ever and require a broader range of job experience and a surprisingly long list of competencies.

In addition to what we typically think of as required leadership skills, the next generation of leaders must bring a sophisticated set of new skills. The next generation must be visionary coalition-builders; internationally astute; quick learners and fast implementers; highly creative; comfortable with change, volatility, and ambiguity; intimately aware of changing customer needs; agile enough to revamp operations instantly; and able to produce rapid results in all areas.

The breadth of required leadership competencies demonstrates that every forward-looking trainer must work to meet this challenge. Ask yourself questions such as: "What am I doing to prepare our next generation of leaders? What skills are required for our organization? Am I prepared to deliver skills and knowledge that will help future leaders learn and prepare for their jobs?"

185

The journey to becoming a good leader may be long and filled with potential potholes—and may even lead to a few dead ends. This chapter will help you prepare leaders by addressing critical topics that will make their journey easier, including skills such as: strategic thinking, setting goals, building trust, addressing values, creating a vision, and focusing on ethics.

All of the activities in this chapter will give your leaders a chance to practice and improve their decision making capacity. The first activity, "The Great Leadership Debate," presented by Lisa Rike, addresses the importance of critical thinking in leaders. Barb Crockett's activity, "What a Difference a Goal Makes," is short but offers a tremendous amount of learning. She introduces an effective experiential learning activity to show leaders the importance of setting specific and measurable goals. Mel Schnapper, from Holland, introduces "Create a Vision," which he has used all over the world. Lisa Rike's second activity in this chapter, "Power of Questions," demonstrates how you can show your leaders the importance of asking questions. Cindy Phillips adds a trust activity.

The last two activities address how leaders make ethical and value-driven decisions. Both are heady and require an investment of time (close to two hours each), but they are well worth the time spent. Jeff Furman introduces us to ethicist Randy Cohen and uses his *New York Times* column, "The Ethicist," as a basis for learning. Abu Dhabi learning professionals P. Sethu Madhavan and Yehya M. Al Marzouqu demonstrate how difficult it can be to make decisions based on values.

Is leadership development on your action list? These activities are sure to help you.

The Great Leadership Debate

Submitted by Lisa Rike

Overview
Leaders in this activity use a traditional debate format to gain insights into critical thinking and looking at both sides of an issue. It's a great activity for leaders and high-potential contributors.

Objectives
- To develop critical thinking skills in leaders
- To practice considering different points of view
- To make informed decisions

Audience
Six to twelve members of a leadership team, with additional participants used as coaches for each side

Time Estimate
45 to 55 minutes

Materials and Equipment
- Flip chart with extra paper
- Markers

Area Setup
Any room in which half of the participants can comfortably sit across from the other half

Process
1. Ask the participants for examples of real issues they face as a leadership team that they believe hinder the team's job performance. Examples include:
   - Unequal company benefits to full-time and temporary employees
   - Leaders showing favoritism to certain staff
   - Whether the employees trust the company leaders
   - Numerous meetings that interfere with leaders' ability to spend "face time" with staff and complete tasks

- Lack of relevant information communicated consistently throughout the organization

2. Describe the goals of the activity and explain that the participants will have an opportunity to practice various aspects of leadership, including the skills needed to make informed decisions, practice critical thinking, and other aspects important for an issue of their choosing.

3. Select or ask the participants to select the issue they will debate. Write the selected issue on a flip-chart page so that all can see it.

4. Randomly divide participants into two equal groups. Arrange the participants' chairs into two lines facing each other. Tables can be used, but they are not required.

5. When the participants are seated, assign one side to debate the affirmative view and the other side to debate the negative view.

6. Explain these rules to the participants:
   - They will debate the group's chosen issue from two opposing points of view, for example, whether or not an issue or situation exists or whether or not the benefits are worth the risks.
   - Explain that each side is allowed to make one statement/point at a time. Once the point or statement is made, the other side has a chance to either refute the statement/point or state something that supports their own assigned point of view.
   - Everyone on each side must stay in character and represent their assigned points of view and make their points as valid as possible.
   - It is not necessary to rebut every single point raised by the opposition. Single out the opposition's main arguments and attack those first. Show the weaknesses in the other team's case and show why your case is better.
   - All members of each side must participate. No one may dominate the debate. Participants should encourage one another to contribute.

7. Ask one side to start. Establish a time limit for the debate, usually 8 to 10 minutes. Stop the debate at the agreed on time.

8. Tell the participants to switch roles so that the side making the original affirmative argument is now on the negative side and the participants on the original negative side will now take the affirmative side.

9. Restart the debate and allow it to continue for approximately 5 minutes.

10. Stop the debate and ask these questions to debrief the experience:
    - How was your experience debating both sides of an issue?
    - Which was easiest to argue?
    - What argument was more difficult for you?

- What did you learn being forced to look at both sides?
- As a leader, what is the value of looking at both sides?
- What skills are required to make informed decisions? What do you consider to be the risks, impact, benefits, or advantages of informed decisions?
- How can this type of activity help you to become better strategic thinkers or to make more informed decisions?
- Why is critical thinking an important skill for leaders?
- How can you continue to practice the skills we've practiced here today?
- What might you do differently on the job as a result of participating in this activity?

11. Make the point that being a strategic leader means seriously considering both sides and all points of view before making decisions.

InSider's Tips

- I've used this activity for years. If the participants struggle to come up with a point to make, don't let them pass. Let them know they are expected to respond as if they were committed to that point of view.
- Many participants tell me that they had an "aha" about the issue during these debates.

Lisa Rike brings over twenty years of experience in the adult learning and development field. Her experience as an instructional designer and facilitator spans multiple topics such as different aspects in leadership skills and team development, interpersonal and behavioral style training, train-the-trainer, communication, coaching, and presentation/facilitation skills. Lisa consults to Fortune 500 companies as well to as small and mid-size organizations. She has designed and facilitated leadership and staff development initiatives that range in scope from improving team performance to permeating company culture to bring about improved business results across organizations.

Lisa Rike
853 West Oak Street
Zionsville, IN 46077
(317) 727.6520
Email: tailoredtraining@earthlink.net or lisar@etindy.com
Website: www.etindy.com
ASTD Chapter: Central Indiana

What a Difference a Goal Makes

Submitted by Barbara Crockett

Overview

Teams of leaders work on an assigned task that is either very achievable or extremely difficult, depending on the assignment instructions, and learn valuable lessons about goal setting.

Objectives

- To demonstrate the benefits of specific and measurable goals
- To discuss the importance for leaders to set specific goals
- To have fun through team competition

Audience

Three teams comprised of five to ten leaders each (If you have more than thirty participants, divide the group into six teams and double the required materials.)

Time Estimate

20 minutes

Materials and Equipment

- Three sheets of paper prepared as instructed below, one question per page
- Pens or pencils for participants

Area Setup

Enough space so that the three teams are far enough away from each other that they cannot easily hear the other discussions

Preparation

Create the instruction sheets by writing one of the following on three separate sheets of paper:

      Sheet 1.   Name as many ideas for incentives as you can.

      Sheet 2.   Name as many ideas for incentives that you can in 10 minutes.

      Sheet 3.   Name fifty ideas for incentives in 10 minutes.

Fold each sheet in half and write the task number on the folded sheets: 1, 2, or 3.

Process

1. Start the activity by saying, "We are going to have a contest. Let's get into three teams by counting off by 3's."
2. Assign a location for each of the three groups and tell the participants to move to the assigned space. Continue by saying, "Each group has an assignment on a slip of paper. After I distribute all three sheets, you may look at them and share them within your team, but don't read the instructions out loud. Talk among yourselves but don't let the other teams hear your task or your ideas." Tell the participants that they will have 10 minutes to complete the assignments listed on their sheets.
3. Ask the group to begin working and start the timing period.
4. At the end of 10 minutes, call time. Ask each group to count the number of ideas they were able to list. Groups 1 and 2 usually have about the same number on their lists. Group 3 typically blows away the competition.
5. Ask each team to read their assignment out loud beginning with Group 1 and to state how many ideas they listed.
6. Summarize with a discussion around these questions:
   - How many of you were surprised that you had different tasks? Why?
   - What were the differences?
   - How do you think the different wording of the tasks affected the results?
   - What were you measuring yourselves against to determine success?
     Note: The members of Group 3 count and measure themselves against the target the entire time.
   - What can you surmise based on the results?
   - What advice would you give leaders about setting goals?
   - How can you apply this to your work? Personal life?

InSider's Tips

- I have tried variations on this activity. For example, I tried one hundred ideas instead of fifty, but one hundred is not attainable. I have tried 5 minutes instead of 10 but have found that 10 minutes works best.
- I have conducted this activity eight to ten times with different groups and have always achieved similar results.

- It is a good illustration of SMART goal setting. Setting the time limit for Group 2 did not make a significant difference, but setting the specific goal of fifty did. Usually Groups 1 and 2 don't even count how many ideas were on their lists until asked to do so.

Barbara Crockett is an independent contractor focused on improving the business and leadership skills of individuals by designing and delivering learning solutions. She is an associate instructor in the Maryville University School of Business School, facilitator for Selsius Corporate and Career Training in Belleville, Illinois, and facilitator for the Center for Financial Training in St. Louis, Missouri. Her personal philosophy of learning is to "make it active" and to always include the question, "How can I apply this to my work/world?"

Barbara Crockett
9857 Berwick Drive
St. Louis, MO 63123
(314) 313.8575
Email: barb0730@gmail.com
ASTD Chapter: St. Louis Metropolitan

Create a Vision

Submitted by Mel Schnapper

Overview

Participants are asked to draw upon their artistic skills to draw pictures that represent a higher functioning, more cohesive group or team. Appropriate for any team, department, or group.

Objectives

- To create a pictorial vision of how a group works together
- To identify ways a group could function better in the future
- To discuss best practices for leaders who are establishing a vision

Audience

Up to twenty participants from intact work teams

Time Estimate

30 to 60 minutes, depending on discussion

Materials and Equipment

- Flip chart with paper for each subgroup
- One set of markers of various colors for each subgroup
- (Optional) Crayons
- Masking tape

Area Setup

Tables arranged so that participants can work in groups

Process

1. Ask the participants whether they have ever had a mental picture of how they would like their group to work. State that this activity will give them an opportunity to create and share their ideas. Ask them to form into their work groups of four or five each. (Divide larger work groups into smaller subgroups.) Give each group a flip chart and a set of markers.

2. Tell the participants to use the markers (and crayons if provided) to create a picture on the flip-chart without words or numbers. Ask half of the groups to draw a picture that represents how they function as a team/department/ organization today. Ask the other groups to draw a picture of how they would like to function in the future. Tell them they have 20 minutes to create their pictures.

3. After the allotted time, ask each group to select someone to present their pictures to the large group.

4. Ask the groups assigned to draw a picture of how they function today to present their pictures first. Hang the flip-chart pages along a wall. Applaud after each presentation.

5. Ask the groups assigned to draw a picture of how they would like to function in the future to present their pictures. Hang the flip-chart pages along a wall. Applaud after each presentation.

6. Lead a discussion about the pictures using some of these questions:
   • What happened as you worked together? What was the atmosphere like?
   • What did you learn about yourself? What did you learn about your group?
   • How does this relate to what happens on a day-to-day basis in this group?
   • What differences do you see in the pictures of how you function today and how you would like to function in the future?
   • What can you do differently that would move you closer to how you would like to function?
   • What did this activity tell you about visions?
   • How could a leader use this concept to create a vision?
   • What advice would you give a leader who is establishing a vision?
   • How can you ensure that you make changes that move you closer to your desired future?

7. Summarize by encouraging the small groups to come together again to establish action plans for future improvement.

InSider's Tips

- You may wish to use an observer to see how each small group handles the assignment. These observations (and your own) can be shared in the debriefing period.
- Be flexible regarding time and allow for discussion going in a direction you did not expect.
- This activity works in every country where I've used it including Nigeria, Indonesia, and China.

Mel Schnapper is an international consultant (native Washingtonian), now working in Lesotho. He has worked in over twenty countries doing organization development, business process analysis, team building, and some traditional personnel work. Mel recently published a book on performance metrics, *Value-Based Metrics for Improving Results,* with a methodology for measuring any kind of performance, especially when people, even colleagues, say "You can't measure it!" He has an extensive career in corporate America with companies such as Quaker Oats, Chicago Board Options Exchange, AT&T, and American Express. Although he prefers the exotic environments outside the U.S., he does miss D.C. now and then and comes back about twice a year.

Mel Schnapper
Meidoornplein 18, 1112 EK
Diemen, Holland
Phone: 31–2040205851
Email: mel@schnapper.com
Website:www.schnapper.com
ASTD Chapter: Metro Washington, D.C.

Power of Questions

Submitted by Lisa Rike

Overview

Participants use role play to switch between the positions of leader and employee and discover the value and appropriate use of an "asking" leadership style versus a "telling" style.

Objectives

- To improve leaders' listening skills and their understanding of others
- To discuss how asking more questions can benefit leaders

Audience

Two to twenty leaders

Time Estimate

30 minutes or more

Materials and Equipment

- Flip chart
- Markers

Area Setup

A room with adequate space for small groups to gather apart from other groups

Process

1. Ask participants for examples of topics leaders discuss with their employees, such as performance or attitude issues. Write these suggestions on a flip-chart page.
2. Divide the participants into subgroups of four or five participants each. Tell participants that each group will designate a leader and an employee. The rest of the group will be the observers. The "leader" will facilitate a discussion with the "employee" based on one of the topics you recorded on the flip chart. During that discussion, the leader may only ask questions. The leader must keep the interaction going and not pause to think for more than a 10 or

15 seconds before asking the next question. Comment on the activity by saying, "Here's a tip: Leaders, listen intently about what the employee is saying and ask each question based on what you hear to probe the situation further."

3. Tell the observers that their job is to keep the leaders honest in asking only questions. If the leader "chokes" and doesn't ask a question or hesitates for more than 15 seconds, one of the group observers should volunteer a question or volunteer to be the leader. Each observer must stay focused on the interaction between the leader and the employee and be ready to ask a question based on what he or she just heard. Observers can volunteer each other to be the next leaders as well. Tell everyone this first interaction will last about 5 minutes. Tell them to select a topic and to begin the discussion.

4. Begin timing the activity.

5. After 5 minutes, call time and ask the small groups to select another topic and switch roles. Tell the groups that they should select another topic to use from the flip chart at any time. Remind them that everyone should have a chance to be the leader and that they should allow each member be in the role of the leader for at least 3 to 4 minutes before switching.

6. Roam around the room during the activity and listen to the interactions. If a group is stuck and not sure of a question to ask, coach the group to ask a very broad, open-ended question such as:
   • "What else contributes to this situation?"
   • "What else can you tell me about how that happened?"
   • "What else have you tried?"
   • "What else can you try?"
   • "What might hinder your progress?"
   Remind the participants that asking broad, open-ended questions allows the leader to learn more about the situation and gather their thoughts about what questions to ask next.

7. Stop the small group activity after everyone in the group has been a leader.

8. Ask the participants to take their seats and summarize the activity using questions like these to debrief the experience:
   • What was it like to be able to only ask questions?
   • Did you find yourself asking leading questions such as "Have you tried. . .?" and broad, open-ended questions such as "What are your ideas to improve this situation?" and closed-ended questions where "yes" or "no" are the only responses?
   • How is being able to use different types of questions useful to a leader?

- What is your natural leadership tendency—to tell more or to ask more questions?
- As a leader, what will you do as a result of participating in this activity when you return to the workplace?

9. Make the point that leaders are also talent managers who develop their employees. Note that asking questions engages employees in the discussion and causes them to think and develop abilities to solve problems. Point out that employees are more likely to buy into what is expected of them when they have a say in it. Also emphasize the appropriate use of "telling" and "asking" questions. (The majority of leaders tend to tell more than ask, which means they are missing opportunities to develop their employees to think for themselves and self-coach.)

InSider's Tips

- One concern typically expressed about asking more questions versus telling employees the answer is the amount of time it takes to have this type of inter-action. While it is true that "asking" does take more time, the value outweighs the investment of time. Here are some points to share about this:
  - This is one of the reasons the leaders only had 10 to 15 seconds before someone else took over for them. This change forced them to see how efficiently they can use questions.
  - In the short term, the interaction does take longer but the long-term potential gains are worth the initial time investment. The employees must come up with answers and ideas that help them practice how to self-coach. Eventually, they will coach themselves without asking for the leaders' help.
- This is not suggesting that leaders should only ask questions. The activity was structured this way to help them remember to seek ways to ask more questions than they do now.
- Asking questions also provides a deeper understanding of the employee's view of the situation.

Lisa Rike provides over twenty years of experience in the adult learning and development field. Her experience as an instructional designer and facilitator spans multiple topics, such as different aspects in leadership skills and team development, interpersonal and behavioral style training, train-the-trainer, communication, coaching, and presentation/facilitation skills. Lisa is a consultant to Fortune 500 companies as well as to small and mid-size organizations. She has designed and facilitated leadership and staff development initiatives that range in scope from improving team performance to permeating company culture to bring about improved business results across organizations.

Lisa Rike
853 West Oak Street
Zionsville, IN 46077
(317) 727.6520
Email: tailoredtraining@earthlink.net or lisar@etindy.com
Website: www.etindy.com
ASTD Chapter: Central Indiana

Vote Trust with Your Feet

Submitted by Cindy Phillips

Overview

Participants explore the issue of trust as well as their own preferences, likes, dislikes, and concerns surrounding the issue by taking sides—literally!

Objectives

- To begin a dialogue about both the positive and negative aspects surrounding the issue of workplace trust
- To demonstrate how everyone has a different orientation toward trust
- To discuss dimensions that impact trust

Audience

Eight to fifty with adequate space

Time Estimate

At least 45 minutes; may vary based on the questions

Materials and Equipment

- One Vote Trust handout for each participant
- Pencils or pens
- Five 8½ × 11 signs taped to the wall or floor in order: "STRONGLY DISAGREE," "DISAGREE," "NEUTRAL," "AGREE," and "STRONGLY AGREE" in large font
- Masking tape

Area Setup

A room large enough for participants to stand in five general areas near five signs posted equally spaced along one wall or in the corners and center of the room

Preparation

Customize the handout for your needs, changing the names of groups or adding other more pertinent statements.

200

Process

1. Provide all participants with copies of the Vote Trust handout and pens or pencils. Ask them to complete the handout quietly where they are seated.
2. Ask the participants to stand, taking their completed handouts with them.
3. Read the first statement you want to discuss. Ask participants to stand under the sign that represents their views on this statement.
4. Ask volunteers from each of the extreme responders ("strongly disagree" and "strongly agree") to explain their views. You may also want to ask someone from the neutral group if it seems relevant. Discuss the responses from the volunteers. You may wish to ask other questions such as:
   - What concerns do you have based on the responses to this question?
   - What positive aspects do you see in the group's responses?
   - What does this tell you about the different orientation each of you has toward trust?
   - What dimension is impacting trust with this statement?
5. Repeat this process with each of the other statements until you have covered all the statements that are relevant for this group. Ask the participants to take their seats.
6. Summarize this activity by asking questions such as these:
   - What did this activity demonstrate about trust?
   - What did you learn about yourself? About your colleagues?
   - How does trust affect what you do at work? Negatively? Positively?
   - What impacts trust?
   - How might this activity explain what happens in the workplace with regard to trust?
   - How do leaders build trust?
   - What is a leader's responsibility in building trust?
   - How can you transfer what you have learned to the workplace?

InSider's Tips

- Don't ask every question on the handout; select the ones that seem most relevant to the group and their culture.
- You do not need to ask the questions in order on the page. Instead, ask questions in a sequence that would likely shift the majority from one side of the room to the other to achieve some physical movement.

- Allow the participants to talk; they will make the case for you.
- Balance the discussion among all participants; sometimes one person has a lot of energy on a topic and could easily dominate the discussion.
- This is my variation of an activity I took from Casey Wilson, who borrowed the concept from someone else.

Cindy Phillips, Ph.D., is the president of Leadership4Change, LLC. She is a consultant and educator with expertise in organization development, leadership development, team building, and change management. With several years of management experience in the technology sector, she specializes in developing and implementing change initiatives, along with coaching and strengthening leaders to guide those efforts. She has worked with a diverse range and size of client systems, including Alcoa, Bosch, Booz Allen Hamilton, Capital Blue Cross, the Department of Energy, Harley-Davidson, Sodexo, SAP, Little League Baseball, and Wells Fargo. She completed a Ph.D. in organization development at the Fielding Graduate University, an MBA from St. Joseph's University, and a B.S. in finance/computer science from Towson University. She is an ICF-certified executive coach and a certified action learning coach.

Cindy Phillips, Ph.D.
2436 Stone Heath Drive
Lancaster, PA 17601
(717) 572.6755
Email: cindy@leadership4change.com
Website: www.leadership4change.com
ASTD Chapter: Central Pennsylvania

Vote Trust

Statement		Scale			
1. People should be trusted until proven otherwise.	Strongly Disagree	Disagree	Neutral	Agree	Strongly Agree
2. In order to receive trust, I need to give it.	Strongly Disagree	Disagree	Neutral	Agree	Strongly Agree
3. I can't work with someone I can't trust.	Strongly Disagree	Disagree	Neutral	Agree	Strongly Agree
4. Once I've lost trust, I cannot get it back.	Strongly Disagree	Disagree	Neutral	Agree	Strongly Agree
5. Some people just cannot be trusted.	Strongly Disagree	Disagree	Neutral	Agree	Strongly Agree
6. Trust is critical to achieving our mission.	Strongly Disagree	Disagree	Neutral	Agree	Strongly Agree
7. Trust at our company is improving.	Strongly Disagree	Disagree	Neutral	Agree	Strongly Agree
8. Trust exists between the field and headquarters.	Strongly Disagree	Disagree	Neutral	Agree	Strongly Agree
9. Trust exists between my team and our customers.	Strongly Disagree	Disagree	Neutral	Agree	Strongly Agree
10. Trust exists between my boss and me.	Strongly Disagree	Disagree	Neutral	Agree	Strongly Agree
11. Trust exists between my staff and me.	Strongly Disagree	Disagree	Neutral	Agree	Strongly Agree
12. The factors impacting trust are within my control.	Strongly Disagree	Disagree	Neutral	Agree	Strongly Agree

You Be the Ethicist

Submitted by Jeff Furman

Overview

Leaders face and discuss current ethical dilemmas and questions using a widely read ethicist column to spur debate.

Objectives

- To discuss and consider various aspects of ethical decisions and social responsibility
- To practice responding to ethical issues from different points of view
- To open the discussion about the ethical role of a leader

Audience

Eight to twelve participants

Time Estimate

90 minutes

Materials and Equipment

- Copies of current and one or two past columns of "The Ethicist," found in *The New York Times*
- An Internet link to the podcast version of the column online, where the letters are read by actors and then columnist Randy Cohen reads his replies to the letter-writer. The link is www.learnoutloud.com/Podcast-Directory/Philosophy/Ethics/New-York-Times-The-Ethicist-Podcast/22321

Area Setup

A room with wireless access with the ability to connect to the Internet. PCs or laptops should have working sound cards.

Process

1. To introduce this topic, ask participants how many are faced with an ethical decision at work. Ask for two examples and how these sometimes difficult decisions are made. Tell the participants that during this activity they will have

an opportunity to discuss and consider various aspects of ethical decisions and to practice responding to them from different points of view. Hand out copies of "The Ethicist" column you downloaded and printed prior to the session to all participants.

2. Ask for a volunteer read out loud one of the letters to "The Ethicist." Tell them that each letter is from a real person who is currently dealing with an ethical issue and that the author sent a letter to Randy Cohen at *The New York Times* asking for his advice on how to handle the problem.

3. Ask the volunteer to read the letter. Stop the reader before he or she reads the columnist's response.

4. Ask participants to think for a few minutes about how they would respond to the letter.

5. Give the participants a few minutes to re-read the letter to themselves and think about their responses.

6. After an appropriate amount of time, ask how the participants would respond. Allow 5 to 10 minutes for discussion, depending on the interest level in the topic.

7. Ask another participant to read Randy Cohen's response and ask for their reactions to the response.

8. Repeat this process for several other letters, depending upon the issues and time available.

9. If possible, ask the participants to use their computers to listen to Randy Cohen and actors read the same podcast letter (s) and response (s) in order to get a new perspective through a different presentation of the issue.

10. Lead a discussion about the ethical issues participants are currently experiencing on the job. Encourage participants to give each other advice about how to handle their ethical dilemmas.

11. Summarize the discussion by asking a few questions such as:
    - What did you discover about making ethical decisions?
    - What aspects come into play when making ethical decisions?
    - What social responsibility do you have in the workplace when making decisions?
    - Why is it so difficult to make ethical decisions? Isn't it just a matter of right or wrong?
    - What is different about a leader's responsibility when making ethical decisions?
    - How do individuals' personal perspectives affect ethical decisions?

- What is the one most important lesson you are leaving here with today? How will you implement it on the job?

12. End the activity by encouraging participants to look for "The Ethicist" and other ethical columns in newspapers and to start to reading them. Tell them that a part of any job is to make good ethical decisions. Remind them that it's an ongoing challenge to come up with the most ethical solutions to any issues.

InSider's Tips

- This always works very well because it involves a great deal of participation without putting anyone on the spot. Participants have fun reading the columns aloud. They find it thought-provoking to review ethical dilemmas that others are facing and to have the opportunity to provide their opinions.

- Hearing various actors reading the letters on the podcasts and hearing the author, Randy Cohen, read his responses adds excitement. This often causes participants to see the letters a little differently from how they read them earlier. You can suggest that participants continue to explore their own answers to ethical columns or blogs. This reinforces the learning objective that there are multiple ways of seeing ethical issues.

- "The Ethicist" column, found in *The New York Times,* addresses ethical current and relevant ethical issues. You may find other columns or newsletters that address ethical issues.

- Reinforce the idea that everyone thinks his or her view is correct on issues of ethics, and point out that we all need to recognize this tendency in ourselves. Emphasize that making ethical decisions is as much an art as a science and that many different points of view exist. State that the person writing the letter is usually unhappy with someone else and feels he or she is ethically right. However, the person on the other side of the issue also usually feels strongly that he or she is right. Try to get participants to think about who is more correct, but also to empathize with both sides.

- Note that "The Ethicist" column is published in *The New York Times,* which is not public domain material. I do have written permission from the author of "The Ethicist" column, Randy Cohen, to use his columns in my classes in this manner. I recommend that you also obtain permission from him to avoid any copyright issues.

Jeff Furman has extensive experience as both a PMP instructor and an IT project manager. He has managed many large IT projects for Fortune 100 companies in the New York metropolitan area. He has trained hundreds of project managers and helped them become PMP certified. He has also trained many instructors and helped them become certified technical trainers. He authored *The Project Management Answer Book,* published by Management Concepts, a book that will help project managers learn the cutting-edge skills to become more efficient on their projects and to pass the PMP exam.

Jeff Furman
123 Willow Avenue
Hoboken, NJ 07030
(201) 310.7997
Email: Jeff@Jeff-Furman.com
Website: www.Jeff-Furman.com
ASTD Chapter: New York Metro

Valuing the Values

Submitted by P. Sethu Madhavan and Yehya M. Al Marzouqi

Overview

Popping a balloon never had as many positive learning opportunities as in this fast-paced, highly interactive activity that also gives the facilitator the chance to mystify and intrigue with a magic trick.

Objectives

- To provide an opportunity for participants to share personal experiences and insights related to dilemmas around values or conflicts experienced at work
- To develop the participants' awareness and understanding about their own value judgments as well as those of others
- To demonstrate how values affect decisions and problem solving at work
- To discuss a leader's responsibility to uphold an organization's values

Audience

Ten to twenty-five participants

Time Estimate

Approximately 2 hours

Materials and Equipments

- One thin sewing needle to demonstrate the age-old "magic balloon" trick (See Insider's Tips below for an explanation of the "trick.")
- Five to ten inflated balloons of any size for the participants to try piercing with the needle without bursting them
- A container with medium-sized balloons of different colors or patterns to divide participants into small groups (If colors are not available, write numbers on the balloons to represent different groups.)
- CD markers for participants to write on the balloons
- One set of roles for each group (The sheet describing the "Member" role may be colored differently.)
- One inflated balloon for each group labeled "Roles" and filled with one set of roles

- Incidents describing the value dilemmas from real life
- One inflated balloon for each group that is labeled "Incidents" filled with critical incidents
- A flip chart or slide showing the questions for the groups to address during the discussion
- One flip chart and markers for each group
- Flip chart and markers for the facilitator

Area Setup
A large room capable of accommodating all groups, which should be able to see and hear each other without disturbing one another

Preparation
Copy the Roles and Incidents on paper and cut them apart as indicated on the handouts. Alternatively, you may create your own incidents based on situations unique to the group or your organization. Prepare two large balloons for each team. Place one folded set of Roles inside one balloon and one folded set of Incidents inside the second balloon and inflate the balloons. Select and post the questions you want the groups to address during the session. You should practice the balloon "trick" before the session as well.

Process
1. Introduce the activity and its goals.
2. Demonstrate the "magic balloon trick" by piercing a balloon using a needle without bursting it. Challenge the participants by asking them whether or not they can pierce an inflated balloon with a needle without bursting it. If someone says yes, ask him or her to keep the secret for now. Allow some participants to try piercing the extra balloons with the needle.
3. Invite someone who claims to know the trick to demonstrate it or demonstrate it yourself. State that the secret will be shared at the end of the session (see Insider's Tips).
4. Introduce the concept of the importance of values at work and invite participants to share the core values of their companies or some of their views regarding the topic. You could start by saying that handling value dilemmas in life sometimes brings up issues that are very difficult and sensitive, similar to piercing an inflated balloon without bursting it!
5. Ask participants to walk to the basket of balloons you have prepared before the session and pick up out one balloon each.

Leadership: What It Takes   **209**

6. Tell them to inflate their balloons. While the participants are engaged in this activity, state that the size of the balloon indicates the level of confidence of the person! Remind them that too much of anything, including confidence, may not be always good! If someone bursts a balloon give him or her another balloon of the same color or number.

7. Ask participants to write short phrases on their balloons related to the issue of living by values and to base the comments on their experience. Share some examples such as difficult choices between rules and compassion, honesty and integrity, fairness and seeing both sides, or other examples. Encourage several participants to share some examples.

8. Ask the participants to form groups based on the color of their balloons (or number written on the balloon) and sit together in small groups, selecting a chairperson to represent each group.

9. Distribute the "Roles" balloons to each group. Tell the groups to burst their balloons and to select one role at random. Request that participants choose the white roles first. Those who do not receive a white role will select the colored paper and play a member role.

10. Explain the roles to the participants and encourage the chairperson of each small group to take over.

11. Ask the participants to introduce themselves to the small groups by sharing their views about values reflected in the words they have written on their balloons. Once everyone has been introduced, encourage all the participants to burst their balloons. Allow about 5 minutes for this step.

12. Give the "Incident" balloons to the chairperson in each group. The groups must burst the balloon to select the incidents. Announce the number of incidents the groups will address (generally, four to six each).

13. Present the flip chart or slide listing the questions you would like the groups to address during their discussion.

14. Tell the groups they have about 40 minutes to discuss the Incidents they selected. Note that they should attempt to come to agreement on how they would deal with each chosen value dilemma. Tell them when you have started the timed period.

15. At the end of the timed period, ask a spokesperson from each group to shares the group's views and highlights of their discussion. You may encourage further discussion by asking additional questions or by encouraging members of other groups to ask questions.

16. Bring closure by asking:
    - How were these value dilemmas and conflicts related to those you experience at work?
    - How do values affect decisions and problem solving at work?
    - How has this activity changed your awareness of value dilemmas?
    - What is a leader's responsibility regarding an organization's values?
    - What is the most important learning you take away today?
17. Summarize the activity by summing up the learning from each group. At this point, you may conclude with the following points regarding handling value dilemmas at work:
    - Handling "black and white" value dilemmas is easy, since one can decide decisively what is "good or bad" or "right or wrong" for the company and the people.
    - It is more difficult to resolve a dilemma when you have to choose between two situations that may be equally right or the solution equally appealing.
    - The most difficult situations are when you are caught between two equally problematic choices.
    - Often there are opportunities to solve even the difficult value dilemmas without compromising one's personal values or the core values of the organizations, through open-minded thinking and creative solutions. Refer to some of the solutions discovered by the groups as examples.

InSider's Tips

- The intention is to create some fun and excitement in the room with the intermittent sound of bursting balloons.
- The tips for piercing a balloon without bursting it require that you prepare a balloon in advance by sticking transparent plastic tape in one spot and then putting the pin through that spot. You should also lubricate the pin in advance. In addition, make sure that the needle is sharp and thin and pierces the balloon in a spot where the surface is not stretched, usually at the base.
- This activity can be done with any number of groups of five to seven participants each. If there are more than five groups, you might require additional co-facilitators to ensure adequate support to the groups.

- To shorten the activity, Steps 6 and 11 may be eliminated and members may be encouraged to burst their balloons to celebrate their success when they finish presenting their group views.
- Participants usually are able to come up with very creative solutions to solve the value dilemmas, without compromising their positive values. For example, in the "Friendship Dilemma" incident, values such as "performance" and "honesty" are in conflict with "concern for the people." One of the most popular solutions to this situation is to help the employees to solve their financial problem through some other methods, such as arranging an interest-free loan, rather than by providing a bonus they do not deserve.
- Some of the values that seem to be in conflict in the incidents are provided as a sample handout. Prepare yourself by generating a set of alternative solutions before you begin the workshop. Normally, each alternative will have some advantages and disadvantages, and the final choice of participants is a matter of values rather than a rational decision.

P. Sethu Madhavan, Ph.D., is an established HRD expert working with the Tawazun at Abu Dhabi. Earlier he worked with Ernst and Young, Larsen and Tubro, Abu Dhabi Company for Onshore Oil Operation, Indian Institute of Management, the Centre for Organization Development, and Academy of HRD (India). He has rendered training and consulting services to many leading companies covering many sectors. He has co-authored a book and has many publications, case studies, psychological tests, and survey instruments to his credit. He has served as the editor of journals and as a member of the board of professional bodies. Currently he is a member of the executive council of the National Academy of Psychology (NOAP). He has spoken regularly at HR events in Europe and Asia.

P. Sethu Madhavan, Ph.D.
P.O. Box 908
Abu Dhabi, United Arab Emirates
+971–50–6673021
Email: drsethu@drsethu.com
Website: www.drsethu.com
ASTD Chapter: International

Yehya M. Al Marzouqi, Ph.D., is a leading HRD expert, speaker, and trainer, working with the Tawazun at Abu Dhabi in a senior and strategic role related to human capital. Prior to joining Offset, he had worked in Abu Dhabi Company for Onshore Oil Operation (ADCO) since 1992. During his career he had led various initiatives such as business process re-engineering, establishing personal development processes and plans, succession planning, establishing assessment centers, implementing competency-based training, establishing training centers, implementing e-learning, 360-degree feedback initiatives, and so forth. Yehya has also facilitated large scale change initiatives such as articulating and establishing organizational values and conducted many training workshops.

Yehya M. Al Marzouqi, Ph.D.
P.O. Box 908
Abu Dhabi, United Arab Emirates
+971–50–6419700
Email: Yehya@yehya.net
Website: yalmarzouqi@offset.ae
ASTD Chapter: International

Sample Incidents in Conflict

Incidents	Some of the Values in Conflict
Friendship Dilemma	Performance, honesty, and integrity vs. friendship, concern for people
Caught in Between	Accountability and ownership vs. externalization and blaming
Never at Desk	Task vs. people
The Indispensable Man	Experience vs. expertise
Time Attendance	Fairness vs. need for protecting oneself
Safety Business	Concern for the task vs. concern for safety of people
Medical Issue	Concern for people vs. honesty
Friendly Vendor	Confidentiality and professional ethics vs. friendship
Bureaucracy	Flexibility/customer friendliness vs. bureaucracy/risk avoidance
Task Master	Task vs. people

Roles

CHAIRPERSON

- Lead the group through the steps
- Encourage participation of all
- Maintain good interaction
- Ensure the group sticks to the task at hand
- Check whether the scribe records the points
- Mediate and resolve differences of opinion

SPOKESPERSON

- Present team views (on flip charts) to the room
- Help the scribe to complete the flip charts.
- Help the group order their thoughts
- Seek clarifications and examples
- Participate in the group discussion

SCRIBE

- Write points raised by the group on flip charts
- Write as large and as legibly as possible
- Help the group order their thoughts
- Seek clarifications and examples
- Participate in the group discussion
- Use darker and visible colors to write

TIME KEEPER

- Ensure that too much time is not spent on a single issue
- Agree with the team regarding the time limit for members to speak and contribute
- Remind people how much time is left
- Participate in the group discussion

MEMBERS

- Share your views openly with the team
- Ensure confidentiality while giving real-life examples
- Seek clarification if needed
- Be kind to others and listen to them
- Ensure that the team views are thoughtful

MEMBERS

- Share your views openly with the team
- Ensure confidentiality while giving real-life examples
- Seek clarification if needed
- Be kind to others and listen to them
- Ensure that the team views are thoughtful

MEMBERS

- Share your views openly with the team
- Ensure confidentiality while giving real-life examples
- Seek clarification if needed
- Be kind to others and listen to them
- Ensure that the team views are thoughtful

MEMBERS

- Share your views openly with the team
- Ensure confidentiality while giving real-life examples
- Seek clarification if needed
- Be kind to others and listen to them
- Ensure that the team views are thoughtful

Incidents

A set of ten incidents is provided here. Modify the incidents for your groups or add new incidents as required. Select four to six of the incidents depending on the time available and group size. Copy and cut them apart to put inside a balloon.

Friendship Dilemma

It is the end of the year and you as the team leader have to ensure that your staff are appraised and given performance ratings. You are aware that the top management has announced a performance bonus for the employees rated as "4" and "5" on the five-point performance rating scale used by the company. Employees who are rated below 4 on performance will not be eligible for the bonus.

Ms. X has been working with you for more than ten years. Unfortunately, she has not been able to perform very well this year due to some family issues. She was also quite disturbed due to some persistent health problems faced by her spouse. Your internal customers have recently complained to you about the poor service they are receiving from her. You have spoken to her on a few occasions throughout the year, but she was unable to improve her performance. She has come to see you today to plead with you to rate her "4," not "3," as she is going through some financial problems. You have known her well for a long time and have interacted with her family outside the office on many social occasions. What will you do?

Caught in Between

You are a contract administrator in the IT department. Timely renewal of contracts is one of your key performance indicators agreed upon for the year with your boss.

Five months ago you requested that the procurement department renew a contract. After a month, the procurement department informed you that another vendor claimed that they are the newly appointed representative for the product for the region and therefore you cannot renew the contract with the existing vendor. It took many weeks for you to clarify this issue with the two vendors and the legal, procurement, and finance departments. However, in the meantime the new vendor settled the issue with your contractor and withdrew the claim. Unfortunately, your assistant handling this case went on his annual leave and it took some time for you to follow up on this. Last week, the final contract was sent to the CEO for signature two months after expiring. The CEO was furious to see that the company was using software without a proper contract in place and asked you to explain why this happened. He stated that it is against the company values and policies to treat a vendor like this. You honestly felt that it was not your fault and that many others had contributed to this issue. The CEO has called you, the head of the procurement department, and your boss to seek an explanation. What will be your stand in the meeting? Why?

Never at Desk

Ms. X often arrives late and she disappears from her desk for lengthy periods of time. Friendly attempts as well as serious counseling have not worked. Ms. X told you that she has a migraine problem as well as an ongoing family problem. She is a fast learner and has full capability of becoming a high performer, but unfortunately she is not able to focus on work. You honestly wish to coach and help Ms. X to improve her performance. Another employee in your section, Mr. Y, who is over-burdened, came to you and complained that the work distribution is not fair in the team. Mr. Y has been working overtime. He told you that his family is requesting him to leave the company and take a job in another company if the situation continues. He is seeking your permission to go to higher authorities to resolve this situation. How will you approach this situation?

The Indispensable Man

You are the IT manager of the company. Mr. X has been working with your department for the last ten years. He has developed good relationships with you and with many other people in the company. Recently, you have received many complaints from your internal customers that Mr. X is arrogant, careless, and not friendly to the customers. You have assigned many young and well-trained IT employees to work with him, but he insists that they are not capable of taking over his role fully as he is handling more complex IT systems. Last month Mr. X took a long leave, and a young employee who was a recent graduate in IT was asked to stand by. One of your customers came to you and shared with you that the service is much better now with the young employee being there. You also heard that the young employee is a wizard when it comes to diagnosing and solving IT issues. You were surprised. What will you do?

Time Attendance

Mr. X, a young engineer, was coming late to the office and leaving early. You issued him a warning notice. After this the employee started coming on time and stopped leaving early. However, you have noticed that in between he is not present in the office. When confronted, he stated that he is too busy with various meetings with the customers. However, the customers were complaining about this employee and his non-availability. You are aware that Mr. X was appointed based on the recommendation of the CEO of the company as a favor to one of his close family friends. The other two members of your team have come to you demanding a fair distribution of work among the team members. They felt that it is unfair for you to allow one member of the team to shirk work and overloaded others. What will you do?

Safety Business

You were in the middle of a very important meeting on the fifteenth floor of your corporate office. Your guests had indicated that they had to finish the meeting in the next 5 minutes, as they had another meeting to attend. You are keen to thrash out some key issues and gain some agreements from your guests within the remaining five minutes. While you were discussing these issues, you were surprised to find a worker cleaning the windows of your meeting room from the outside without wearing a helmet. You noticed also that he had not fastened his safety belts properly. What will you do?

Medical Issue

Mr. Y has been working with you for the last seven years. Unfortunately, he has been diagnosed with a medical condition requiring surgery. He is requesting a long leave, beyond what is allowed under the company's medical and leave policies. He shared that going on leave without salary is going to be very difficult for him. In addition to the medical leave, he would like you to grant him a week away from the office unofficially, without any leave application. He promised that he can do some work while he is in the hospital. You feel very much inclined to help him. However, you are also concerned about questions from higher authorities, as it is against the policy of the company. What will you do?

Friendly Vendor

One of your old friends now working with an engineering company contacted you after a long time and invited you for dinner. He convinced you that his company can be a valuable supplier to your company. You helped him to register with the procurement department of your company and also to be short-listed as a possible vendor for an upcoming project. However, the evaluation committee selected another vendor. Your friend was upset with you and requested you to reveal who was given the contract and why. What do you do next?

Bureaucracy

You are working in a bank that has listed "non-bureaucratic way of working" as one of its core values. Five years ago, the bank had simple forms and processes for its mortgage customers. However, the mortgage department has been revising those forms based on the problems and legal issues they have faced over a period of time. Currently, the bank has a lengthy mortgage application form, which requires the customer to sign in fourteen places. You have been working in the customer service section for many years and have seen many customers become furious about the lengthy process and complicated application forms. Recently, you have been transferred to the mortgage section and were given the task to review the forms. You wanted to simplify the forms and the process, but experienced colleagues in the mortgage section cautioned you, citing the legal problems they have faced in the past due to the use of "simple" forms. What will be your approach?

Task Master

You are the administration manager in a bank. Mr. X who had spent eight years in the army, has recently joined your department as your assistant manager. You observed that Mr. X is a talented administrator and highly experienced at handling various administrative issues. He is a hard worker, high performer, and a tough task master. However, the culture of your company is very different from that of the army, which is usually a "command and control" culture. Your company has a more participative style of management. The team members have complained to you about the dictatorial approach of Mr. X. You have tried to counsel Mr. X and persuade him to change his style. However, Mr. X refuses to buy in, as he strongly believed that his style is the best way to get work out of people. You also observed that some of your employees have started working harder recently, as they were under pressure from Mr. X. In the meantime, one of your team members who is a low performer came to you and stated that he is resigning, as Mr. X is putting unreasonable demands on him. What will you do?

Questions to Address

Sample questions for the groups to address during the discussions and while presenting the groups' views are listed below. Modify the questions to suit your groups or add new questions as required. Select three to five questions and present them to the groups during the briefing stage.

- Share your group's decisions regarding each situation and explain the rationale.
- What disagreements occurred among the group members regarding their choices?
- Briefly summarize the views of group members.
- What values seemed to underlie the group's final decision?
- How did you feel when someone agreed/disagreed with your values?
- Do you think that the similarities in team members' values help decision making at work? Why?
- What is the impact of having similar values on team work?
- Is "shared values" among the team members good for organizations? Under what circumstances could it become a threat to an organization?
- Is there any right or wrong or black or white solutions to value issues? How do you handle shades of gray?

Chapter 9

Solving Problems: Find Practical Solutions

Problems, problems. . . . Wouldn't it be nice if there were no problems? Did you know that the ability to solve problems is one of the key reasons people are promoted?

Solving problems and implementing solutions do not come naturally to many of your participants. Some people panic when faced with a problem or even a situation in which the possibility that something is wrong exists. On the other hand, some people love a good problem—just as some people fear dealing with problems!

As a trainer you will appreciate the practicality of the activities in this chapter and the ideas offered for teaching problem-solving skills. The contributors to this chapter are true problem solvers and share their best, tried and true, road-tested activities with you. One of the best ideas from this group of problem solvers is to tap into individuals in your organization who collectively can help you identify real-life organizational problems and use the logical approaches presented here to solve them.

Laurie Friedman generously shares the DIG UP methodology, a five-step process that ensures your participants will not go straight to the conclusion, but instead will consider the facts along the way. In "Consult the Experts," Pam Nintrup suggests that you tap your participants to submit scenarios as pre-work to obtain real-life examples.

Erin Miller also uses scenarios for problem-solving practice and provides you with some examples to help you start. Jo Lynn Feinstein creates a comprehensive activity to examine service or performance gaps. It is a good activity to prepare for a strategic planning session.

These activities will be solid additions to your next problem-solving training. You should really take one for a spin the next time you need a solution in your training room.

Dig It Up

Submitted by Laurie Friedman

Overview
This activity shows participants a methodology that will allow them to "dig up" the right solution to a problem in a methodical and logical way using a five-step process.

Objectives
- To improve problem-solving skills and effective decision making
- To learn to separate an issue from its potential causes
- To identify metrics to measure and evaluate problem-solving outcomes/solutions

Audience
Twenty or fewer

Time Estimate
50 to 60 minutes for a relatively simple problem

Materials and Equipment
- One copy of the DIG UP Methodology handout for each participant
- Flip chart and extra paper
- Markers
- Paper for participants
- Pens or pencils for participants
- Masking tape

Area Setup
A room that offers writing surfaces

Process
1. Provide each participant with paper and a pen or pencil for writing and the DIG UP Methodology handout Explain that DIG UP is a five-step problem-solving technique. State that the acronym represents a problem-solving

method in which the steps are followed in sequence to ensure that you define the problem accurately and brainstorm all possible solutions.

2. Ask the participants to read through the five steps on their handouts. Allow about 5 minutes for this. State that they will have an opportunity to work on a problem. *Note:* You may ask participants for a problem or use one that you have identified prior to the session.

3. With the problem clarified, ask the participants to select partners to work with to specifically *Define* and write down the problem. Tell them that the "D" step in their handout may be the most challenging because sometimes the problem defined is not the actual or real problem.

4. Post the following questions on the flip chart and tell the participants they have about 5 minutes to discuss them as they work with their partners to define the problem:
   - What exactly is the problem?
   - Is everyone experiencing the problem?
   - What words help to clarify the problem?

5. At the end of 5 minutes, ask participants for their suggestions for defining the problem. Agree on a definition and post it on a flip-chart page. Tape this page to the wall.

6. Announce that the next step, "I," is to *Identify* all the causes of the problem. Say that it is important to identify all the possibilities. For this step ask the participants to brainstorm all the possible causes. Be sure that you accept all ideas, the wilder the better at this point. Allow about 10 minutes and post these pages on the wall.

7. After the participants have completed the "I" step, explain that the "G" noted in their handout requires that they *Gather* every possible fact about the situation. Ask what facts the participants know about the problem. After they have stated a few facts, say that the next step is to identify all the possible solutions.

8. Have the pairs join with another pair to create groups of four.

9. Give each group a sheet of flip-chart paper and a marker and tell them to take about 10 minutes to list all the possible solutions to the problem they have identified.

10. After 10 minutes give groups masking tape to hang their charts on the wall. Tell the participants to walk around and review the solutions from all the other groups. Give them a few minutes for this review, then ask them to return to their own solutions and cross off any they do not think are possible.

11. State that the "U" stands for *Umpire*. Tell the participants that they will now put on their umpires' caps and review all the possible solutions that have been

posted. They are to use markers and put a check mark in front of the ONE solution they think will work the best. *Each participant may select only one answer*. Allow a few minutes for this part of the activity.

12. When the participants have put check marks beside their preferred solutions, spend some time discussing the results. You may find more than one solution was selected. If so, make the point that in real life, they would need to review the facts again or use another tool such as an advantages/disadvantages listing to help decide on a final solution. Put all solutions that have been selected on one flip-chart sheet and help them decide which to implement, if necessary.

13. State that the "P" stands for *Put into Effect*. Their task for this step is to make sure the solution is implementable and measurable. Lead a large group discussion to identify a set of metrics. Ask the participants how they will know whether the solution chosen has been successful. Remind them that they must also monitor the outcomes. Ask what they think a logical monitoring plan might be for this solution. Who should monitor it? How often? To whom should the solutions be reported?

14. Summarize by asking questions such as:
    • What did you learn about problem solving?
    • What will be the easiest step for you to use? The most difficult?
    • In what situations do you think you will use this tool?
    • What is the most important lesson you have learned from this activity?

InSider's Tips

• More participants can be included by using more than one large group and adjusting the time. The activity can also be used for self-directed learning purposes.

• The DIG UP methodology is especially valuable to help separate the problem from the person or to ensure that the problem being solved is the "real problem" and not just a symptom of the problem. For example, if someone concluded that the paper towels stored under a counter were wet because someone was putting excessively wet sponges next to the dry towels when the real problem was a leaky pipe, more work would be necessary. The DIG UP tool provides a process to accurately identify and problem-solve using brainstorming techniques.

224

- Do not skip steps. The tool is a process to clarify on the "real" problem, to gather facts, and to make informed decisions.
- Ask specific questions to investigate facts and bring clarity.
- Remember that the best solution includes input from the people who are knowledgeable about the problem and who may be impacted by the solution.
- This activity has been previously published in *The Sherpa Guide: Process-Driven Executive Coaching* by Brenda Corbett and Judith Coleman.

Laurie Friedman is a certified Sherpa executive coach who has been a senior consultant for a large consulting firm and has her own consulting firm, Strategic Business Consulting, in Bethesda, Maryland. Her expertise is in leadership development, team building, strategic thinking, communication skills, and change management. She is a certified Myers-Briggs Type Indicator and Action Learning facilitator. She has published numerous articles and book chapters on leadership challenges such as managing organizational agreement, retention and engagement, and strategic thinking. She holds a master's degree in human resources and organization development from George Washington University. She is passionate in her belief that coaching is an essential business strategy for achievement of business results and personal fulfillment.

Laurie Friedman
Strategic Business Consulting
6808 Algonquin Avenue
Bethesda, MD 20817
(301) 320.3960
Email: laurie@sbcstrategy.com
Website: www.sbcstrategy.com
ASTD Chapter: National

DIG UP Methodology

DIG UP is a five-step problem-solving technique. The letters in "DIG UP" are an acronym for a problem-solving method and provide an easy-to-remember tool. The steps are followed in sequence to ensure that you solve the real problem. The DIG UP tool can be used by individuals or in groups to brainstorm problems and solutions collaboratively. The fives steps are:

D = *Define the problem*. Write down specifically what the problem is. This is the most challenging step because sometimes the obvious issue is not the actual or real problem. Sample questions to ask yourself: What exactly is the problem? Is everyone experiencing the problem? Write a summary problem statement that succinctly defines the problem.

I = *Identify and list all the possible causes of the problem*. It is important to identify *all* the possibilities. Make sure you think big and think "out of the box."

G = *Gather every possible fact about the situation and identify all the possible solutions*. Collect solutions from anyone who is able to provide you with information. If working in a team environment, share all possible solutions and then cross off solutions that are not practical. The items left on the list should provide workable solutions and information to support effective data-driven decision making.

U = *Umpire to assess all the solutions*. Review all the possible solutions and evaluate your choices. Select those that match your criteria best or what is most important, for example, time, cost, or quality.

P = *Put into effect*. Be confident that your decision is implementable because your solution was derived from a data-driven process and includes input from everyone involved. Make it measurable; identify metrics to track the solution. Create a monitoring plan so you know whether decisions are being implemented successfully and results have been obtained. Your monitoring plan should include what you will report, how often, and to whom.

Consult the Experts

Submitted by Pam Nintrup

Overview

In this activity, participants tap into the power of collective wisdom to solve real-life problems posted around the room on flip-chart paper.

Objectives

- To gather a variety of opinions on how to solve specific organizational problems or scenarios
- To solve problems in a non-threatening atmosphere
- To take advantage of collective wisdom in a way that makes everyone feel valued

Audience

Up to thirty members of the same organization

Time Estimate

45 minutes

Materials and Equipment

- One flip-chart easel with paper for each small group
- Masking tape
- Two to three markers for each flip chart

Area Setup

A room large enough for small groups to work at separate flip charts

Preparation

Before the session, decide what you will use for problem statements. These will depend on the purpose of the training. You may ask the participants to submit problem statements prior to the session that reflect organizational issues, a learning topic, or team or project objectives. Print the chosen statements in large letters that can be read from a distance and tape one to the top of each flip chart. Space the flip charts around the room so there is room for small groups to gather at each one.

Process

1. Break participants into small groups (same number of groups as flip charts) and have each group gather at one of the flip charts.

2. Provide directions by saying, "We are going to gather the wisdom of our world. Each flip chart contains a different problem our organization is facing. We need your ideas to solve them. Each person should write *one* possible solution for the posted problem. Each idea must be unique; avoid 'agree' or 'ditto' comments. Building on previous ideas is encouraged. Once you have finished with one chart, move to another as a group and provide your individual ideas again. Continue until you have visited each flip chart. When complete, we will have (number of participants) ideas for solving each problem that was posted."

3. Debrief by having a volunteer for each flip chart read the problem statement and the ideas that were listed. Ask whether people have any ideas to add. Encourage them to apply the suggestions to solve the problems or to develop action plans when they return to the job.

4. Following the session, take all ideas from the flip-chart pages, type them, and send them to all participants so everyone gains from the wisdom of the group.

InSider's Tips

- This activity gets the creative juices flowing and encourages group problem solving and interaction in a way that allows everyone to contribute. You will find participants discussing posted ideas as well as spontaneously coming up with more ideas. Participants enjoy moving around and sharing their expertise.

- This activity is flexible and can be used for problem solving, brainstorming, or gathering ideas on any topic.

- Editing the pre-work submissions is sometimes required to ensure anonymity and clarity. Everyone should be encouraged to submit at least one problem or scenario prior to the session.

- This activity can be done without flip charts by listing problems on separate sheets of paper and passing them around the table group for suggested solutions, then moving the sheets to a different group. While this method takes a little less time, the interaction is also limited.

Pam Nintrup is president of Project and Process Professionals, a company formed to provide education and coaching on project and process management, with a strong focus on soft skills, productivity, and efficiency. Pam has helped many organizations and individuals improve their abilities to deliver projects, improve processes, and manage life. She has over twenty-five years of experience and is certified in project management, process improvement, and coaching and is passionate about helping others. Pam is past president of PMI Southwest Ohio and is the 2011 president of the Greater Cincinnati chapter of ASTD.

Pam Nintrup
6660 Westchase Park Drive
Cincinnati, OH 45248
Phone: (513) 519.1392
Email: pnintrup@ppprofs.com
Website: www.ppprofs.com
ASTD Chapter: Greater Cincinnati

Scenario Cards

Submitted by Erin Miller

Overview

Identifying common themes, solutions, and skills for solving real-life problems and challenges is the goal of this activity, based on issues and challenges contributed by participants. Works best as a closing activity in a problem-solving workshop.

Objectives

- To apply specific skills and knowledge to solve problems
- To discuss common challenges and solutions when problem solving

Audience

Three to twenty participants from the same organization or work group

Time Estimate

10 to 15 minutes

Materials and Equipment

- Three to six Scenario Cards
- Flip chart
- Markers

Area Setup

Normal classroom setup

Preparation

Develop the Scenario Cards. Select three to six situations based on the topic of the class or current organizational issues. Describe the situations on separate index cards, but in a generic way that will not cause embarrassment or put someone on the spot in case a similar situation exists. (An example is provided at the end of the activity.)

Process

1. Begin by explaining that this activity is about building problem-solving skills. Tell the participants that they will look at some common, real-life situations and identify practical ways to apply various solutions.

2. Ask a volunteer to select one of the Scenario Cards and read the card out loud. Ask the volunteer to share one idea of how he or she might approach the situation. Then ask the rest of the group to add their ideas. Capture ideas on a whiteboard or flip chart.

3. When you've posted a few key ideas for solving the first scenario, ask for a different volunteer to read another card and follow the same procedure as before.

4. Continue working through all the Scenario Cards in the same manner.

5. After the last Scenario Card has been read and discussed, ask the group to identify the themes they've heard from the discussion. List these themes on the flip chart.

6. Ask the group to discuss common skills required to solve problems. List them on the flip chart.

7. Point out that many of the ideas that have been suggested could work in many situations. Make the point that participants should become adept at using their problem-solving skills back on the job.

InSider's Tips

- This activity is useful for applying new concepts and skills to real-life scenarios. Attendees at training on project management, customer service, leadership, and other topics often comment that the theories and concepts sound great, but they want more time to focus on applying them to the "real world." Use this technique for any topic when you want participants to be able to problem solve or think on their feet.

- I've found this worked best if I created scenarios that were very realistic, that would get an "oh yeah, that happens all the time!" reaction from participants. However, it's important to remain generic enough that you're not targeting groups, individuals, or projects within your organization. A generic example is something like, "Suppose you are assigned to lead a project, and you learn that a critical resource will be leaving the team for another position.

What can you do to keep your project on track?" However, this example is too specific: "Suppose you have a team member who is always late on Thursdays and derails team meetings with stories about her cat . . . ."

- You can use this activity for distance learning as well. Simply substitute PowerPoint slides for the index cards, and facilitate brainstorming and discussion via the webinar.

Erin Miller, assistant director of training and development at The Hartford, holds a master's degree in organization learning and development from the University of St. Thomas and a bachelor's degree from St. Olaf College. She spent three years teaching high school biology and has thirteen years' experience in the training and development field, including new hire training program management and classroom delivery, instructional design, project management, and web-based design and development. Erin currently manages a top-notch team of instructional designers at The Hartford with a focus on consistent improvement, high quality standards, and applying best practices to the design role.

Erin Miller
Assistant Director, Training and Development
The Hartford
500 Bielenberg Drive
Woodbury, MN 55125
(651) 738.5338
Email: erin.miller@hartfordlife.com
ASTD Chapter: Twin Cities

Sample Scenario Cards

These sample situations will help you develop your own Scenario Cards for this activity.

Project Management
- Suppose you are leading a project, and the due date has moved up a month. How would you alter your project plan? How would you communicate with your project sponsor and team members? What risks and opportunities would you focus on?
- Imagine you are a team member on a large strategic project. Your direct manager has described your role and expects you to spend 25 percent of your time on the project. When you attend the kickoff, you learn that the project manager has a much larger role in mind and expects 75 percent of your time. What do you do? Who do you work with? What solution do you propose, and why? What are the possible risks and rewards of your solution?

Leadership
- Imagine the CEO of your company has just announced major strategic changes. Your direct reports received an all-employee email and attended a meeting announcing the new "Future Forward!" initiative. How do you help them link this broad corporate initiative with their day-to-day work? What kind of communication plan might you put in place? How will you act as a champion for this change?
- Some days you feel as if you are leading a soap opera cast rather than a production team. A half-dozen people have recently come to you with private complaints about their co-workers, ranging from quality and production concerns, to slights over lunch invitations, to truly inappropriate behavior. How do you approach this situation? What are your goals? Who will you work with, and what will be your approach? What are the risks and possible rewards of what you're suggesting?

Customer Service
- Three team members have called in sick, and the phone queues are overloaded. After some customers have been on hold for many minutes, several are upset

before you even greet them. How do you maintain your composure? What are some ways you can continue to deliver excellent service?

- A customer comes to your service counter who is clearly confused and frustrated about the product he recently purchased. It has features he doesn't understand, and he isn't even sure how to ask the right questions. How could you put such a customer at ease? What phrases, body language, and tone would be most effective?

Through the Looking Glass

Submitted by Jo Lynn Feinstein

Overview
A rainbow of Post-it® Notes is the defining feature of this activity, which methodically leads participants to discover solutions to organizational problems and challenges from the perspective of important stakeholders.

Objectives
- To identify service and/or performance gaps
- To prepare for strategic planning

Audience
Minimum of eight to ten from the same organization or work group

Time Estimate
2 to 3 hours

Materials and Equipment
- Post-it® 4 × 6–inch note pads of different colors, one for each table
- Fine-point marker for each table
- Tent cards of different colors that match the note pad colors
- One flip chart for each group, plus one for the facilitator
- Masking tape
- Whiteboard and markers

Area Setup
Set up the room with tables and chairs arranged for small groups of three or four. Place one note pad and one marker on each table, making sure that each group has a note pad of a different color. Leave sufficient open space in front of the whiteboard for three or four participants to stand and move around comfortably. Wall space near the whiteboard is needed to display multiple flip-chart sheets. Tent cards of various colors that match the color of the Post-it pads should be positioned on a table at the entrance.

Preparation

Send an invitation to participants at least one week in advance explaining the purpose of the workshop and ask them to come prepared to discuss how they and others see their organization. (If this activity is used for a single business unit or department, alter the wording of the invitation accordingly.)

Process

1. Greet participants upon arrival and ask them to select tent cards and print their names on both sides. Tell them they are free to sit wherever they like.
2. Open the session by reviewing the purpose of the activity. Explain that participants will be working together based on the color of their tent cards. Point out the different color Post-it Note pads on the tables. Tell the participants to find a table with a Post-it pad that matches the color of their selected tent card and move to that table.
3. After all the participants have relocated to the appropriate tables, ask each formed group to identify a recorder. This person will use the marker to capture ideas on the Post-it pad. Ask the recorders to write only one word, short phrase, or idea per sticky note.
4. Explain that the task of the groups is to determine how stakeholders (pick a stakeholder group, if you wish) would describe their organization (or their business unit or team). Allow 2 minutes for this step. Remind the recorders again to write only one or two words per sticky note.
5. Bring the large group back together and select one group and a volunteer to report out their ideas and suggestions.
6. After the group shares its ideas about how the organization is seen, take the notes from the group's reporter and place them on the whiteboard. Begin by roughly grouping the notes into categories based on the area of the business addressed. For example, you might have clusters of notes for topics such as customer service, efficiency, cost structure, culture, or others. If an idea applies to more than one topic, ask the group recorder to create another sticky note with that word or idea and post the idea in both clusters.
7. Repeat Step 6 for each group of participants. As you proceed, encourage participants to share "aha!" moments or make note of the similarities and differences among their ideas. You will end up with a multi-colored patchwork of sticky notes clustered loosely into common topic groupings.
8. Summarize the information that can be gleaned from this patchwork. Encourage observations and comments from the group.

9. Now tell the participants that they will examine this information from a different perspective.

10. Ask the participants to identify the top stakeholders whose views are critical for their organization's success. For example, the stakeholder might be customers, vendors, the board of directors, staff, or even competitors. List each stakeholder group at the top of its own flip-chart page and post the pages so they are visible to all participants and within easy access for you. At this point you may be working with four or more stakeholder flip-chart pages.

11. Select a cluster of sticky notes and peel one note at a time from the whiteboard. Ask the large group which of their stakeholders would describe the organization (or unit or team) in this way. Paste the sticky note on the flip-chart page with that stakeholder group heading. If more than one stakeholder group would describe the organization in that way, ask the recorder with the note pad color matching that sticky note to make another note with the same word. Attach that note to the flip-chart page for the second stakeholder group.

12. Continue through the sticky note clusters, allowing for questions and discussion as participants explore their views and the views of others in the room.

13. Ask each small group to go to one of the stakeholder group flip-chart pages and make a "T" to divide the sheet into two columns. Label the left column "current" and the right column "desired." Tell them to place the sticky notes in the appropriate columns based on how they think that stakeholder views the group/organization now and how they hope they view in the future. List the additional words/descriptions in each of the columns using additional sticky notes: current in the left column and the desired or "how we want this stakeholder group to describe the organization" in the right column.

14. After 10 minutes have the small groups move to different charts. Repeat this process until each small group has worked with each stakeholder chart.

15. Have the small groups return to their tables. Address one stakeholder flip-chart page at a time, identifying the gaps of each.

16. Summarize the gaps for each stakeholder on another flip-chart page. You may wish to have participants rank each entry based on criticality. This may take an additional 20 minutes.

17. Identify action items to address the most critical gaps. This step may take as long as an hour or more.

18. Prioritize the action items and list next steps for participants to take back to the job.

Solving Problems: Find Practical Solutions

InSider's Tips

- This can be a long and intense activity. Do everything you can to ensure that you and the participants are fully present and prepared. Take stretch breaks as needed.
- Sufficient discussion time is critical to the success of this activity, so plan accordingly. Do not shortchange the process.
- If participants are a mixture of line workers, supervisors, managers, and executives, or any combination of these, it will be crucial to create trust and safety around the entire process. Use your best judgment to determine whether you will meet with key players in advance or whether there are other ways you can build a safe environment.

Jo Lynn Feinstein, Ed.D., CPLP, has been actively engaged in individual and organizational performance improvement for nearly twenty years, including successful contributions to public and private organizations from startups to Fortune 500 companies. She was part of the pilot and among the first to earn the Certified Professional in Learning and Performance (CPLP) designation. Jo Lynn has been an invited speaker at conferences and workshops and was recognized as Educator of the Year by the Ventura County Economic Development Association. She remains active in ASTD and is on the Board of Hiring for Hope, a not-for-profit, offering staffing and other HR services.

Jo Lynn Feinstein, Ed.D., CPLP
3303 Storm Cloud Street
Thousand Oaks, CA 91360
(805) 551.5494
Email: jolynn@metro805.com
Website: www.jlfeinstein.com
ASTD Chapter: Los Angeles

Chapter **10**

Professional Development: Skills for the Workplace

As a trainer, most of what you do likely falls in the professional development category. This chapter focuses on those activities that help your participants learn skills that enhance their work every day and ultimately lead to career advancement.

It is your job to construct intellectually challenging and innovative learning experiences in a safe, supporting, and inclusive environment. Often the skills required don't fit tidily into a specific workshop topic. For example, you may not be teaching a stress management course, but that doesn't mean your learners don't need to know how to overcome the stress of learning new skills or taking on additional responsibility in their jobs.

The learning required may be more attitudinal than skill-based or more about professional values and commitment than knowledge. For example, being positive makes a huge difference in how people feel in the workplace and that "can do" outlook impacts their productivity. Yet few training programs include an opportunity for learners to improve their attitudes, unless you include positive thinking content tangential to an established course or during formal or informal one-on-one conversations during breaks or even after class with selected learners.

Although the activities in this chapter are written as workshop activities, they can be the bud of activities that go beyond the workshop to mentoring or coaching events, one-on-one discussions, or any of the other ways that you support your learners.

Key to any professional development is your own personal attitude, how you model the skills you advocate, and how you reinforce your learners. Antoinette Webster addresses the topic of enthusiasm. She says that "enthusiasm is to a person what gasoline is to the engine of an automobile: the vital moving force," and that fits with our road-tested theme. Your participants will like her activity. Sarah Hurst's "Stress Symphony" will have you laughing when you read it. It works! Activities from both Renie McClay and Jennifer Fetterhoff offer a way to have difficult discussions about how well your participants work both as a team and with other departments.

Cynthia Solomon demonstrates how a "graffiti wall" can be used to change behaviors and create a new culture. Her activity involves the entire organization. Sharon Dera's activity will help your participants see the value of their jobs. Barb Murray's activity makes its point quickly. The activity takes just 10 minutes to show us that we may be completing many tasks all day, but we don't remember much of what we did! Ruth Soskin's activity will help you ensure that your participants are prepared for their next interviews.

This broad array of activities can be woven into many different training program you design and deliver for your learners.

Activating Enthusiasm

Submitted by Antoinette S. Webster

Overview

Participants actively work to close their enthusiasm gap and learn how a lack of enthusiasm may impact their own success, the success of their organization, and their own long-term happiness.

Objectives

- To experience and become more aware of the dynamics of enthusiasm
- To identity the various ways enthusiasm can be expressed and experienced

Audience

Six to thirty participants, but has been successfully implemented with a group of more than 180

Time Estimate

20 to 30 minutes

Materials and Equipment

- Flip chart or PowerPoint slide with the letters: **P E M S** vertically on the left side
- Flip-chart paper and markers or blank paper and pens or pencils for small group discussion
- Enthusiasm Quotes wall chart, handout, or PowerPoint slide with the quotes used for the session
- Masking tape

Area Setup

Room arranged so that participants are able to form subgroups of three to six people and move about the room

Process

1. Introduce the activity with a brief discussion about enthusiasm. First ask the participants how they define it. Ask why they think enthusiasm is important.

Allow a couple of comments, providing positive nods. State that enthusiasm may be more than what people think. Direct participants' attention to the Enthusiasm Quotes you have posted or provide a handout and read them aloud. Solicit comments from the group.

2. Refer to the **P E M S** flip chart or slide. Ask whether participants have any idea what the letters stand for in relation to enthusiasm. As you fill in the words, state that this activity will help participants understand that enthusiasm is holistic—it is experienced and expressed **P**hysically, **E**motionally, **M**entally, and **S**piritually.

3. Invite participants to think about a time when they felt enthusiastic. Or they can think of a time when they observed others who were enthusiastic. Ask the participants what they remember about how the emotion affected them. Solicit three or four responses.

4. Ask participants to stand. Tell them that you want them to move around the room and demonstrate enthusiasm to the rest of the group. Allow 2 to 4 minutes for this, depending on the size of the group. Mention that the participants may feel silly or goofy at first but say that emotion is okay since everyone is doing this together. You may also ask them to act like someone they consider to be enthusiastic and demonstrate the behaviors or say the words that represent enthusiasm.

5. After the allotted time, ask the participants to form four small groups (more if you have a large group). Assign **P** to one group, **E** to one group, **M** to one group, and **S** to another group, repeating as necessary. Distribute flip-chart paper and markers or blank paper to each small group to enable them to capture and report their ideas.

6. Ask the small groups to develop a list of characteristics, behaviors, and traits for their respective quality as it relates to the experience and expression of enthusiasm: **P**hysical, **M**ental, **S**piritual, or **E**motional. Tell them they have 5 minutes for this activity.

7. At the end of the 5-minute period, call time and ask each of the small groups to report back to the larger group. Post flip charts on the wall for later reference if you wish.

8. Guide participants in linking this activity to the overall topic or focus of the session. Invite participants, as they go about their day-to-day activities, to notice how others express and experience enthusiasm.

InSider's Tips

- The majority of responses will be positive, but occasionally there are negative responses to the activity. This is natural, as participants are focusing on their direct experience and expression of enthusiasm and/or their observations of others.
- This activity creates awareness of how people show up (engaged) in the workplace and in life.
- Everyone has enthusiasm; it is innate within us, although for some, earlier experiences or messages may have caused their enthusiasm to become subdued.
- Activating enthusiasm directly relates to creativity, increased energy, clarity, productivity, and engagement along with a variety of skills and abilities.
- You may wish to spend a couple of minutes toward the end polling the group on the benefits of or connection between enthusiasm and the overall program topic and their role within the organization.
- The dynamics of enthusiasm are personal in addition to how a lack of enthusiasm affects teams, clients, and the organization.
- As an alternative, ask participants to demonstrate the *lack* of enthusiasm. If time is a consideration, have half the group demonstrate enthusiasm and the other half the lack of it.

Antoinette S. Webster is a dynamic, practical professional speaker, facilitator, coach, and author. She is president of A System That Works^{SM}, a speaking, training, coaching, and consulting company that applies an integrative approach for transformational growth and development. A System That Works offers quality, practical programs, products, and services targeted to the unique organizational culture and personal preferences. Antoinette is the author of *Enthusiasm! How to Draw It to Yourself and Keep It, Igniting the Spark of Enthusiasm!, Targeting Business Success, Effective Meeting Facilitation,* and *10 Steps for Training the Trainer . . . EFFECTIVELY.* She earned her MBA from Xavier University.

Antoinette S. Webster
LEAP II, SGM (and ME! ~ Master Enthusiast!)
A System That Works
640 Foster Avenue
Hamilton, OH 45015
(513) 887.0600
Email: Antoinette@ASystemthatWorks.com
ASTD Chapter: Greater Cincinnati

Enthusiasm Quotes

"Enthusiasm is in every person, it's just brought out in various ways."

—Unknown

"Enthusiasm is a state of mind that inspires and arouses a person to action; it is contagious and affects not only the enthused, but everyone with whom he or she comes in contact. Enthusiasm is to a person what gasoline is to the engine of an automobile; the vital moving force. . . .

"If you mix enthusiasm with your work, it will never be difficult or monotonous.

"It will be fun and exciting."

—W. Clement Stone

Stress Symphony

Submitted by Sarah E. Hurst

Overview

Participants take part in a colorful stress-reduction symphony that demonstrates how laugher and having fun are the best remedies to redirect our stress-filled lives toward a more relaxed pace.

Objective

- To practice ways to reduce stress

Audience

Ten to twenty-five participants

Time Estimate

10 to 15 minutes, more if you want to use the activity for a larger group

Materials and Equipment

- One sheet of yellow, blue, or green paper cut into squares or rectangles no larger than 6" × 6" for each participant

Area Setup

Any room or setting in which participants are able to see each other

Process

1. Bring your stack of colored paper to the session ready to distribute with the colors mixed in the stack. Explain to the participants that they are going to do a stress buster.
2. Pass the stack of papers and ask each participant to select one piece of any color. Ask the participants to stand and hold their selected papers.
3. Next, ask participants for examples of unrelieved stress. Expect them to respond with headaches, stomach aches, or illness. Explain that this easy activity often will help them reduce their stress levels.
4. Ask the participants with the blue paper to hold up their sheets; you hold a blue sheet up as well. State that when we are stressed we sometimes forget

to breathe. Ask this group to breathe with you by following your breathing example.

5. Holding up the blue paper, inhale loudly followed by a loud exhale. Push your shoulders up and down in an exaggerated motion when you inhale and exhale. Tell them that when you hold up the blue paper they must follow your example and inhale and exhale loudly.

6. Hold a piece of blue paper up and let those who chose the blue paper practice breathing, loudly inhaling and exhaling. Thank the participants and tell them they can stop for now but to hold onto their blue papers.

7. Ask the participants who chose the yellow colored paper to hold up their choice. Explain that these participants will sing with you, because singing loosens the diaphragm and allows more air into the lungs and the brain, thus reducing stress.

8. Loudly sing the vocal scale, "la, la, la, la, la, la, la," flinging your right and left arms out to your sides. Explain to the yellow paper holders that they must sing when you hold up the yellow piece of paper.

9. Allow the participants holding the yellow paper to practice singing and flinging their arms. Tell the yellow paper holders to stop singing for now, but remind them to hold onto their yellow papers.

10. Ask the participants who chose the green paper to hold up their choice. You hold up a green paper as well and tell them that stress can be relieved with movement, relaxing their body tension.

11. Tell the green paper group that they must follow your example as you shake your body and hum loudly. Allow the green colored paper participants to practice your given example. Then tell them they may stop but, like the others, hold onto their green paper for later use.

12. Now announce that you will conduct a symphony of stress relief. Remind the group that when their chosen color of paper is lifted up they must sing, breathe, or move as they have just practiced.

13. Lift up one color at a time, waiting for the response from the group. Repeat this exercise in several sequences—yellow, green, blue or green, blue, yellow.

14. Lift up two different colors of paper, waiting for the response from the group. Repeat this symphony prompt with different combinations of colors several times. Interject single pieces of paper several times selecting colors faster and faster.

15. Finally, put up all three pieces of paper at one time.

16. By now the entire group should be laughing and joking about the activity.

17. Debrief by asking the participants whether they are now relaxed. Ask what made them relax. Ask them what they could do to relax in the future.
18. Remind participants that any time they feel stressed they can easily just breathe, move, sing, or laugh to relax. Suggest that they can always think back on this exercise and laugh causing instant stress relief.

InSider's Tips

- This exercise is for fun and relaxation; be prepared to laugh at yourself.
- Be sure to set a loud example when showing the participants what is expected when the papers are held up. Overdramatize the examples for better results.
- Hold up each color of paper at least two times before beginning the symphony; this gives each group equal time to practice.
- Move the participants through the exercise faster and faster when they begin the symphony; this creates a jovial mood and more relaxation.
- Laughing is a great stress reliever, so encourage the laughter and camaraderie that occur during this activity.
- This activity can be used as part of a stress class or in any other program to reduce stress and refocus the group.

Sarah E. Hurst is the training manager of Stewart & Stevenson LLC, Houston, Texas, and has been in training for over eighteen years. She is responsible for researching, developing, creating, and presenting classes on leadership, communication, project management, and more. Sarah's participant activity "Project Change Challenge" is published in Pfeiffer's 2008 resource book, *Trainer's Warehouse Book of Games: Fun and Energizing Ways to Enhance Learning*. Sarah's ASTD membership began in 1996 and she is currently president-elect of the Houston chapter.

Sarah E. Hurst
27222 Yale Street
Pasadena, TX 77502
(713) 477.8587
Email: s.hurst@ssss.com
ASTD Chapter: Houston

Zoom!

Submitted by Renie McClay

Overview

A team of participants must figure out how to reassemble a book with no page numbers or other easily discernable way to complete the task to demonstrate the advantages of good team communication, the nature of leadership, and other group dynamics.

Objectives

- To experience working as a team with little vision or direction
- To identify team dynamics that will help or hinder results

Audience

Four to twelve participants who work together

Time Estimate

15 to 30 minutes

Materials and Equipment

- Two copies of the book *Zoom*, by Istvan Banyai

Area Setup

Any area

Preparation

Purchase two copies of the *Zoom* book from your favorite retailer or bookstore. Cut out pages from one of the books and put them in random order before coming to the session.

Process

1. Give the random pages to the team with few verbal instructions.
2. Let the team figure out what needs to be done.
3. Once the team has the pages in the order they feel is right, give them the intact book to check their work.

4. Summarize the activity with questions such as these:
   - What team behaviors helped you to complete this activity?
   - Did any team behaviors hinder the process?
   - How was this activity similar to what occurs in real life?
   - How was communication, did you felt listened to, heard?
   - What team dynamics were occurring?
   - Who was leading the process? How was leadership occurring? Was that helpful?
   - What could have made this activity go more smoothly?
   - What is the future application to the team of what happened here?
   - Did you see anything you should continue doing as you work together in the future? Stop doing? Start doing?

InSider's Tips

- This book is perfect for this activity. It has images on only one side of the page and has no page numbers.
- The team needs to discuss and decide what to do; they often break into sub-groups and sequence sections of the book.
- The book will generally be sequenced correctly, however, they may confuse the front and back.

Renie McClay has managed training for three different Fortune 500 companies, including Kraft, Gerber, and Pactiv. She has written *Fortify Your Sales Force* (Pfeiffer), *The Essential Guide to Training Global Audiences* (Pfeiffer), and *10 Steps to Successful Teams* (ASTD Press). In addition to helping companies strengthen their teams and their sales forces, she helps them to successfully on-board new employees by creating effective new hire orientations and mentoring programs. She facilitates around the world in a classroom as well as virtually. Renie is a past president of SMT: Center for Sales Excellence.

Renie McClay
1177 Russetwood Court
Wheeling, IL 60090
(847) 215.2364
Email: rmcclay@inspiredtolearn.net
Website: www.inspiredtolearn.net
ASTD Chapter: Chicagoland

Puzzled Prospects

Submitted by Jennifer Fetterhoff

Overview

Assembling a child's puzzle helps team or group members find new and improved communication pathways while learning valuable problem-solving skills.

Objectives

- To use teamwork to develop communication and problem-solving skills
- To explore the challenges of interdepartmental communication when one department cannot see all the information
- To discuss ways to improve interdepartmental communications

Audience

Five to fifteen members of a project team or senior management composed of members from multiple levels or departments (More than fifteen participants require more puzzles.)

Time Estimate

20 to 45 minutes, depending on the size of the group

Materials and Equipment

- Children's large floor puzzle that can be found anywhere toys or educational learning supplies are sold
- Two blindfolds
- (Optional) Large table if participants cannot sit on the floor easily

Area Setup

A room with enough space for an open team activity on the floor or a large table

Process

1. Place the puzzle pieces upside down on the floor in front of the participants.
2. Recruit two individuals as volunteers to be blindfolded. Ask them to sit on the floor next to the puzzles before they are blindfolded.

250

3. Ask the remaining participants to provide instructions to the two blindfolded participants for assembling the puzzle. Explain that there are two rules:
   - Only the blindfolded participants can touch the puzzle pieces and move them around.
   - Both blindfolded participants must work together at the instructions of their team to complete the entire puzzle.
4. Tell participants that they have approximately 15 minutes to complete the puzzle. (Option: If time permits, continue until the puzzle has been put together successfully.)
5. When the time is up or the puzzle has been successfully put together, debrief using questions such as these:
   - Ask the blindfolded participants, "Can you share what was easy about the task or what was challenging about the task?"
   - Ask the other participants, "What was easy and what was challenging for you?"
   - How was this activity like your daily work? Utilize the participants' responses and examples to return to the essence of communication and teamwork, not only within their specific team, but also when other teams may be involved, such as with projects or other departments or companies.
   - How does it feel when other departments or teams do not accurately communicate with you? Have you ever been blindsided?
   - Use your own observations of what occurred and explain how what you observed may have helped or hindered the efforts.
   - Based on what was easy and what was challenging, how could you transfer those lessons to the workplace?
6. If time permits, undo the puzzle, place upside down, shuffle the pieces around, and ask for two more volunteers to repeat the process.
7. After the puzzle has been completed a second time, ask these additional questions of the blindfolded participants:
   - Was it easier or harder for you to do this activity compared to the first participants?
   - What advantage or disadvantage did you have (they were able to see what the finished puzzle looked like prior to becoming blindfolded)?
   - Use the participants' answers to compare how what happened relates to their positions/departmental communications. Does it help to have a "vision" of what the final outcome is supposed to be, even if there is still a "blinder" feeling when working on a project?

- Help participants compare the first attempt and the second attempt at the activity and how it may have helped or hindered their efforts. Then ask:
  - How is putting the puzzle together like interdepartmental communication?
  - What have you done to inhibit good communication between your department and others?
  - What can you do to improve interdepartmental communications?
  - What the greatest lesson you've learned here?

InSider's Tips

- Using the participants' specific examples and playing off of their conversations helps drive the debriefing portion of this activity.
- Any time I have used this activity, the participants have loved it. It is really an eye-opener for those departments who may have to work with numerous other departments on projects. It helps them to understand how important communication is and, although the vision may be clear to them, those they are communicating with may not have that same vision.
- The activity works best if you can use a table rather than the floor. The larger the group is, the harder it is to see what is happening with the puzzle.
- The activity works best with ten to twelve participants. If you have a larger group, you may want to have several puzzles available to keep the size of the groups to ten or twelve per puzzle. When debriefing the activity though, use the observations from all groups and allow the participants to share how each experience may have differed or what similarities there may have been.
- No matter how you choose to conduct the activity, debrief the same way, always bringing the conversation back to how each team contributes to the overall success of the ultimate vision and each contributes an important part to its success.
- As additional variations, take one of the puzzle pieces out of the activity so that participants cannot complete the entire puzzle. You could also have one participant hide a puzzle piece and not participate until the end, then surrender the piece to the group. You could also break the participants into groups with only certain puzzle pieces, and each group must first put their pieces together and then regroup as a whole to complete the puzzle.

Jennifer Fetterhoff is the training coordinator with Belco Community Credit Union. She is responsible for ongoing strategic employee development, including leadership, service, and technical skills. She is currently working on her associate's degree in business. Jennifer is passionate about learning and educating others, spending time with her daughter, Kerri Anne, and her two dogs, Buttons and Kevin. She is also active within her church and community and is the 2010 co-editor of the Central PA ASTD chapter newsletter, "Hello Central."

Jennifer Fetterhoff
Training Coordinator
Belco Community Credit Union
449 Eisenhower Boulevard
Harrisburg, PA 17111
(717) 720.6232
Email: fetterhoffj@belco.org
Website: www.belco.org
ASTD Chapter: Central Pennsylvania

Performance Graffiti Wall
Submitted by Cynthia Solomon

Overview

This activity represents the intersection of old-world technology (think "town crier" or community bulletin board) and 21st century social networking as participants post what they are doing to achieve organizational or team goals in "real time."

Objectives

- To engage in continuous daily identification and share ideal organizational behaviors
- To display individual successes in accomplishing the highlighted behavior of the week
- To establish a new culture of improved behavior that becomes the new norm

Audience

Any number of people who share some scope of work, a department, team, or other work unit

Time Estimate

Initial instructions take 10 to 15 minutes. Because this is a "real time" workplace activity, the bulk of the time required happens during the week as the participants carry out the instructions provided.

Materials and Equipment

- A place appropriate for participants to write on over the period of one week. This area is the "graffiti wall." Examples of an appropriate surface include a flip-chart sheet or poster board taped or tacked to a wall at a comfortable height to accommodate all participants.

Area Setup

This is a "real time" activity that does not occur in a room. The "graffiti wall" is best located in a central hallway where the most participants will see it daily or very often. The idea is that individual members of a work group write instances of observing a chosen set of ideal behaviors for that week.

254

Process

1. Select a particular behavior that the organization values as an important part of its culture. An example might be: responded to a request for information within XX minutes/hours/days; helped another person solve a problem; identified and mitigated a potential safety hazard; gave some expression of genuine gratitude for the service provided by another; identified and reported a way to save money for the organization. The behaviors should support the organization's mission and strategic goals.

2. Agree at the organizational leadership level on the set of cultural behaviors that will be demonstrated across the organization each week. This will engage the entire organization in focusing on the same behavior in different departments.

3. At the weekly department meetings, conduct a brief 10-to-15-minute in-service session that explains the purpose of the graffiti wall. Stress these points:

   - We are focusing on identifying, reporting, sharing, and celebrating the behaviors we value as part of our organizational culture. Discuss how the identified behavior helps the organization meet its mission and/or strategic goals.
   - For the next week, you are asked to write, draw, or chart something that represents how you demonstrated the "behavior of the week" that is marked at the top of the graffiti wall.
   - You may add as many behaviors as you like, but be specific each time. You may also add something positive you experienced or viewed a colleague doing.
   - At each weekly meeting, we will acknowledge and celebrate our efforts to implement our desired organizational culture and values.
   - Everyone is expected to add something each week.

4. Place the "Graffiti Wall" in a prominent place where all will pass by during the day. Place pens or markers so that contributors can add their behaviors.

InSider's Tips

- The graffiti walls can be displayed at a quarterly or biannual meeting as a reminder of how members of the organization are working toward living the organizational culture and behaviors.
- If the graffiti wall becomes full, add another page or board for the week.

Cynthia Solomon, Ph.D., is an associate professor of education and coordinator of the graduate program in human resource development at Tusculum College, Greeneville, Tennessee. In addition to her primary academic responsibilities, Cynthia manages her own consultant service, CSolomon and Associates, specializing in leadership and team development skills, organizational performance management, organizational culture studies, and change, all functions of the instructional systems design model, and train-the-trainer workshops. Her work has been published in two ASTD *Info-lines* and Pfeiffer's *Team and Organization Development Annual.*

Cynthia Solomon, Ph.D.
114 Walosi Way
Loudon, TN 37774
(865) 408.1520
Email: csolomonphd@att.net
ASTD Chapter: Smoky Mountain

Part of the Big Picture

Submitted by Sharon Dera

Overview
This activity underscores the vital connections between the individual players in organizations and teams through the creative use of a puzzle metaphor.

Objectives
- To understand what effect one's actions have on others
- To understand how helping others obtain what they want helps us

Audience
Twenty to fifty participants in groups of six to eight

Time Estimate
20 to 25 minutes

Materials and Equipment
- PowerPoint slide of puzzle pieces (see the example)
- Projector and screen
- Flip chart and markers

Area Setup
Any setup

Process
1. Project the puzzle piece image.
2. Ask the participants to form small groups and discuss the posted question: "If I stopped doing my job, who would it affect?"
3. Ask each small group to select a leader to ensure all participants provide input. Also ask each group to take notes to share with the entire group. Allow 5 to 7 minutes.
4. After the time is over, ask everyone to gather as a large group. Ask for one example from each small group and write examples on the flip chart.

5. Ask, "Do we have any individuals in the room whose job affects someone else's?" When a participant answers, probe deeper by asking "how" the other individual would be affected. Ask the rest of the group, "What would happen if one of you stopped doing your job?"

6. If a number of people are in the large group whose jobs affect others in the room, ask participants to physically move to show the relationships. For example, Person A affects B and C. The participants might form a triangle in the middle of the room as a demonstration. You could ask, "Does anyone else's job relate to A, B, or C?" If yes, these participants could join the group in the middle. If there are no more relationships to the first triad, start a second one, keeping A, B, and C in their positions.

7. After you've found all the relationships in the room, debrief the activity by asking:
   - What have you discovered about your job?
   - What does the statement "helping others obtain what they want helps you" mean?
   - What might you do differently in the future?

InSider's Tip

- This activity works well by helping participants to understand the importance of their jobs, how they relate to others' jobs in the organization, and how everything fits into the "big picture."

Sharon Dera, CPLP, has more than seventeen years of experience in needs assessment, human performance, process improvement, and organization development. Her broad experience was acquired by working in the retail, finance, healthcare, government, manufacturing, hospitality, and travel industries in operations, business management, customer service, sales, communications, marketing, succession planning, leadership, coaching, and training. Sharon is owner and CEO of The Proficience Group, Inc., working in partnership with organizations to identify the root cause of performance deficiencies and determine the best solutions/interventions that close the performance gap. Her company lends a "fresh set of eyes," exposing possible blind spots. Sharon is currently serving on the National ASTD Chapter Recognition Committee. The earned an MBA from Dallas University.

Sharon Dera, CPLP
8948 Random Road
Fort Worth, TX 76179
(817) 236.7594
Email: sdera@charter.net
Website: www.proficiencegroup.com
ASTD Chapter: Fort Worth Mid-Cities

Sample Puzzle Pieces

If I stopped doing my job, who would it affect?

Multitasking Stressors

Submitted by Barbara Murray

Overview

This activity explores the downsides and risks of keeping "lots of balls in the air."

Objectives

- To discuss how expectations in the workplace may lead to stress
- To experience how we may complete many tasks but not really know what we did

Audience

A minimum of ten or twelve

Time Estimate

10 to 15 minutes

Materials and Equipment

- Small item for each participant (paper clip, eraser, pen, stir stick, rubber band, or other small items)
- Blank sheet of paper and a pencil for each participant
- Bag or container to conceal the items

Area Setup

A room large enough for the participants to stand and to create a large circle

Process

1. Ask participants to stand and form a circle close enough for them to pass a small item to the next person.
2. Hand each participant one small item such as a pen, paperclip, or eraser. Tell participants that this activity will re-create a situation not unlike what happens at work.
3. Have the participants pass the items to the left, faster and faster, until someone drops one. When someone drops an item, ask the participant to step out of the circle to discontinue play. Pick the dropped item up and place it back in play.
4. Have the remaining participants pass the items to the right, faster and faster, until someone drops an item. Ask the participant to discontinue play and step out of the circle. Pick the dropped item up and place it back in play.

5. Keep the passing game going until you have one or two people left.
6. Ask everyone to sit down while you gather the items and conceal them.
7. Hand out blank sheets of paper and pencils. Ask participants to silently list what items were passed around. Identify who has the most correct items. You may need to dump the items out of the container to "prove" some item was included.
8. Announce that there are two winners: one for the last people standing and one for the most items listed correctly. Lead applause for both.
9. Summarize with these questions:
   • What did you observe during the activity?
   • How does this relate to what occurs daily on the job?
   • What could be done differently in the activity and on the job?
   • How could this discussion help you in the future?
   • What is significant about the fact that we passed the items over and over and still could not remember all of them?

InSider's Tips

• Participants are surprised when they have to remember what they passed.
• This activity is lively and yet meaningful. We can be passing things in a frenzy and don't even take the time to see what we are doing.

Barbara Murray is currently president of the ASTD Great Plains chapter (GPASTD). She has been a dual member of ASTD for nine years, actively serving on the GPASTD Board for six years. Barbara has worked in training and development for more than eleven years. She is responsible for PREMIER Bankcard Management Development, serving more than three hundred managers and key personnel. She prides herself on being a servant leader. She has developed and delivered numerous management development courses to serve the needs of the PREMIER team. Barbara provides the tools and training necessary to assist the managers in becoming great PREMIER leaders.

Barbara Murray
4902 South Oxbow Avenue
Sioux Falls, SD 57106
(605) 357.3401
Email: bmurray@premierbankcard.com
ASTD Chapter: Great Plains

Get Ready for Interviewing

Submitted by Ruth Soskin

Overview

Sometimes the smallest details have the greatest impact on the successful outcome of a job interview. This activity helps participants to avoid overlooking these possible job-killing details.

Objective

- To identify areas of the interview process that participants need to improve to be effective in finding employment
- To provide insight into how to prepare for an interview

Audience

Fifteen to thirty participants who are seeking a new job

Time Estimate

30 to 40 minutes, with more time for discussion if schedule permits

Materials and Equipment

- Flip charts
- Markers
- Masking tape

Area Setup

A room with enough space that small groups can stand or sit around a flip chart for a discussion

Process

1. Begin the session with all participants in one group. State that many interviewees overlook that the interview process begins before meeting with the interviewer (whether the interview is on the phone or in person). This may be obvious to the seasoned interviewer but provides an "aha" moment to others. For example, those going for an interview should consider how they feel on the inside as well as how they look on the outside. What you feel like on the

inside and look like on the outside impact the first impression that you make. If you have a negative attitude because your job search is going badly, you may need to change your "inward appearance" to make a positive impact. Ask participants what overall steps they use to prepare for an interview.

2. As participants contribute to the conversation, translate their statements into general categories such as:
   - What I need to know about the company
   - Questions for the interviewee
   - Questions for the interviewer
   - Appearance—how I feel on the inside as well as how I look on the outside
   - Differences in interview preparation for telephone versus in-person interview
   - Post-interview etiquette

3. List one heading each at the top of separate flip-chart pages.

4. Divide participants into at least three groups of three to five participants each.

5. Give each group one of the flip-chart pages from the previous discussion. (If you have a small group, give each subgroup more than one flip-chart sheet.)

6. Tell participants they have about 10 minutes to brainstorm all ideas applicable to the topic assigned to them.

7. Each group should select a recorder to log ideas on the flip chart and a spokesperson for sharing the ideas with the large group.

8. After 10 minutes, ask each group to report out. Add other ideas as they come up in the discussion.

9. Summarize the discussion by asking:
   - What steps, if any, did you overlook in preparing for your interview?
   - What will you do differently next time?

InSider's Tips

- Although this activity seems basic, it starts participants thinking about how to prepare for an interview.
- I created this for first-time job seekers, but this activity will also work well for job readiness training.
- This activity exposes participants to group work and collaboration.
- This activity is an effective "warm up" for behavioral interviewing.

- Interviewing is a stressful process. This activity gives participants a chance to prepare for the interview process and feel more confident about it.
- The interviewing process involves more than anxiously waiting for the phone to ring or an email message inviting the job seeker to an interview with a potential employer.
- This activity demonstrates proactive behaviors.

Ruth Soskin, Trainology, Inc., is an energetic, goal-oriented training and development consultant. Learning should be collaborative and fun! She has fifteen years' expertise in adult learning in telecommunications, computer applications, and soft skills. Ruth has an M.A. in counseling. Her counseling skills contribute to her ability to work with people of diverse backgrounds and aptitudes. She earned certifications in Myers-Briggs Type Indicator (MBTI), Developmental Dimensions International (DDI), Blessing White's Managing Personal Growth, and Helping Others Succeed. She is also a certified customer service instructor for the National Retail Association.

Ruth Soskin
835 Ridge Avenue #303
Evanston, IL 60202
(847) 866.8604
Email: ruthsoskin@trainology.com
ASTD Chapter: Not a member yet

Section II

Training Tools and Techniques

Chapter 11

Icebreakers: Getting to Know You

The key purpose of an icebreaker is to introduce your group members to each other and to introduce your training session topic. A well-planned icebreaker ensures that a training session will start with more involvement and focus. When planning your icebreaker, remember these guidelines.

Never ask anyone to do anything you would not want to do. All of your activities, including icebreakers, should maintain participants' self-esteem, build trust, and enhance what they are learning. Select an icebreaker based on the type of group you are training. You are not likely to use the same icebreaker with a group of engineers that you would with a sales team. Relate the icebreaker to the content.

If your icebreaker introduces the training session's content, it ensures that you are making every minute count. You use the icebreaker as another training tool to help your learners focus on what's important right from the start of your session. Use your icebreaker to set the tone of your session and to establish an environment for learning. Icebreakers also give you an early indication of the participation level you can expect from your participants.

Observe the group during the icebreaker to learn something about the group as well as the individual participants. The time you spend conducting an icebreaker activity is also a perfect opportunity to determine who among the participants you might tag as the natural-born leaders, who might have a tendency to dominate, and who will likely need some coaxing to speak up. This information will help you to manage the group later. Watch the time during an icebreaker. If you have designed an exciting icebreaker, it is easy to lose control and either exceed the time limit for the activity or squander the positive energy created by the activity.

Participants learn as much from each other as from the program, so start quickly with introductions that are directly tied to an icebreaker. Knowing something about the other individuals in the session will make it easier for them to listen, to contribute, and to become involved.

This chapter presents you with a wide selection of icebreakers. The first four provide you with options to solve a classic icebreaker issue: whether you want participants to conduct their introductions from their seats to save time or whether you want them to stand up and engage in a more one-on-one activity. "What's Under Your Bed?" (The title of this activity makes you want to turn to it immediately!) by Christi Gilchrist is an icebreaker that ensures a few laughs. Sharon Dera shares two of her favorite icebreakers and, to pique you interest, she uses candy and toilet paper! Lisa Downs asks participants to reveal their nicknames in her icebreaker.

Davis Robinson and Sharon Dera provide two icebreakers that are conducted in small groups. Each takes only 20 minutes and both are appropriate for very large groups. In "Immodest Interview," J.T. Kostman instructs participants to introduce each other in a novel way. This tried-and-true, road-tested activity always works. Amanda Luster gets energy flowing with "Who's Snowball?" Kenneth Stein shares an icebreaker that lasts throughout the entire session. Finally, Emily Crouch starts participants thinking about the subject matter as part of their own introduction to the class.

These icebreakers can be used and adapted in many ways for almost any audience. Choose one that is right for your audience.

What's Under Your Bed?

Submitted by Christi Gilchrist

Overview

Revealing, humorous, interesting, and "too much information" possibilities reside in this simple but effective activity.

Objectives

- To initiate discussion for participants who need to know each other better
- To learn interesting facts about other participants in a workshop setting

Audience

Appropriate for groups of any size

Time Estimate

20 to 30 minutes, depending on group size

Materials and Equipment

- One What's Under Your Bed? handout for each participant
- Pens or pencils for all participants
- (Optional) Fine-point markers

Area Setup

Any appropriately sized room

Process

1. Give each person a copy of the What's Under Your Bed? handout and a pen or pencil. If you want to encourage participants to draw pictures or be creative, give them fine-point markers.
2. Tell participants that they should try to answer as many questions on the handout as possible. Tell them that they have 2 minutes for the task. *Note:* If you encourage them to draw pictures, allow 5 or 10 minutes for this step.
3. After the appropriate amount of time has elapsed, discuss the first question on the handout and ensure that everyone responds. Go on to the next question, making comments along the way and ensuring all respond, until all the questions have been answered.

4. If you ask participants to draw their responses, you could collect them and hold one up at a time. Ask participants to guess what the picture(s) might be. After participants have had a moment to guess what a picture represents, the artist of the picture can introduce him- or herself and explain the drawing.

5. For very large groups you can ask participants to circulate around the room meeting other people using their responses as discussion starters.

InSider's Tips

- This is a very simple and quick activity for introductions and for expressing and revealing personalities. Give participants time to think and write on their handouts.

- The activity may be adapted for other types of questions. The optional step of drawing answers to the questions is fun, but takes more time. Having participants guess the item that is drawn adds an element of creativity.

- If you are flexible with the distribution, number, and size of a small group activity, you may use this activity to put people into small groups. For example, when asking the question, What's under your bed? three people say books, four say dust, five say dirty clothes, and two say they don't know. You can use these answers to form four small groups.

Christi Gilchrist is an organization development consultant at CenterPoint Energy in Houston, Texas. She has over thirteen years of diverse experience in human resource management, education and training, curriculum development, classroom instruction, internal consulting, and organization development. Christi is passionate about driving company retention through large-scale company initiatives and helping people find and fit their strengths to combat their organizational challenges. Christi graduated from The University of Texas at Austin with a bachelor's degree in sociology and from The University of London External Program with a master of arts degree in applied educational leadership and management.

Christi Gilchrist
509 Avondale Lane
Friendswood, TX 77546
(713) 207.6923
Email: christi.gilchrist@centerpointenergy.com
ASTD Chapter: Houston

What's Under Your Bed?

What's Under Your Bed?

What's in Your CD Player?

What's in Your Pantry?

What's in Your Car Trunk?

Tell Me Something Good

Submitted by Sharon Dera

Overview

Candy color choice determines the question participants must answer, and the information shared in this activity is designed to encourage engagement in your session's content.

Objectives

- To encourage people to share something interesting about themselves
- To encourage participation right from the start

Audience

Ten to fifty participants

Time Estimate

5 to 20 minutes

Materials and Equipment

- Colored candies (any brand or variety such as Spree, Mentos®, jelly beans, suckers, or M&M'S®)
- A PowerPoint slide with list of questions that correspond to the candy colors you selected
- LCD projector and screen

Area Setup

Any room or activity area

Process

1. Distribute rolls, packages, or wrapped candy to each person.
2. Ask participants to open the candy and select one piece.
3. Display the PowerPoint slide with color-coded questions.
4. Ask for a volunteer to begin the activity by introducing him- or herself.
   The volunteer should state his or her name, title, and department
   (or company if appropriate) and answer the question that matches the color of
   the candy piece selected.

274

5. Ask for another volunteer. Request the same basic information from the participant and ask the individual to answer the question that matches the color of the candy piece selected.
6. Follow this pattern for the rest of the participants before ending the activity.

InSider's Tips

- Individually wrapped candies are the least messy.
- Be sure to have participants select their candy color before you display the questions.
- If you don't have candy available, you could have the participants select a favorite colored candy before displaying the questions. For example, "What is your favorite color Life Saver®?"
- The following questions are examples of what works well:
    - (Red) If you could have dinner with three people, who would they be and why?
    - (Yellow) What is your idea of an ideal vacation?
    - (Green) If you were stuck on a deserted island, what three items would you like to have with you and why?
    - (Pink) If you won one million dollars in the lottery, what would you do with it?
    - (Orange) If you were a car, what type would you be and why?
    - (Blue) What is your favorite dessert and why?
    - (Purple) What cartoon character are you most like and why?

Sharon Dera, CPLP, has more than seventeen years of experience in needs assessment, human performance, process improvement, and organization development. Her broad experience was acquired by working in the retail, finance, healthcare, government, manufacturing, hospitality, and travel industries in operations, business management, customer service, sales, communications, marketing, succession planning, leadership, coaching, and training. Sharon is owner and CEO of The Proficience Group, Inc., working in partnership with organizations to identify the root cause of performance deficiencies and determine the best solutions/interventions to close performance gaps. Her company lends a "fresh set of eyes," exposing possible blind spots. Sharon is currently serving on the National ASTD Chapter Recognition Committee. She earned an MBA from the University of Dallas.

Sharon Dera, CPLP
8948 Random Road
Fort Worth, TX 76179
(817) 236.7594
Email: sdera@charter.net
Website: www.proficiencegroup.com
ASTD Chapter: Fort Worth Mid-Cities

Getting to Know You ... Getting to Know All About You

Submitted by Sharon Dera

Overview
A roll of toilet paper becomes a humorous "talking stick" as each tissue sheet rolled off by the participant requires one bit of information be shared.

Objectives
- To encourage people to open up and feel comfortable with the group
- To introduce participants and learn more about them

Audience
Fifteen to twenty-five

Time Estimate
15 minutes

Materials and Equipment
- Roll of toilet paper

Area Setup
Any room arrangement

Process
1. Hand the roll of toilet paper to someone in the group you've determined to be an outgoing individual, stating, "Take as much as you think you'll need. Then pass the roll to the next person." (*Note:* This usually gets some strange looks and also a lot of laughs.)
2. Encourage the participant to pass the toilet paper to the next person and then say, "Take as much as you think you'll need. Then pass the roll to the next person."
3. Facilitate this toilet paper sharing and passing activity until all participants have had an opportunity to take some of the toilet paper.

4. Roll off a few squares of the toilet paper yourself (three or four squares) and set the roll aside.

5. Explain to the participants that they will use the paper to introduce themselves by giving one piece of information for each square.

6. Demonstrate the activity by tearing off one square at a time while providing a piece of information about yourself. For example (1) your name; (2) job title/function; (3) number of years in profession; (4) the kind of pet you have and its name.

7. Select one of the participants to follow your lead and provide one piece of information per square of toilet paper.

8. Select another participant to share his or her information in the same manner and continue by moving around the room until everyone has had an opportunity to introduce him- or herself.

InSider's Tips

- Be prepared with information-sharing suggestions to assist those who may have taken a long strip of the toilet paper and need some helpful information-sharing ideas, for example, birthplace, marital status, children/names/ages, pets/names/ages, hobbies, favorite foods/songs/vacation spots, to keep the communication pace going.
- This activity gets people talking and laughing and is always well received.

Sharon Dera, CPLP, has more than seventeen years of experience in needs assessment, human performance, process improvement, and organization development. Her broad experience was acquired by working in the retail, finance, healthcare, government, manufacturing, hospitality, and travel industries in operations, business management, customer service, sales, communications, marketing, succession planning, leadership, coaching, and training. Sharon is owner and CEO of The Proficience Group, Inc., working in partnership with organizations to identify the root cause of performance deficiencies and determine the best solutions/interventions to close performance gaps. The company lends a "fresh set of eyes," exposing possible blind spots. Sharon is currently serving on the National ASTD Chapter Recognition Committee. She earned an MBA from the University of Dallas.

Sharon Dera, CPLP
8948 Random Road
Fort Worth, TX 76179
(817) 236.7594
Email: sdera@charter.net
Website: www.proficiencegroup.com
ASTD Chapter: Fort Worth Mid-Cities

What's in a Name?

Submitted by Lisa Downs

Overview

Participants play a game of nickname guessing that encourages connection and camaraderie at the start of a training session.

Objectives

- To allow the participants to introduce themselves at the start of a training session
- To learn about the other participants in the training session for better camaraderie

Audience

Fifteen or more

Time Estimate

Approximately 10 to 15 minutes

Materials and Equipment

- One index card for each participant
- One pen or pencil for each participant

Area Setup

A U-shaped or circular arrangement

Process

1. Ask participants to write a nickname they either currently have or had as a child on the index cards you hand out and, when finished, place the index cards face down in front of them. Tell participants not to let anyone see what they wrote.
2. Collect the cards, shuffle them, and read the first nickname aloud. Ask the group to guess who the nickname belongs to.

3. Once the nickname and the person are revealed, ask the individual to share how the nickname came about.
4. Repeat this process until everyone has been paired with his or her nickname.

InSider's Tips

- Include your nickname in the mix to build rapport.
- This activity also works well with items like favorite foods, hobbies, unique interests, past vacation experiences, or favorite music styles or artists.
- This is a great icebreaker for a group of learners that will be in a multi-day session or one that will be highly interactive, as participants enjoy using each other's nicknames (respectfully). It helps to bond a new group.

Lisa Downs is a learning consultant with Intrepid Learning Solutions in Seattle, Washington. Previously, she was a leadership development manager with T-Mobile USA, where she conducted and developed manager, leader, and personal effectiveness training and coaching. Before working at T-Mobile, she worked in the accounting industry as a training manager and consultant. In addition to serving as the 2008 president and 2006–2007 vice president of membership for the ASTD Puget Sound chapter, she is the 2010 chair of the ASTD Chapter Recognition Committee and a member of the National Advisors for Chapters committee. Lisa is the author of three books in the ASTD Trainer's Workshop series: *Listening Skills Training*, *Time Management Training*, and *Negotiation Skills Training*.

Lisa Downs
16207 NE 90th Court
Redmond, WA 98052
(425) 216.3015
Email: lisa@developmentwise.com
Website: www.lisadowns.net
ASTD Chapter: Puget Sound

Roll of the Die

Submitted by Davis M. Robinson

Overview

The roll of the die determines the order and amount of information each participant shares in this fun introduction activity.

Objectives

- To engage learners and let them have fun while introducing themselves
- To facilitate relationships and enhance networking

Audience

Any number of participants

Time Estimate

20 minutes

Materials and Equipment

- One die for each group

Area Setup

Enough space for small groups to work around tables

Process

1. Introduce the activity by stating that participants will work in small groups and have an opportunity to learn about each other. Ask them to form small groups of five or six around or near a table. Give one die to each small group.
2. Ask participants to choose a number from 1 to 6 and to say that number out loud for all in the group to hear. Once participants select their numbers, provide additional instructions.
3. Tell them that one of the participants in each group will roll the die. If the number selected by a participant is rolled (that is, is in the top position), that individual states his or her name and then reveals something about him- or herself, such as hobbies, work experience, education, or family data. Tell the

participants to be careful not to disclose too much because they may need more information later if their number is rolled again. After someone discloses information, he or she then rolls the die.

4. If a number is rolled again, the person keeps providing information until a different number is rolled. Ask for one volunteer at each table to be the first roller of the die. Allow 10 minutes for the activity.

5. At the end of the time period, call a halt to the activity. If someone's number was never rolled, ask the participant to introduce him- or herself to the entire group.

6. If you wish to bring closure to the activity, involve the entire group in the introductions and make a transition back to the larger group. You could ask questions such as:
   - What was the most surprising information you learned?
   - Who has an interesting background? What is it?
   - Which team had the most similarities? What were they?
   - What was the most exciting information you learned?
   - What was the funniest thing you learned about a colleague?
   - What was one of the most impressive things you learned about a colleague?

InSider's Tips

- You will need strong facilitation skills if your group is large.
- If the collective group is large and people have not introduced themselves because their numbers were not rolled, you may wish to have them introduce themselves at their tables.

Davis M. Robinson, Ph.D., is the president and CEO for Horizon Consulting Services, LLC, which specializes in training and organization development. He obtained his doctorate of philosophy in organization development and educational leadership and master's of education in human resource development from the University of Louisville. He obtained his bachelor of science degree in psychology from Western Kentucky University. He has over fourteen years of experience in the training and organization development disciplines and has worked in leadership roles for various industries including finance, retail, human services, and healthcare.

Davis M. Robinson, Ph.D.
7312 Brook Meadow Drive
Louisville, KY 40228
(502) 541.1755
Email: dmr30@yahoo.com
Website: www.horizonconsultingserv.com
ASTD Chapter: Kentuckiana

Guess What We Have in Common

Submitted by Sharon Dera

Overview

A simple activity that uses pen, paper, and a bit of intuition and guessing to explore commonalities among participants while encouraging involvement.

Objectives

- To invite participation and stimulate inclusion in the group
- To meet participants and learn something in common with others in the group

Audience

Ten to twenty-five, in small groups or four or five

Time Estimate

15 to 20 minutes

Materials and Equipment

- Paper and pencils for group leaders or recorders

Area Setup

An area that is large enough to accommodate small groups standing at different places in the room

Process

1. Divide the participants into small groups of four or five. Assign a designated spot for each group.
2. Ask the group members to determine things all members of the group have in common and write them on the paper to share with the large group. Tell them that they can't use simple/obvious things such as "we all have a nose" or "we are all wearing clothes." Tell the participants that they must communicate with each other to determine and gain agreement on substantive things the entire group has in common.

3. Hand out the paper and pencils and ask someone to record for each group. Tell participants that they have 5 to 7 minutes for the task.
4. When time is up, have the groups take turns sharing commonalities.

InSider's Tips

- Walk around the room to observe, encouraging input from each of the small group members.
- This activity encourages involvement of all group members in providing ideas.
- This activity is always well received.

Sharon Dera, CPLP, has more than seventeen years of experience in needs assessment, human performance, process improvement, and organization development. Her broad experience was acquired by working in the retail, finance, healthcare, government, manufacturing, hospitality, and travel industries in operations, business management, customer service, sales, communications, marketing, succession planning, leadership, coaching, and training. Sharon is owner and CEO of The Proficience Group, Inc., working in partnership with organizations to identify the root cause of performance deficiencies and determine the best solutions/interventions to close performance gaps. The company lends a "fresh set of eyes," exposing possible blind spots. Sharon is currently serving on the National ASTD Chapter Recognition Committee. She earned an MBA from the University of Dallas.

Sharon Dera, CPLP
8948 Random Road
Fort Worth, TX 76179
(817) 236.7594
Email: sdera@charter.net
Website: www.proficiencegroup.com
ASTD Chapter: Fort Worth Mid-Cities

Immodest Interview

Submitted by J.T. Kostman

Overview
Interviewer and interviewee switch roles to draw out participant information in this always effective icebreaker format.

Objectives
- To get to know other participants in a group
- To strengthen the connection between the members of an existent group or team

Audience
Five to thirty participants

Time Estimate
25 to 60 minutes

Materials and Equipment
- Instructions written on a PowerPoint slide, flip chart, whiteboard, or handout
- Watch, stopwatch, or timer
- Pen and paper for participants

Area Setup
Optimally, participants should be able to wander about

Process
1. Announce that the purpose of this activity is to get enough information about someone so that you can introduce him or her. Tell the participants that you will be timing the activity and that they have 5 minutes to gather information about others. Tell everyone to find someone with whom to partner, preferably someone they don't know.
2. When you say "Go" participants will have 5 minutes to interview their partners and get answers to each of the questions you post or hand out.

Icebreakers: Getting to Know You

287

After 5 minutes, the interviewer becomes the interviewee and the roles are switched. The new interviewer will have 5 minutes to obtain the same information.

3. Post or hand out the following list:
   - Name/organization/department
   - How long with the organization
   - A professional or personal accomplishment
   - An interesting or unusual fact
4. Answer any questions.
5. Say "Go!" and time the activity for 5 minutes.
6. Call time and tell the partners to switch roles and the new interviewer will have 5 minutes to obtain the same information.
7. When the two rounds are over, pick someone at random and ask who he or she interviewed. Have the person you picked introduce the other person to the group. Ask for another pair of volunteers. To make things more fun, remember odd bits and facts about the participants and occasionally ask the group who it was later in the training session.

InSider's Tips

- This works great with established groups, as well as those that are meeting for the first time.
- Have you ever been to a meeting when everyone went around the room introducing themselves? Did you enjoy it? Does anyone? This alternative is more meaningful, memorable, and just plain fun! I have used this activity with groups of more than two hundred people and it worked.
- Most people in a professional setting tend to get to know one another only superficially: names, titles, roles, and responsibilities. By humanizing the members of the group, we can see what truly interesting people our colleagues are. We see them as real people, not just as roles.
- The key to success is to not give those being interviewed enough time to be modest (hence the name of the game). I will often expand or contract the amount of time to keep things moving at a frenetic pace (Just 1 minute left!).

J.T. Kostman, Ph.D., has advised senior-level executives in organizations ranging from the federal government to the Fortune 500 on the development of effective organizational transformation, leadership development, and performance improvement solutions. He is a consultant, coach, and professor. J.T. holds a Ph.D. in industrial and organizational psychology, which he earned after leading a distinguished career as a paramedic, police officer, deep-sea rescue diver, and team leader of an elite scout/sniper reconnaissance team with the U.S. Army. He lives in New York City and D.C., where he consults primarily to the defense and intelligence communities.

J.T. Kostman, Ph.D.
LSR Alliance, LLC
313 Wills Avenue
Stanhope, NJ 07874
(703) 403.2555
Email: JTKostman@yahoo.com
Website: www.LSRalliance.com
ASTD Chapter: Metro Washington, D.C.

Whose Snowball?

Submitted by Amanda Luster

Overview
Participants face each other in a paper snowball fight that is part guessing game and part introduction and learning tool.

Objectives
- To provide an opportunity to learn about each other with active participation
- To encourage involvement and group discussion

Audience
Two to twelve participants

Time Estimate
15 minutes

Materials and Equipment
- Paper for each participant
- Pens or pencils for participants

Area Setup
A room with a small open space for everyone to stand in a circle

Process
1. Tell participants that to start the workshop they are going to learn more about each other and get active in the process.
2. Hand out the paper and pens or pencils.
3. Have each person write two non-business things about themselves on the paper and then wad it up into a "snowball." Model what you mean.
4. When everyone has completed the task, have them stand in a circle with their snowballs. Start by yelling "Snowball fight!" and throw your paper across the circle. Everyone should join in naturally, but if they don't, tell them to. Pick up a "snowball" near you and toss again. Do this for a couple of minutes and then ask everyone to stop.

5. Have each of them pick up a snowball close to them and open it. One by one, go around the circle. Ask a participant to read the two things written on the paper and try to guess to whom the information belongs. If the guess is correct, have the owner of the "snowball" expand on the two items. If the guess is incorrect, move to the next participant who reads the "snowball" he or she picked up After you've moved around the circle once, allow the participants who guessed incorrectly to try again. If the second guesses are still incorrect, ask the participants who wrote those "snowballs" to introduce themselves.
6. Thank everyone for participating and have them return to their places.

InSider's Tips

- Start the activity with energy and excitement so people want to join in.
- This activity also works well with pre-written questions and can be used as a learning tool. You can create questions that reinforce a section of material covered in your training and use the snowball fight activity as a creative way to ask questions about the topic just covered.
- You can also have the participants create their own questions about a topic just covered, write these on sheets of paper, and initiate a snowball fight.

Amanda Luster is an active training manager at a financial institution, including supervising the e-learning team. Amanda has a BSE from the University of Arkansas, with a focus on adult education. Her interest is learning new things about facilitating and online education and facilitating the process of moving from "teaching" to "facilitating" and from "e-reading" to "e-learning." She enjoys learning from the newest generations and believes they bring great value and excitement to the trade.

Amanda Luster
P.O. Box 799
Lowell, AR 72745
(479) 770.1600
Email: aluster@arvest.com
ASTD Chapter: Northwest Arkansas

Look What I Can Do!

Submitted by Kenneth R. Stein

Overview

A posted list of "interesting facts" about each participant encourages session break and post-training networking and connections.

Objectives

- To identify common interests among the participants
- To provide a basis for continued relationship building

Audience

Groups of thirty-six or fewer

Time Estimate

Approximately 30 seconds per participant

Materials and Equipment

- Flip chart or other medium to capture participants' names and skills
- Markers
- Masking tape

Area Setup

Any room or area

Process

1. As participants introduce themselves, ask them to add something that they do well as a part of their introductions. It could be a hobby, interest, or skill that they would be willing to discuss with others during the event. It may be work focused (I'm good at PowerPoint) or unrelated to work (woodworking, gardening, private pilot, SCUBA diver, world traveler).
2. Capture the name and interest or skill on a flip-chart page. At the first break in your training session, post the list on a wall in the room.

3. During the training event, encourage participants to review the skills or experiences that interest them and contact the self-identified "expert."
4. As part of the learning process, stress the importance of building relationships and how sharing personal information begins building trust.

InSider's Tips

- The activity may be used as stand-alone icebreaker or added on to a different icebreaker.
- You may adjust this to use as energizer; ensure that participants have time to interact with each other after the activity.
- People love to talk about their hobbies and interests, so make sure you set aside time to let this happen. For example, you may need to plan for a longer break to allow time for people to make initial contact.
- Give participants a few minutes to think about what they want to share.

Kenneth R. Stein, Ed.D., CPLP, is with the learning organization of the Boeing Company. He has presented programs at American Society for Training and Development International Conferences, been involved in live television and talk radio shows, and participated in numerous learning events. Kenneth is a past president and serves on the board of directors for the Space Coast chapter of ASTD. He is part of the OneVoice Team and winner of the 2009 ASTD Volunteer-Staff Partnership Award. Kenneth has a doctorate in adult education from Nova Southeastern University, is a Certified Professional in Learning and Performance (CPLP), and a Senior Professional in Human Resources (SPHR).

Kenneth R. Stein, Ed.D., CPLP
430 Messha Trail
Merritt Island, FL 32953
(321) 704.9384
Email: kstein@digital.net
ASTD Chapter: Space Coast

Spell It Out!

Submitted by Emily Crouch

Overview
This activity proves that there is a lot more in a name than you think!

Objectives
- To warm up the group and introduce participants
- To help participants to think about the subject matter and realize they already possess knowledge about the topic

Audience
Fifteen or fewer

Time Estimate
10 to 15 minutes, depending on group size

Materials and Equipment
- One page of colorful typing paper for each participant
- Flip chart or whiteboard
- Markers
- Pens or pencils for participants

Area Setup
An area large enough for the participants to see each other

Process
1. Tell all participants to write their names vertically down the left side of a sheet of paper you will hand out.
2. Demonstrate by writing your own name vertically on a flip chart or whiteboard:

   E
   M
   I
   L
   Y

3. Ask participants to use each letter to identify an action related to the topic you are teaching: sales, customer service, leadership, policies and procedures, or others. These examples relate to sales:

   Exceeds expectations

   Motivated to sell

   Informative about our product

   Listens to their needs

   Yearns to assist prospects

4. Ask the group to share what they came up with. Usually these examples will relate to your material and you can refer to their examples throughout the training.

InSider's Tips

- You might ask the participants to post their names and corresponding action lists on the wall so participants can review them during a break.
- This activity may also be carried out by asking the participants to use their table tents to display the name/action list.
- It is fun and gets participants talking early, while at the same time helps participants remember each other's names.

Emily Crouch is a regional trainer for GID/Windsor Property Management Company and supports the Mid-Atlantic and West regions. She is responsible for classroom and on-site training within assigned regions and assists with developing, coordinating, and organizing a variety of activities resulting in increased policy standardization, efficiency, and employee motivation. Emily transitioned from leasing to management over a thirteen-year career in property management. She is originally from Tampa, Florida, and holds a BA in public relations from the University of South Florida.

Emily Crouch
3000 S. Randolph Street, Suite 100
Arlington, VA 22206
(703) 379.9696
Email: ecrouch@windsorcommunities.com
Website: www.windsorcommunities.com
ASTD Chapter: Metro Washington, D.C.

Chapter 12

Openings:
Start with a BANG

One of the most important parts of your training session is the opening. You want to start your training with a BANG. The contributors to this chapter offer you solid, time-tested activities to ensure that you do exactly that. When you open your session, you will want to:

Build interest in the session.
Ask what participants know and what they want to know.
Note the ground rules and what to expect.
Get them involved.

Build interest immediately. Start your session on time and grab participants' attention right from the start. Save the ground rules and housekeeping details for later. Be creative with your opening.

Ask your participants about what they want to know. Sometimes a simple listing of expectations on a flip chart is all that is needed. At other times you may want to use small group discussions to help them formulate their thoughts.

Note the ground rules. This is an important part of the opening, but I prefer to present them after a warm-up activity. One of my favorite ground rules is about breaks. I like to tell participants that the session includes planned breaks, but I emphasize that they are adults and should feel comfortable to get up at any time for something to drink, to use the restroom, or to just stand if the chair isn't that comfortable.

Get your participants involved right from the start. Participant introductions and discussions about expectations or the topic are perfect ways to prime the pump for interaction among participants.

This chapter addresses everything you might want to include in your next opening. Paul Terlemezian offers two ways you can start off with a BANG and grab attention right from the start. Linda Kulp uses a creative technique to ask what learners want out of the session. Patsi Turner's "Level the Playing Field" helps establish ground rules and balance participation when your training session includes learners from different organizational levels such as managers and line workers. Make sure you check out Beverley Taylor's "Make a Wish" if you are looking for a novel approach to addressing ground rules and expectations. Diana Hauman shares her "Great Expectations" activity that encourages participants to begin working together right from the start of your session. Mark Boccia's "Definition BINGO" creates a foundation of knowledge and helps participants know what to expect.

Three contributors, Lou Russell, Sandi Ruther, and Antoinette Webster, help participants focus on the topic by addressing stress and other concerns that participants may bring with them to your learning event. "Jazzed," offered by Barb Murray, demonstrates that we each own our own attitude and it uses this important life lesson to involve your learners right from the start.

All eleven of these activities will help you open all your sessions with a BANG and ensure that you take advantage of this time to establish a participative climate, build interest and excitement, and to establish your credibility.

Rapid Rate of Change

Submitted by Paul Terlemezian

Overview
Delivering an apology right up-front in your presentation not only gets a laugh but encourages audience engagement and participation.

Objectives
- To grab an audience's attention at the start of a presentation
- To engage participants by using humor

Audience
Any size from one to one thousand, ideally managers, executives, or trainers and others for whom effective communication is a high priority

Time Estimate
5 minutes or less, depending on the laughter and interaction

Materials and Equipment
- None

Area Setup
No required room size or setup

Process
1. Begin by stating that you have an apology to make, or actually you have two apologies to make.
2. Continue by saying that the first apology is because you've heard that you should never start a presentation with an apology so you are apologizing for doing so. This always gets a laugh and sets the expectation for curiosity as to what the second apology will be.
3. The second apology is related to the fact that you only recently started working on the presentation and you finished it just minutes before you arrived. Therefore, you are apologizing for the likelihood that it is already out-of-date!

4. Deliver an awesome presentation that is timely and references things that happened very recently.

5. Remember to invite the participants to add more updated information as you go along in your presentation.

InSider's Tips

- Always provide your sources of information; don't pretend to be smart. Admit to being smart enough to know that you don't know everything and willing to learn new things from others every day.
- Let the audience participate and contribute content. You want to establish credibility as an expert, a facilitator, and a dynamic learner. The best presentations are ones during which you also learn something new.

Paul Terlemezian retired after a successful career in technology and training with a focus on customer training and business development. In June 2003 Paul came out of retirement to start iFive Alliances. In addition to developing revenue-producing alliances, iFive Alliances provides consulting services, go-to-market strategies, and keynote speeches on the future of learning as a business. Paul serves on the board of several organizations and founded the TAG (Technology Association of Georgia) Workplace Learning Society. The organization's focus is the effective combination of technology and learning in the workplace.

Paul Terlemezian
125 Laurian Way
Atlanta, GA 30328
(404) 252.8330
Email: pault@ifivealliances.com
Website: http://ifivealliances.ning.com
ASTD Chapter: Greater Atlanta

Focus Einstein Style

Submitted by Paul Terlemezian

Overview

This activity uses a humorous story about a very smart scientist who was notoriously absentminded to focus learners and make sure the right questions are asked and answered.

Objectives

- To engage the audience early with humor
- To set the expectation that questions are desired and welcome
- To determine needs and expectation of the participants

Audience

Twenty to one hundred

Time Estimate

15 to 25 minutes to create the list of questions

Materials and Equipment

- Index cards—at least one for each participant
- Pens or pencils
- Flip chart
- Markers

Area Setup

No required room size or setup

Process

1. At the start of a training presentation, state that you have created the mandatory boring PowerPoint presentation and that you expect the group to ask so many good questions that you never have a chance to use it. Warn them that if the presentation is boring, it will be their fault.
2. Tell this story to make your point. "You do know about the time that Albert Einstein lost his train ticket—right? It seems he was on a train outbound from

his home when the conductor came by to collect tickets. When the conductor reached his seat, Einstein was on the floor searching for his ticket. The conductor spoke up and said, 'No problem, Mr. Einstein. No need to find your ticket. I trust that you have made your purchase.' Einstein mumbled something and waved in appreciation while continuing his search. About 15 minutes later, the conductor came by again and Einstein was still searching. The conductor stated, 'Don't you understand? You don't need to find your ticket. We are satisfied that you have paid.' At which point Einstein impatiently stated, 'No, you don't understand. I need to find my ticket. I've forgotten where I'm going!'"

3. Explain that, like Einstein, the PowerPoint slides will keep you on track and help you remember where you are going. State that you fully expect their questions to be more interesting than what you have planned!

4. Tell participants to use the index cards and pens or pencils that are around the room. Give them a couple minutes think of their questions and write each one on an index card. Ask the participants to form small groups of six to ten to present their questions without discussing answers in the small groups. Have each group select the best question and present it aloud to the larger group.

5. Post the questions on a flip chart and tell participants you will respond to each as you deliver your presentation. Adjust your presentation to weave in your answers.

InSider's Tips

- At the end of your session, collect the index cards with the unanswered questions. After the session post the PowerPoint, the questions, and your responses on your website or other social networking services you use. Posting the information in this way ensures that you communicate all the answers to all the questions.

- You may also ask participants to write their questions on the backs of their business cards, thus giving credit to the individual who asked the question when you post them on your website.

Paul Terlemezian retired after a successful career in technology and training with a focus on customer training and business development. In June of 2003, Paul came out of retirement to start iFive Alliances. In addition to developing revenue-producing alliances, iFive Alliances provides consulting services, go-to-market strategies, and keynote speeches on the future of learning as a business. Paul serves on the board of several organizations and founded the TAG (Technology Association of Georgia) Workplace Learning Society, focused on the effective combination of technology and learning in the workplace.

Paul Terlemezian
125 Laurian Way
Atlanta, GA 30328
(404) 252.8330
Email: pault@ifivealliances.com
Website: http://ifivealliances.ning.com
ASTD Chapter: Greater Atlanta

Learning Is Valuable

Submitted by Linda Kulp

Overview

Participants write a pre-session learning outcome wish on the back of play money and store their wishes in a container to be discovered and read at the end of the session.

Objectives

- To determine and incorporate participant learning objectives
- To use results to evaluate whether learning objectives were accomplished

Audience

Groups of fewer than twenty-five

Time Estimate

20 to 30 minutes

Materials and Equipment

- Small plastic tubes or plastic eggs that are hollow and can be opened and filled (purchased at a novelty or dollar store)
- Play paper money (must have one unprinted side) that can be folded and placed in the plastic holders
- Pen or pencil for each participant

Area Setup

None required

Process

1. At the start of a session, hand out the plastic eggs/tubes and money slips, along with pens or pencils. Ask the participants, "What is one valuable learning objective you hope to accomplish in this program? Write it on the back of the play money, along with your name." Have all participants state their objectives out loud. Ask them to place their valuable thoughts inside the tubes/eggs.

2. Collect the filled tubes/eggs.
3. At the end of the training program, hand out the tubes/eggs randomly. Each person reads the note inside. Ask the person who wrote it whether he or she realized the desired learning objective. This not only helps the participants to realize what has been learned over the training period but is also a way for you to evaluate the training program.
4. If the person does not feel his or her training objective was accomplished, ask why or why not and how you can assist. You may wish to discuss this in the class or follow up later with the person. How far you go with this depends on how much time you have allotted for this activity.

InSider's Tips

- Another way this exercise can be done is to have the plastic tubes/eggs and slips of paper handed out at the end of a training program that is one of several classes. Ask participants, "What is the one most important thing that you learned in this program and that you wish to share with the next group that starts this program?" Hand out the filled tubes/eggs to the new group of participants and have each read aloud what a previous participant said about the program. This helps set the stage for discussion of some of the learning objectives you are trying to accomplish.
- The activity helps participants focus on at least one important reason they are taking the workshop/program. It's a wonderful jump-start and/or reflection time.

Linda Kulp is an experienced learning professional with more than ten years of experience. Her previous experience was in the field of human resource management and education. She has a master's degree in human resources management, is certified in human performance technology, color code instruction, and holds various other related credentials. Linda is a member of ASTD National and ASTD Orange County in California. Linda was president of her local chapter in 2008 and held other board positions before and after that time. She is a current member of NPELRA, PELRAC, and IPMA. Among her recent accomplishments is the creation of an online university for her employer that has provided the opportunity to continue an aggressive employee learning function in spite of budget limitations.

Linda Kulp
27943 Chiclana
Mission Viejo, CA 92692
(949) 716.6339
Email: lindaymay@hotmail.com
ASTD Chapter: Orange County

Level the Playing Field

Submitted by Patsi R. Turner

Overview

Participants throw away their hard-won job titles and well-tended egos in this activity to focus on learning and real engagement with the topic.

Objectives

- To level the playing field for all participants
- To minimize the focus on rank and title of participants

Audience

Fifteen to twenty participants

Time Estimate

20 minutes

Materials and Equipment

- Large plastic trash can with trash bag (one that you can carry easily)
- Several blown-up balloons tied and placed inside the trash bag in the trash can (so that no one can see them)
- One name tag for each person with an imaginary title, such as "president," "big cheese," etc.
- Index cards with imaginary versions of each participant's ego, such as "brilliant," "perfect," or "know-it-all"
- One trash bag tie to close the trash bag

Area Setup

Any size room or activity area

Process

1. Welcome all participants and introduce yourself.
2. Review the day's agenda.
3. Look around the room and cite the value of having a diverse group of people by age, gender, and years of service, experience, education, marital status, religion, and so forth to learn from.

4. Follow by stating that there are two dimensions about every individual that are not needed in a classroom because these dimensions do not add value. Suggest that this activity will remove these unnecessary dimensions before you get started. State that these dimensions are the participants' ranks or titles and egos.

5. Give people the index cards with their name tags with imaginary titles and index cards with imaginary egos. Tell participants that you are coming by with the trash can and you want them to state their titles and egos as they toss them into the trash bag. Move quickly to each person and have fun with those with BIG egos and impressive-sounding titles.

6. Tie the bag and remind them that everyone has an equal rank and you have all the egos. Pull the bag out and display the puffed-up bag filled with balloons.

InSider's Tips

- This activity is ideal for mixed groups of managers/directors/employees or boss/subordinates.
- This activity is unexpected because you start out seriously, following the printed agenda.
- You may add fun by using scissors to cut up huge egos into small parts.
- Be careful not to lose track of time; move quickly from one person to the next.
- I created this based on work done with salespersons whom I was told over and over had big egos.

Patsi R. Turner is a working principle and managing director for HR Performance, Inc., an Atlanta-based management and human resources consultancy. She is the owner and founder of the company and has been serving clients since 1999. The company's focus is on enhancing the capabilities of employees and improving organizational processes. Patsi's strong professional background is steeped in leadership and organization development, strategic and human capital planning, employee relations, and process improvement. That combination of skills makes her valuable and resourceful to both clients and colleagues. Patsi thrives on her work and believes in life-long mastery learning.

Patsi R. Turner
6105 Rock Springs Road
Lithonia, GA 30038–1510
(770) 482.5946
Email: pturner@HRPerformanceinc.com
Website: www.HRPerformanceinc.com
ASTD Chapter: Greater Atlanta

Make a Wish

Submitted by Beverley Taylor

Overview

Participants in this activity gain new powers that allow them to make sure their time is valued and they learn exactly what they expect to learn.

Objective

- To empower individuals to express a positive vision

Audience

Works best with fewer than fifteen participants

Time Estimate

15 to 30 minutes

Materials and Equipment

- One magic wand purchased at a party or toy store (hidden until it is introduced in the activity)
- Flip chart and markers
- Masking tape

Area Setup

A room that allows seated participants to see one another

Process

1. Introduce the topic of conversation and ground rules. Display the magic wand. Ask them what their wish is for the training session.
2. Tell them that, during this session, anything can happen. However, you want them to know that there are no obstacles, no mountains too high, no complaints that cannot be overcome, no negative attitude that cannot be turned around.
3. Hand someone the magic wand and ask him or her to make a wish about the training session. Once the participant has made a wish, the participant may select the next person who will make a wish. Capture these wishes

The Book of Road-Tested Activities

on a flip-chart page and post them. They become the participants' expectations and ground rules for the session.

4. After everyone has made a wish, place the magic wand on the table in the front of the room and tell participants that it is available for anyone to use at any time during the session.

InSider's Tips

- The magic wand gives individuals the "power" to speak their minds and turns negatives into positives.
- As a prop, the magic wand adds humor, even when participants have complaints or may be adversarial.
- Select a wand that is plain silver or gold, without too many feminine frills.
- I've seen this "idea" in more than one place; however, I had never used it until this past year. It was the easiest preparation and most rewarding small table activity I have ever used!

Beverley Taylor states that if she was holding a magic wand, she'd wish her bio was already written . . . oh wait, it is! It's on LinkedIn! She is a learning strategist who works collaboratively with organizations to create optimal blends for communicating and learning (email, e-learning, m-learning, simulations, gaming, teleconferencing, podcasting, intranet, online documentation, face-to-face interactions). She conducts needs analysis and provides design, development, implementation, and evaluation support to enhance high-visibility projects and initiatives.

Beverley Taylor
4355 Cobb Parkway J603
Atlanta, GA 30339
Email: Beverley.m.taylor@gmail.com
ASTD Chapter: Atlanta

Great Expectations

Submitted by Diana Hauman

Overview
Both the learners and the facilitator benefit using this activity that guides learners through a process that puts them in charge of their learning experience and expectations.

Objectives
- To set expectations for the environment, content, and the facilitator at the beginning of a program
- To model how the workshop will be conducted

Audience
Nine to twenty-five participants in three small groups

Time Estimate
10 to 20 minutes

Materials and Equipment
- Three flip charts, one per group
- Markers

Area Setup
Enough space for three groups to form around the three flip charts

Process
1. Divide participants into three small groups. Ask participants to move to their assigned flip charts and to determine recorders and reporters for their groups.
2. Assign each group one category: Content, Facilitator, or Environment. State that they are to identify all their expectations for each category for this session and to list their expectations on their flip charts. Use the following to further define and provide examples for the three different groups.

- *Content:* "What do you need to know and be able to do with regard to this topic? What knowledge do you need? What skills? Be as specific as possible."
- *Facilitator:* "What can I do to make this a valuable learning experience for you? How can I help build your confidence and competence?"
- *Environment:* "Describe the learning environment that will help this group be productive. What are some best practices from other experiences you have had?"

3. Circulate among groups to answer questions and to ensure they are completing the activity in a timely way.

4. Reconvene as large group and ask each group to present its information. Ask questions to clarify. For example, if "be respectful" is on the "Environment" chart, ask what respect looks like or how they would know whether they are being respectful. Ask for additional ideas from the other groups.

5. At the conclusion, explain that this is an example of how the program will be conducted as they will seek answers among participants and share experiences.

6. If this is a multi-day program, review the charts at the end of each day for feedback and suggestions.

InSider's Tips

- This activity engages participants early and provides an example of how the session will be interactive. It also provides an opportunity to indicate whether or not a topic/question will be addressed. If not, say whether it can be addressed one-on-one during a break or before/after class.
- If the class is smaller than nine participants, divide the group in two and have one group address the Content and the second the Facilitator. The environment can be discussed by the entire group.
- As a facilitator this early activity provides you with an opportunity to see how individuals are interacting in small groups: who is quiet and reticent, who is outspoken, who takes charge, or who is negative.

Openings: Start with a BANG

Diana Hauman established DDH Enterprises, Inc., in 1990 to help organizations achieve their goals through their most valuable assets, productive employees. She is an experienced facilitator and she brings her own or the clients' material to life using real-world examples, activities, and humor to keep the learners engaged. Her process, "PROMISE TO PERFORMANCE . . . MAXIMIZING CUSTOMER SATISFACTION" helps enhance an organization's level of customer satisfaction. She also develops award-winning new hire orientation and training programs. Diana finds personal and professional satisfaction in seeing others grow and develop and hearing, "Oh, I know how I can use this!"

Diana Hauman
48 Kenfield Circle
Bloomington, IL 61704
(309) 838.1320
Email: ddhentinc@aol.com
ASTD Chapter: Central Illinois

Definition BINGO

Submitted by Mark Boccia

Overview

This variation on the classic game of BINGO not only engages learners early in your session, but allows everyone to begin to win the knowledge game before your training even begins.

Objectives

- To introduce twenty-four key terms and phrases related to your session so everyone has a similar foundation
- To provide learners an opportunity to interact with one another

Audience

Works best for up to thirty participants

Time Estimate

7 to 10 minutes

Materials and Equipment

- One BINGO card for each participant: 5 columns, 5 rows with a "Free Space" in the center. The remaining 24 spaces have terms that will be defined during the workshop. Make various BINGO cards by moving some of the terms to different spaces on the sheet.
- Twenty-four index cards with one term and its definition typed on each
- Two prizes for winners
- Pens or pencils for participants

Area Setup

Any setup that allows learners to move around

Preparation

Design the BINGO cards and definition cards before the session.

Process

1. Announce the BINGO event with excitement. Emphasize: "This isn't just any old BINGO!"

2. Hand out a BINGO card and one definition card to each participant. *Note:* If you have fewer than twenty-four participants, some may have more than one definition.

3. Explain the rules of BINGO. Participants will write definitions in the boxes to complete a horizontal line, vertical line, or diagonal line.

4. Model the game with a participant by saying, "Ms. X, what term do you have on your index card?" Ms. X says, "I have ABC." "Great, what does it mean?" Ms. X reads the definition and you write it down on your BINGO sheet in the correct space. Tell participants that after you have put her definition on a sheet, Ms. X will want the definition from the index card you have. So you read your card and she writes down the definition. You then thank one another and make your way around the room to find other people who have definitions that will help either of you get BINGO.

5. Emphasize that a prize will be given for the first two participants who have BINGO; however, note the caveat that participants must have the correct definitions listed because they will be asked to report out and explain to the class.

6. Say, "Ready, Set, Go!"

7. Most participants will begin by writing their own definition on their sheets and then speak to others immediately around them. This is okay if you have a variety of BINGO sheet layouts. All participants are likely to make their way around the room to find participants with definition cards they need and to exchange information. The reality is that most participants will end up with only ten or twelve out of twenty-four definitions as they try to get BINGO.

8. Stop the game after two participants announce they have BINGO.

9. Ask the two winners to read their definitions. Encourage the rest of the group to write those definitions on their cards. This is an opportunity for you to explain why the definition or phrase is important and tell learners when the topic will be discussed further.

10. Use the most important definitions as a transition into your presentation. For example, "Maria had ABC on her BINGO sheet" or "No one had XYZ, so let's review that in greater detail."

InSider's Tips

- This activity is great within the first hour of class or as a test preparation activity.
- Usually two or three individuals will start speeding ahead to find the right definitions. This encourages others to get up and do the same. Introduce the activity with excitement and encourage people to work quickly but accurately.
- Be sure to have a duplicate set of definition cards available, especially for larger classes. For smaller classes, participants might be responsible for one or two cards. Be sure all definition cards are held by participants. Sometimes the "winning" card someone needs is left on a table unattended while everyone is scurrying around.

Mark Boccia, director of training for the Global Lodging Operations, is in his twelfth year with Marriott International and has a variety of leadership experience in the hospitality industry from both the hotel operations and sales side of the professional learning and development discipline. Mark leads a start-up training and development team charged with creating and sustaining all lodging operations training initiatives for rooms, food and beverage, and engineering as the various disciplines and Marriott brands roll out new programs, products, and services to the market. Mark's scope encompasses twelve Marriott brands representing nearly 300,000 hourly, supervisory, and management associates from Marriott's managed and franchise hotel portfolio worldwide.

Mark Boccia
8864 Blade Green Lane
Columbia, MD 21045
mark.boccia@marriott.com
www.marriott.com
ASTD Chapter: Metro Washington, D.C.

I Said I Need to Learn

Submitted by Lou Russell

Overview

A three-step process offers a pleasant, easy, and effective way to connect learners in a significant way to encourage trust, creativity, and learning.

Objectives

- To open discussion and establish trust among participants using an icebreaker
- To identify and discuss personal triggers that may block learning and creativity

Audience

Fifteen to twenty-five

Time Estimate

20 to 30 minutes

Materials and Equipment

- One blank piece of paper for each participant
- Pens or pencils for participants
- (Optional) A small bell or other noisemaker to close sections of the activity
- Flip chart and markers

Area Setup

Tables that allow learners to sit in groups of four to six

Process

1. **Intrapersonal step:** Give everyone paper and pens or pencils. Ask the learners to think of a project (or your topic) from the past and focus on a negative emotion they experienced during this project. Ask them to write down the emotion but not share with others. Ask them to rate this emotion's severity by writing a number between 1 (hardly any emotion) and 10 (extreme emotion). This part of the exercise should be done fairly quickly and is not too important other than helping people think very clearly about their experiences so they get more depth of understanding.

318

2. Ask them to think about what triggered that emotion for them. In other words, what happened that provoked their reaction. Ask them to list three things, although some may only write one or two. Give them a minute or two to do this.

3. **Interpersonal step:** Ask the learners to take their papers and pair up with someone at another table whom they don't know very well.

4. When the participants find partners, explain that you are going to carefully orchestrate the discussion. Tell them to share their negative emotions with their partners, as well as the triggers that caused them. Explain that each person will have 1 minute to tell his or her story. The person listening cannot ask any questions and should just nod knowingly and listen carefully (demonstrate this). Tell them you will announce when it's time to switch roles. If you do not have an even number of people, you may need to have a group of three, in which case you may have to push them along a bit due to time constraints. Begin this step.

5. Call time after 2 minutes.

6. Ask each pair to find another pair of storytellers so that they form groups of four. If you have an odd number of pairs, it's okay to form groups of six.

7. In this round, task each set of partners with telling their stories to the new people. This time, the time limit is 30 seconds per story. Once again, you will indicate when it is time to switch and you may have to remind any team of six that they have less time.

8. State the timing again and call time after 2 minutes.

9. Finally, give each team 1 minute to identify one common emotion that all their experiences brought out. Once the teams have completed this step, use the following questions to debrief:
   - What emotion did your team agree on in common?
   - What were some of the triggers that participants mentioned? (There will be some laughter because many teams will probably say "frustrated.")
   - What can I do to prevent these triggers from occurring during this session? What can you do? What can we all do together?

10. Note these ideas on a flip chart if you wish and build them into your content and the delivery.

11. **Kinesthetic:** To finish the activity, ask the teams formed during the activity to gather their belongings and move to a table together to begin the workshop session.

InSider's Tips

- There are three parts to this exercise:
  - Intrapersonal—learners analyze their own experiences by themselves.
  - Interpersonal—learners share their experiences with three or four other people.
  - Kinesthetic—learners move to sit with their new friends.
- This is my favorite opening activity. It's simple, inexpensive, and helps prepare participants to learn new techniques and skills. It also gives me an easy, non-threatening way to move learners around so they meet other people (not just those they came with), establishing trust between learners which is critical to learning.
- I use this opening for our leadership and project management workshops, but it could easily be adapted to any topic, including customer service, communication, teamwork, or any topic that involves working with others.

Lou Russell, CEO of Russell Martin & Associates, is a consultant, speaker, and author whose passion is to create growth in companies by guiding the growth of their people. In her speaking, training, and writing, Lou draws on thirty years of experience. She is committed to inspiring improvement in leadership, project management, and individual learning. Lou is the author of six popular books, including *Leadership Training* and *10 Steps to Successful Project Management.*

Lou Russell
Queen
Russell Martin & Associates
9084 Technology Drive
Fishers, IN 46038
(317) 475.9311
Email: lou@russellmartin.com
www.russellmartin.com
www.lourussell.com
@nolecture (Twitter)
LinkedIn and Facebook: Lou Russell
ASTD Chapter: National

Let Go of Your Fears

Submitted by Sandi Ruther

Overview

The simple act of naming a fear or mental roadblock and throwing it away is a powerful metaphor to enable participants to engage with your session and release inhibitions that get in the way of creativity or change.

Objectives

- To enable participants to identify emotional fears or roadblocks
- To provide a physical vehicle for releasing fears or roadblocks

Audience

From two to two hundred

Time Estimate

4 to 7 minutes

Materials and Equipment

- A slip of paper or an index card for each participant
- Pen or pencil for each participant
- Large industrial-size garbage can
- Poster board with words "Fear Disposal" or "Roadblock Dump" attached to the garbage can

Area Setup

Any size room or activity area

Process

1. Say that, in many skills training sessions, participants need to overcome their fears or remove roadblocks in order to change behaviors or practice new skills. Explain that during the training, the fear(s) or roadblock(s) need to be "neutralized" so that participants are able to engage their creativity and be open to the ideas and options generated during the session.

2. Give everyone index cards or slips or paper and pens or pencils. Invite participants to spend a few minutes writing down their biggest fear(s) or mental roadblock(s). *Note:* Participants may write down more than one fear or roadblock or just the single biggest obstacle or fear.
3. Ask participants to fold or crumple their papers.
4. Wheel or drag the industrial-size garbage into the room. As it passes by have participants throw their papers in the trash can, symbolically releasing the fear(s) or roadblock(s).
5. If appropriate, let participants know that if they still want the fear(s) or roadblock(s) at the end of the session, they are welcome to retrieve their papers from the trash.
6. Leave the can at the back of the room (or at the front of the room off to the side). If you need to refer to it (or let participants throw additional fear(s) or roadblock(s) away), it is within eyesight.

InSider's Tips

- Inviting participants to physically release something emotionally binding can be very powerful.
- Don't force participants. Make the environment safe.
- Keep the papers anonymous by ensuring that papers or cards are the same size and blank.
- You may substitute a common wastebasket; however, it will not have the same dramatic effect.

Sandi Ruther is the founder and principal of ProGold Consulting, LLC, a successful documentation, training, and consulting firm whose mission is to help businesses improve employee morale, operational efficiency, and business profitability by aligning people, processes, and systems. Bringing more than eighteen years of experience in business process optimization, internal auditing, technical writing, technical and business skills training, facilitating, and consulting, ProGold Consulting, LLC, helps clients eliminate organizational roadblocks and implement cost-effective solutions. Sandi is also an expert communicator, delivering dynamic and persuasive keynotes and seminars on the topic "Polished, Not Perfect! A New Definition of Success."

Sandi Ruther
P.O. Box 632156
Highlands Ranch, CO 80163–2156
(303) 593.0025
Email: sandiruther@comcast.net
Website: www.progoldconsulting.com
ASTD Chapter: Rocky Mountain

Purging the Potholes

Submitted by Antoinette S. Webster

Overview

Eliminating and fixing potholes is a metaphor used in this activity to encourage participants to let go of life's stresses that get in the way of being present and engaged on the job, at home, and during training sessions.

Objectives

- To eliminate the mind chatter and stress that takes attention away from being present and focused on the training topic
- To open more fully to the learning experience by freeing up mental and physical energy

Audience

Six to thirty participants

Time Estimate

10 to 15 minutes

Materials and Equipment

- One Potholes handout for each participant (ideally copied on orange paper)
- Pens or pencils for participants
- Garbage can, without a lid
- (Optional) Slide or flip chart with a relevant graphic or cartoon

Area Setup

Garbage can centered either at the front or back of the room so all participants may toss their Potholes away

Process

1. After opening comments, let participants know you want them to get as much as they can from the session. State that you are aware they have many demands on their time, energy, and attention, which can distract them from being present to the program.

2. Distribute the Potholes handout and pens or pencils, stating that you want to help them eliminate the nags, mind chatter, and stressors that they brought with them. Reassure them that doing so will help them focus on being present and attending to the topic.

3. Set the activity up by using a road construction/potholes and orange barrel analogy. Ask how many of them drove through a road construction site in the past month. Ask whether this added stress to their drive. State that the circles on the handout represent potholes in a road and the orange paper represents the orange barrels or cones often seen at road construction sites.

4. Display the optional slide or flip chart with a relevant graphic/cartoon to further emphasize your point. State that this activity will help them be more open to the learning experience by freeing up mental and physical energy.

5. Tell participants that they have 3 minutes to jot down their pothole equivalents on the handout. State that each circle represents a different pothole, or one of the stressors they brought with them. Tell them that they should write a brief phrase or word describing the cause of their stress; there is no need for the entire story or details.

6. After 3 minutes, ask who would like to share one of their "potholes" or stressors. Remind participants that that there is no need to share the details. Listen to the responses, commenting, as appropriate, on items relevant to the whole group and/or themes you notice.

7. After a few responses, instruct participants to crumble up their pothole pages into balls.

8. Instruct them to toss their stressors into the trashcan to temporarily get rid of them. They can do this either one at a time or all at once.

9. If time permits, facilitate a debriefing step noting any particular observations or asking questions such as:
   - What was it like acknowledging your stressors and writing them down?
   - What did it feel like to throw them away?
   - What did you notice as you heard some of the other participants' responses?
   - How might this help you . . . (begin to segue into the topic or focus for the learning session)?

InSider's Tips

- Keep the tone light and upbeat.
- Consider doing a pothole handout for yourself.
- For fun you can stand near the trashcan to facilitate their aim.
- This activity was originally designed for use at the beginning of a training program. Other applications include for use with programs related to stress, conflict resolution, change, teams, barriers to success, project management, or problem solving or use when meetings become stalled or unfocused. Adapt it as appropriate for your unique situation.
- Suggest to participants that this is a tool they can use back on the job or in their personal lives, especially when feeling stuck or to gain clarity.
- If time permits, this activity could be expanded to include 5 minutes of small group discussion on what might be done to reduce stressors or find ways to resolve them.
- For smaller groups, have each person walk up to toss their potholes directly into the trashcan, doing so with drama and flair.
- The activity works because it is an objective process whereby participants acknowledge what's going on in their lives in a more productive way. Most people easily relate to and have had experiences with potholes, construction delays, orange barrels, or cones slowing them down or causing various challenges along the way, making the activity relevant, practical, and fun. Tossing the pothole ball in the trashcan is a healthy form of release and often creates competition to see who can shoot one into the can.
- During the sharing segment, participants often relate to the responses, realize they are not alone, or note that some people have worse problems.
- The activity is easily adaptable to meet specific needs within and outside of the training/learning environment, whether in-person or virtual.

Antoinette S. Webster is a practical professional speaker, facilitator, coach, and author. She is also president of A System That Works, a speaking, training, coaching/consulting company that applies an integrative approach for transformational growth and development. A System That Works offers quality, practical programs, products, and services targeted to the unique organizational culture and personal preferences—not just for today but for tomorrow as well. Antoinette is the author of *Enthusiasm! How To Draw It to Yourself & Keep It*, *Igniting the Spark of Enthusiasm!*, *Targeting Business Success*, *Effective Meeting Facilitation*, and *10 Steps for Training the Trainer. . . EFFECTIVELY*. She earned her MBA from Xavier University.

Antoinette S. Webster
A System That Works
640 Foster Avenue
Hamilton, OH 45015
(513) 887.0600
Email: Antoinette@ASystemthatWorks.com
ASTD Chapter: Greater Cincinnati

Potholes

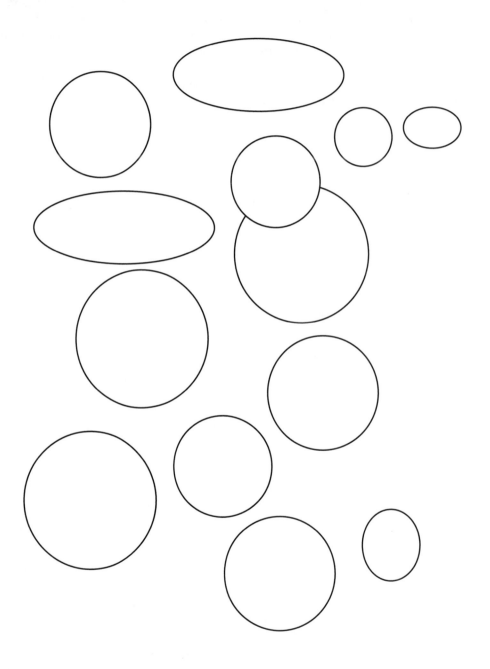

Jazzed

Submitted by Barbara Murray

Overview

Participants use a simple role-play that demonstrates that being happy, engaged, or joyous is a choice. They then connect this lesson to the choice to take advantage of learning opportunities.

Objectives

- To instill excitement, energy, and anticipation by using an icebreaker
- To demonstrate that attitude is up to each participant

Audience

Two or more participants

Time Estimate

8 to 10 minutes

Materials and Equipment

- None

Area Setup

Any room or activity space will work, but the partners formed during the activity need some space between them to interact.

Process

1. Assign everyone a partner. Ask partners to spread out throughout the room.
2. Tell the partners to stand back-to-back.
3. Next ask the partners to turn to face one another and greet each other by stating how much they Do Not want to be here today. When everyone has finished, draw attention to the negative aura this greeting creates. Ask, "What was the atmosphere during this exchange? How did you feel?"
4. Ask the partners to turn and stand back-to-back again. Then ask the partners to turn to face one another, but this time greet each other as if they are

greeting long-lost loved ones returning after a long absence. Ask, "What was the atmosphere this time? How did you feel this time?"

5. After you have heard some comments, ask the partners to return to a back-to-back position.

6. Once again, ask the partners to turn and face one another, but this time react as if they had just won the lottery for $10 million. (There will be screaming shrieking and jumping up and down.)

7. Explain that this is the kind of excitement everyone should expect to see during this session. Ask, "Who is responsible for this excitement?"

8. Briefly discuss the differences in the way they felt with each greeting. Ask whether the participants are jazzed now. Suggest that partners high-five each other and return to their seats.

InSider's Tips

- The participants will be confused by the first greeting. Many may *want* to be there. The tone will be negative and pitch will be low. (A negative aura.)
- The participants will think the second greeting is the last and contrast it to the first. When the third greeting is introduced, they are surprised.
- Keep focused on the third greeting for the most excitement. Keep the energy flowing.

Barbara Murray is currently president of the ASTD Great Plains chapter. She has been a dual member of ASTD for nine years, actively serving on the Great Plains ASTD board for six years. Barbara has worked in training and development for more than eleven years. She is responsible for PREMIER Bankcard Management Development; serving over three hundred managers and key personnel. Barb prides herself in being a servant leader. She has developed and delivered numerous management development courses to serve the needs of the PREMIER team. Barb provides the tools and training necessary to assist the managers in becoming great PREMIER leaders.

Barbara Murray
4902 South Oxbow Avenue
Sioux Falls, SD 57106
(605) 357.3401
Email: bmurray@premierbankcard.com
ASTD Chapter: Great Plains

Chapter 13

Reviewing: Make It Fun

Many trainers build participant review opportunities into their training sessions. After all, your participants' recall of what you just taught is clearest while they are still in your training session. And unfortunately, they will forget more and more of what you taught as time goes on. By creating opportunities to review knowledge and skills just learned, those lessons will remain fresher longer and be easier to recall long after they leave your session.

As you create reviewing options, build a foundation for recall for your learners. Find connections and linkages to make it easier for them to recall information with a minimum of effort. Also consider different learning styles (auditory, visual, and kinesthetic) when designing your review sessions. Encourage participants to review their material. Being able to quickly find the correct information is as important as memorizing it. Select review activities that require the learners to review their notes taken during the session.

The creative reviewing activities presented here are fun, action-oriented, and practical. If transferring learning to the workplace is one of your concerns, try a review activity in your next training session.

Competition is often a fun way to set up a review of materials. Deborah Thomas provides a review using a PowerPoint game board, while Rebecca Judd shows you how to create a card game. Both are competitive and fun. Sarah Burke uses learning stations to ensure that everyone is a teacher and everyone is a learner in her activity. Lori Spangler shares a review activity called "Answer the Question and Keep the Card" that works for small and very large groups alike. Sue Weller creates simple but excellent reviews you can use at the end of your class. Your Gen-Ys will love the review that Kella Price describes using Twitter.

Whether you review your material in a large group or small, use paper or electronics, your review time is calm or rowdy, your learners will benefit from well-designed and executed reviews.

PPT Board Game Review

Submitted by Deborah Thomas

Overview

Competition is always a good way to engage learners, but a knowledge and retention competition based on key content presented in your session is a big win for your learners as well.

Objective

- To review course objectives using a game board

Audience

Ten to twenty-four participants

Time Estimate

15 to 25 minutes at the end of a module or at the end of a workshop

Materials and Equipment

- PowerPoint Game Board (see the example)
- One set of index cards with questions on one side and the answers on the other
- Dice (use free electronic dice or real dice)
- LCD projector
- Timer

Area Setup

Any room configuration

Preparation

Build a board game in MS PowerPoint (see example at the end of the activity). It's easy and cheap! Once it's built it can be displayed on the projector. Build the game using the drawing tools in PowerPoint. Keep in mind that you don't have to be an expert artist to draw a board game. Games are meant to be fun and the lines can be a little off. Create a set of questions that are true-false, multiple choice, short answer, long answer, or yes-no. Of course, the questions should always be based on important learning content objectives. Write one question per index card and put the answers on the other side, being aware not to show them to participants.

Process

1. Introduce the activity by saying, "It is time to review what we have learned." Project the game board.

2. Divide the participants into teams (up to four teams). Decide which team should go first. Perhaps ask who has a birthday coming up. The team that has a team member whose birthday is soonest goes first.

3. Ask the teams to designate team captains. Explain the rules. Tell them that you will draw questions from the stack of cards and will start the timer after you ask each question. Each team will have 45 seconds to respond. The team members can discuss and agree on the answer; then the team captain will answer for the team. You will determine whether the answer is correct. If the answer is correct, you will mark an X on the game space that indicates the number of spaces that team is allowed to move based on the dice roll.

4. Ask whether everyone understands the rules. Clarify if needed. Roll the dice for the first round.

5. Draw a card. Ask the question and begin the timer. As the team huddles to agree on an answer, you might wish to do a countdown. Ask the team captain for the answer.

6. Read the correct answer and determine whether the team's answer was correct. If the answer is close but not exact, ask the other teams to decide whether it should be counted as correct. Remind other teams that their teams will be afforded the same opportunity. That ensures fair play.

7. If the answer was correct. Use the pointer pen in PowerPoint (right click to access) and choose a different color for each team. Mark an X on the game space to indicate the number of spaces that team moves based on the dice roll.

8. Have the next team roll the dice and answer the next question you draw.

9. If a team does not give the correct answer, they don't move any spaces. In this case, ask the entire group for the correct answer. Although no one moves ahead on the board, they do "move ahead" by acquiring more knowledge.

10. The first team to reach the end of the game board wins.

InSider's Tips

- This is a great way to ask review questions. The element of team competition ensures that all team members participate.
- The timer is a critical component of the game. This helps people forget that it is a review and instead evokes a sense of play.
- If the competition gets too heated, remind them that it's a game and that everyone is a winner.
- The game board can be used at various points throughout the session to review. There could be several rounds and the team that wins the most rounds wins the game.
- Be sure to include some very simple, very difficult, and everything in between type of questions. The simple questions will offset the difficult questions. When a team is given a simple question, it may infuriate the other teams. Discuss that all is fair in love and games.
- You may actually want to have simple and difficult questions as a life lesson. Some teams do have an easier time of it in real life. Generally, teams in a workshop are comprised of colleagues. This sense of chance and "luck of the draw" will help offset any ill feelings.

Deborah Thomas, owner of SillyMonkey, LLC, a game-based learning boutique, started her career as a teacher at one of the worst-performing middle schools. She drove student SAT scores up 30 percent by creating and using innovative techniques. She applies that same passion for helping people retain learning objectives through games as a designer for Fortune 500 companies, including the Coca-Cola Company. She provides services for manufacturing, energy, retail, pharmaceutical, sales, and finance companies. She is president of the Atlanta chapter of the Georgia Game Developers Association, board member of the Technology Association of Georgia Workplace Learning Society, and past president of NASAGA.

Deborah Thomas
1453 Ashwoody Court
Atlanta, GA 30319
(404) 966.2372
Email: sillymonkey@mindspring.com
Website: www.sillymonkeyinternational.com
ASTD Chapter: Greater Atlanta

Sample Game Board

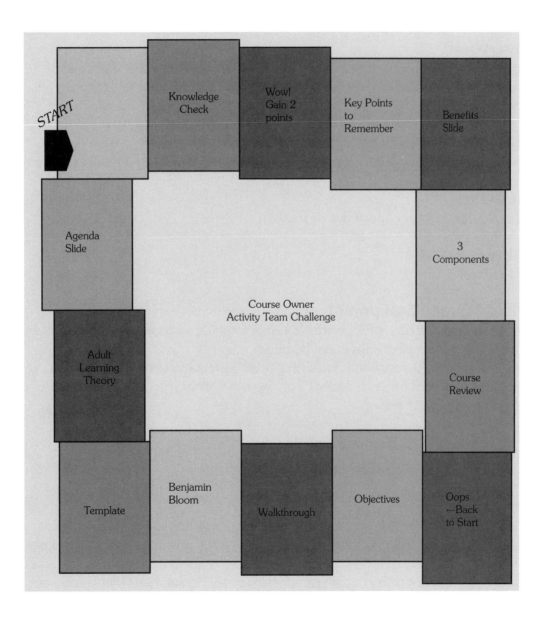

Throw Down Your Answer

Submitted by Rebecca Judd

Overview
Participants play a competitive card game and discover that a friendly round of cards is the perfect way to encourage participants to store away key learning for later recall.

Objective
- To reinforce the recall of correct data or desired action from a training session

Audience
Six to thirty, in subgroups of five or six

Time Estimate
30 minutes

Materials and Equipment
- One complete deck of Throwdown Cards for each subgroup (a question on one side and the correct answer on the other)
- One deck of Answer Cards for each player, each correct answer on its own card
- One blank card for each deck of Throwdown Cards
- (Optional) Small prizes

Area Setup
Up to five tables arranged for groups of five or six

Preparation
Create decks of Throwdown Cards for your topic by listing twenty to twenty-five questions on one side of index cards and placing the correct answers on the other side. Create one deck for each group. In addition, create a deck of Answer Cards for each participant with just the correct answers to the questions written on individual index cards.

Process

1. Say that participants at each table will review content from the workshop playing the Throwdown Card game.
2. Place a Throwdown Card deck in the middle of each table, with the questions up, but place a blank card on top of each deck so that those at the table cannot read the scenarios prior to starting the game.
3. Provide each participant in the room with a deck of Answer Cards.
4. Explain the rules of play:

   A volunteer at each table will remove the blank card and the players will read the first question together. As soon as one of the participants in a group knows the correct answer, that person will yell, "Throwdown!" and all other members of that group must find the answer in their Answer Card decks and place it face up on the table. Once all participants have played their Answer Cards, the scenario card is turned over to reveal the correct answer. Those who "threw down" the correct answer receive 1 point for that round. At the end of play, the person with the most points wins.
5. Answer any questions participants have and start the play. When every group has finished all of the questions, declare a winner for each table group. In case of a two- or three-way tie, declare all of them winners.

InSider's Tips

- Have a subject-matter expert review your questions for accuracy and job relevancy.
- Test the activity to make sure you've developed enough questions to support the desired time allotted.
- Award small prizes to the winner(s) in each group if you wish.
- You may wish to award prizes to the group with the most total points if groups have equal numbers of participants.
- Play the game multiple times for additional reinforcement of learning.
- This activity was co-developed with Lori Landy.

Rebecca Judd is a senior instructional designer. She has been designing and delivering training for more than twenty-four years. She holds a master's degree in human resource development and is passionate about eradicating the "training is boring" stigma.

Rebecca Judd
1901 Chouteau Avenue
MC 340
St. Louis, MO 63166
(314) 206.0938
Email: rjudd@ameren.com
ASTD Chapter: St. Louis Metropolitan

Learning Stations

Submitted by Sarah Burke

Overview

Participants in this activity pair up and switch roles between trainer and learner and in the process give important content an anchor point for later recall.

Objectives

- To increase participants' retention of difficult subject matter
- To identify additional teaching opportunities through observation

Audience

Eight to twenty participants

Time Estimate

30 to 45 minutes, depending on the number of participants

Materials and Equipment

- Preselected materials or training aids for each topic
- Post-it® Notes to label each station with the learning topic or objective
- A bell or whistle
- (Optional) The song "Switch" by Will Smith (verify with your legal department that this falls under "fair use" and does not infringe on any copyright)
- (Optional) A CD or cassette player or way to play the music

Area Setup

Tables set up as learning stations so that participants can move from one station to the next in a logical path

Preparation

The number of stations will equal half of the class size; for example, for twelve participants prepare six stations. Assign a topic/objective to each learning station and label it with a Post-it Note.

Select key information that you wish participants to retain. If you wish, you may create learning aids for some. Identify where the content resides in the participants' materials.

Process

1. Tell participants that they will have an opportunity to easily review several of the important aspects of what they have learned. Have the participants form pairs. Assign each pair one of the review topics. Tell them where they can find the content in the materials and let them know whether you have developed a learning aid for their topic. Tell them to take 10 minutes to design a 2-minute review of the content, identifying the key points, critical steps, or other important information. Call time after 10 minutes.

2. Have the pairs decide who will be the trainer and who will be the learner first. Have the "trainers" find their stations based on the name on the Post-it.

3. Tell the "learners" that they are to position themselves in front of the trainers. The trainers will spend 2 minutes reviewing the key concepts. At the end of the 2 minutes, you will play music (or ring a bell or blow a whistle) signaling that the learners should move to the next learning station in a clockwise direction.

4. When everyone is in position, ask them to begin. At the 2-minute mark, signal that the learners should move to the next station.

5. After all learners have moved through all stations, have the current learners take the trainer positions at their assigned learning stations. The trainers become the learners and position themselves in front of trainers. Begin the rounds, signaling at the end of the 2-minute segments, and continue until all learners have moved through all of the learning stations.

InSider's Tips

- An adult retains information much better when able to teach it to someone else.
- As the facilitator, move around the room to ensure that everyone is providing accurate information. Erroneous information should be corrected.
- The song helps motivate and engage the participants (as well as signal to them that it is time to move to the next station). Use it if possible.

Sarah Burke is a training supervisor at CarMax Auto Finance. She has over nine years of experience in instructor-led facilitation, instructional design, e-learning development, LMS, intranet, and project management. Sarah also volunteers for the ASTD Atlanta chapter, primarily in professional development.

Sarah Burke
225 Chastain Meadows Court
Kennesaw, GA 30144
(770) 792.4750, ext. 8592
Email: sarah_c_burke@carmax.com
ASTD Chapter: Greater Atlanta

Answer the Question and Keep the Card

Submitted by Lori Spangler

Overview

In this simple card game, the winners in each group receive a round of applause, but in the game of recall, all the participants are winners.

Objective

- To review concepts and information learned during the training session

Audience

Any number in groups of five or six

Time Estimate

20 to 30 minutes

Materials and Equipment

- One deck of twenty-five to forty question cards for each team

Area Setup

Enough tables to seat participants in groups of five or six

Preparation

Identify twenty-five to forty questions that relate to your training topic. Write each question and the correct answer on one side of an index card. Questions may be open-ended, multiple-choice, or true/false. You may include a few creative questions that don't relate to the topic. Make multiple sets, one for each team of five or six participants.

Process

1. If participants are not already seated in teams, ask them to form teams of five or six and sit at tables. Ask the individuals from each team who came the farthest distance to raise their hands. These people will ask the first question and play the role of the reader first.

2. Give each table group one deck of cards with questions and answers. Explain to participants that some of the questions are open-ended, some are multiple-choice and some don't even relate to the topic. Tell them to spread the cards randomly on the table, written side down.

3. Tell them that each "reader" should choose a card and read the question. Once the reader reads the question, the first person to answer correctly takes that card. Tell them to take turns reading cards. The goal is to obtain more cards than others at the same table. The objective is to answer as many questions correctly as possible.

4. If no one has the correct answer, the reader keeps that card (so be sure they take turns as the reader). Tell the participants they have 10 minutes for the activity. Tell them to begin.

5. During the activity, walk around the tables and respond to questions.

6. After 10 minutes (or however much time you allowed), call time and ask the participants in the groups to count the number of correct cards each person has collected. State that the person with the most cards wins. Invite the winners at each table to stand and lead applause for them. Tell them that in the end, they are all winners for retaining so much of the knowledge from the workshop.

InSider's Tips

- This is excellent for large groups with just one facilitator.
- Most learners like to be active when they learn; the competition is an extra bonus.
- If you laminate the index cards, they can be easily reused.
- If you have a large group and need to create multiple decks, enter the questions on your computer and print four or six to a page on card stock. Cut the cards apart to create a deck for each group.
- The activity requires little participation from the facilitator, although you do need time before the session to prepare questions.

Lori Spangler is a lead performance consultant at Deluxe Corporation, where she works with a remote sales force, consulting, assessing, and implementing sales training strategies. Lori loves to facilitate training when she can adjust "on the fly" to meet the needs of her learners, either in person or online. In addition to being certified in SPIN Selling, Strategic Selling, and IMPAX Strategic Account Sales, she holds master of arts degrees in adult education and communication.

Lori Spangler
205 Primrose Court
Vadnais Heights, MN 55127
(651) 483.1172
Email: Lori.Spangler@Deluxe.com
ASTD Chapter: Twin Cities

I'll Say It Myself

Submitted by Sue Weller

Overview

Participants articulate key learning points from your training session and make commitments on how they plan to put the most important "aha" moment to use.

Objectives

- To help learners articulate what was most important or meaningful to them during training
- To provide an opportunity for learners to share their "aha" moments

Audience

Any size group that has completed a training session together

Time Estimate

15 to 20 minutes for an average size group, about 30 seconds per person

Materials and Equipment

- PowerPoint slide or flip chart with three statements pre-printed on them:
  - One thing that surprised me was . . .
  - Starting tomorrow, I will . . .
  - I plan to tell someone that . . .
- A means to display the slide
- Paper and pencils for participants

Area Setup

No special arrangements

Process

1. At the end of the session, show the learners the three statements (either pre-printed on your flip chart or on a PowerPoint slide).
   - One thing that surprised me was . . .
   - Starting tomorrow, I will . . .
   - I plan to tell someone that . . .

Reviewing: Making It Fun

2. Ask the learners to think about everything they've learned and to complete one of the statements above on a sheet of paper. Suggest that they look through their notes. Reiterate that the learners must answer only *one* of the statements.

3. After several minutes, either ask for volunteers or go around the room, making certain to have each learner answer one of the statements. Don't allow your learners to take the easy way out. If the first person says he or she can't come up with anything, pass and tell him or her you'll come back (but make sure you do!).

4. If someone says he or she was going to say the same thing as the someone else, ask the person to think of something else. If you are not rigid on this point, you'll get a lot of people saying "ditto" as opposed to really thinking about what the workshop meant to them.

5. If you have certificates to hand out, you can hand out each certificate as that person shares his or her statement, thereby allowing participants to "earn" their certificates and allowing you to better keep track of who has commented and who still has to contribute.

InSider's Tips

- Often, at the end of a class, a facilitator summarizes the class and the key leanings. In this activity, you allow the learners to summarize and tell everyone what was important. Furthermore, it allows the learners to hear from their peers, thereby reinforcing the value of the session.

Sue Weller is the senior manager, training development, for Baxter Healthcare, where her instructional design team specializes in the design and development of regulatory and compliance training. Sue holds an undergraduate degree in organizational communications from Loyola University, Chicago, and a master's degree in training and development/instructional design and e-learning from Roosevelt University, Schaumburg, Illinois. Sue is also adjunct faculty at Oakton Community College, Des Plaines, Illinois, where she teaches various training, human resources, and management courses. Sue holds the Senior Professional in Human Resources designation and is the 2012 president for the Chicagoland chapter of ASTD. She is in the process of studying for her CPLP designation.

Sue Weller
1325 Regency Lane
Lake Villa, IL 60046
(847) 270.3970
Email: susan_weller@baxter.com
ASTD Chapter: Chicagoland

Tweet! Key Learnings

Submitted by Kella B. Price

Overview

This real-time recall and reinforcement activity not only helps keep the learners in your session connected and learning, but it also keeps those not in attendance in the learning loop as well.

Objectives

- To identify key learning points from an activity
- To share learning with others (either participants or absentees)

Audience

Any number of participants with Internet access

Time Estimate

10 or 15 minutes

Materials and Equipment

- Participants must bring their smart phones or laptops
- Access to the Internet
- One copy of What Is This Thing Called Twitter? for each participant

Area Setup

Wireless access

Preparation

Notify participants in advance of your intent to use Twitter and the benefits of sharing key learning points with others. Be sure they know they will need to have an account to access the site. State that they will maximize their learning, walk away with notes to reference at a later date, and share learning with those not present. Send the participants a copy of the handout, What Is This Thing Called Twitter? via email.

Process

1. Set guidelines at the beginning of the session about tweets. Remind participants about the hashtag that corresponds to the session.
2. Tell those who do not have access to the Internet to pair or group with others for posts. Be sure they know that, without an account, they will not be able to access the tweets later. Give everyone the handout (the same one you sent prior to the session) with information on how to set up an account, how to post tweets, and the hashtag that will identify the session.
3. At the conclusion of an activity or module, pull up the dialogue on the screen as a summary for discussion.
4. Encourage participants to revisit their tweet dialogue at a later date. If the session included a call for action for participants to implement, follow-up Twitter discussion can keep participants connected, identify obstacles, and help them find ways to overcome the obstacles.

InSider's Tips

- This activity can be done throughout a session or as part of a closing/re-cap of key learning points.
- This works best if participants are already familiar with Twitter, but since Twitter is easy to use, this can be used with any group that has access to a computer or phone with Internet capability.
- Notifying participants in advance of your intent is critical to maximizing the use of Twitter as a tool.
- I have found it to be beneficial to have participants, when possible, share their Twitter usernames in advance so that they may "follow" each other prior to the activity. This makes it easier for novice users to track live tweets. You can even have Twitter open on a training room screen for audience viewing if you want to maximize live tweet comments.
- Remind the participants of the hashtag at the beginning of the session.
- This is a great way for maximizing knowledge-sharing across users. It will also increase visibility of the session and valuable key learning points for those who did not attend. It may also increase future enrollment.

Kella B. Price, CPLP, has thirteen years experience in training and development and talent management functions. As CEO of Price Consulting Group, she is a trainer and facilitator. Kella has designed training and development tools and published content on diversity, expatriates, stress, job satisfaction, employee turnover, and virtual training. Kella is adept at using Web 2.0 technologies, including blogging, Twitter, bookmarking, and social media networks. She regularly conducts training on how to use these technologies as a business tool for collaboration and building relationships.

Kella B. Price, CPLP
10579 E. 37th Place
Yuma, AZ 85365
(928) 276.3009 or (252) 622.8119
Email: KPriceConsulting@aol.com
Website: www.thepriceconsultinggroup.com
ASTD Chapter: San Diego

What Is This Thing Called Twitter?

I will ask you to post key ideas you have gained from our discussions in Twitter. If you have questions about the content, this would also be a great place to post your question or to start a discussion with your fellow participants.

Twitter is a "micro blog," a message that is 140 characters or fewer.

When using Twitter, consider your goals:

- "Why are you there?"
- "Why do you want to be there?"
- "Why do you want to connect with other people?" "Is it for friendship, or as part of your business?"

Twitter is a powerful tool that can be used to build your personal brand through personal connections. Carefully select the username and picture you will use as part of your branding.

Once you've set up your account, find other people from the workshop or others and "follow" them. Your goal is to build personal connections and stay informed. You can find people you already know, friends or business colleagues, and those you may not know personally, but know of.

Your posts on Twitter should be personal interest (a quote or something interesting you did in a particular day), a brag (accomplishment highlighting your work), an interesting link, or a data nugget. These elements will keep others interested in your "tweets."

Check out www.tiny.cc to make links shorter to facilitate posts.

How to Build Your Following and Followers
- Find on Twitter: Search by Twitter username
- Find on other networks: Gmail, Yahoo, AOL, Hotmail, MSN
- Invite by email: Send invites to another email or contact list
- http://twitter.grader.com: Enter your Twitter username and get your ranking and "Suggested Folks to Follow"
- http://twinfluence.com/index.php: Top fifty Twitters in three different areas

Hashtags are keywords with number signs (#) in front of them, used for searching for conversations in Twitter. Be sure to follow @hashtags and the service will track and catalog the hashtags you use.

Retweet is used to repeat/quote someone's tweet so that people who are following you receive the information also. Start with RT (retweet) followed by the username of the person who tweeted it (e.g., @User) and the content of the actual tweet.

Example: kellapriceRT @relth New Blog: Leaders: Social Media Is Here to Stay: Learn to Maximize Its Benefits. http://tinyurl.com/kq6fty

Two items to check out to improve the functionality of your Twitter account:

- *Tweetdeck:* Breaks Twitter into manageable pieces
- *Twhirl*: When opened on it sends you "tweet mail"

Now you're ready to start using Twitter!

For this workshop, please use the hashtag #. This will connect all information about the workshop with the other participants' Twitter accounts.

Chapter 14

New Tools: Add a Twist
to Your Techniques

Active learning! Participation! Involve your learners. As a training professional, you have heard these directives a hundred times and you know why the concept is emphasized over and over.

First, activities are energizing. Using them gives learners a break from just words. Activities stretch participants' minds and relax their bodies. Activities also involve people working together. They provide an avenue to build rapport and increase knowledge retention. Activities promote learning by doing. Your participants retain knowledge better if you engage as many of their senses as possible. Activities provide you with a way to reinforce information in a variety of ways. Your training style would be pretty boring if you just stated the same things over and over in the same way, even though repetition *is* good. Finally, activities are motivational. Learners respond because they are actively involved. It is a pleasant way to learn.

I recently used one of the activities from this book (consider it a trial run) in one of my team-building sessions. I was so excited to try this one new idea it buoyed my attitude for the whole two days! So if training is your dream and you find that you don't have the energy or enthusiasm you once had, perhaps you have taught the same training session one too many times. Perhaps the travel schedule or the long hours are getting you down. While you might try many remedies to help you build a more positive attitude, one that works for both you and your learners is to experiment with activities or methods you've never tried before.

The road-tested learning techniques shared here are all new training twists you should try. We all say that we learn from participants, but Laura Mendelow practices it with "Speedy SMEs." Sharon Dera contributed two ideas for this chapter.

"Remember Me?" is a short but powerful experiential learning activity that will help both trainers and supervisors understand why employees retain some but not all information. "Product Knowledge Scramble" could easily fit in the review chapter as well, but we have chosen to locate it here. Check out alternate uses for this activity. Lori Spangler shows you how knowledge about a topic can come from many places in "Key Ideas."

Paul Terlemezian opens with a contradictory comment that gets immediate attention and encourages participation throughout your session with "Give Them the BlackBerries." Kella Price offers an activity with a dual purpose: to divide participants into small groups and to learn more about them. Tina Pressley uses scenario cards in a competitive format that will add fun to your session. Lisa Haneberg has been blogging for six years and tells you how you can use blogs as a training tool. J.T. Kostman and Sandi Ruther explain two ways that you can ensure transfer of learning after your session. Both activities are creative and good ways to end your session.

Finally, Todd Whisenant shares a very interesting train-the-trainer activity.

Here are some great new ideas! Your colleagues have shared several excellent ideas. Why don't you try something new next week! Make it fun for both you and your learners.

Speedy SMEs

Submitted by Laura Mendelow

Overview
Everyone is both an SME and a learner in this engaging activity, with the goal of sharing the collective knowledge of the group and making new organizational connections.

Objectives
- To share information quickly on a variety of topics
- To demonstrate the value of learner participation

Audience
Twenty to sixty participants, depending on the number of topics

Time Estimate
30 to 40 minutes

Materials and Equipment
- Markers or table tent cards
- Paper for participants
- Timer or your watch
- Index cards for all participants
- Pens or pencils for participants

Area Setup
Tables in a U-shape

Preparation
Before your training session begins, select the topics for discussion. You will need about one topic for every four or five people. These topics are based on the areas of expertise of your audience so it is recommended that you know your audience ahead of time. If you don't know your audience, you can poll them in advance and have them submit the three topic areas in which they have the greatest expertise or knowledge. Write the topic names on table tents and place them around the U-shaped table arrangement.

New Tools: Add a Twist

Process

1. As the participants enter the room, ask them to find a table with their expertise area identified on the table tent.

2. Explain to the group that there are many experts in the room (meaning the participants themselves) and often we don't take time to learn from each other. Explain that this activity will allow them to learn from each other in a fast but meaningful way.

3. Try to evenly distribute the participants. The ideal group size is six, but you can still do the activity with two people in a group. Ask participants to move around if the groups are unevenly sized.

4. Hand out paper and pencils and ask each group to write their top best practices, resources, or models (depending on content and topic area) that relate to their topic areas. Allow 5 to 10 minutes for the activity and let the participants work in their small groups.

5. Distribute index cards to all participants and ask everyone to look around the room at the other topics on the name tents. Ask them to write one or two questions on their index cards that they would like to ask the participants in the other groups. Ask them to think about something relevant, possibly information that will help them perform their current or future work.

6. After everyone has finished, ask the participants in each group to count off by 2's so the audience is now split into two groups—"1's" and "2's."

7. Ask the "1's" to move to the center of the room (inside the U-shape table arrangement). Explain that when the activity starts the "1's" will refer to their index cards and will roam freely in the room and ask questions to any of the other participants (the "2's").

8. The "2's" will stay at their stations as the subject-matter experts (SMEs). They will give advice or answers to the "1's" as the "1's" walk around the room. The "2's" can rely on the current list of tips and best practices they just developed.

9. Start the activity and allow 7 to 10 minutes.

10. After you call time, have the groups switch. The "1's" become the SMEs at their stations and the "2's" walk around the room to ask questions.

11. Once the second round is over, debrief by asking the participants to share some of the new knowledge they learned.

InSider's Tips

- Allow people to self-select as much as possible at the beginning.
- Don't structure the roaming part of the exercise; let everyone roam around as if they were visiting booths at a conference. The less structure, the better.
- It is important to know your audience ahead of time and select topics for which you know you will have participants who are knowledgeable.
- You may wish to begin a wiki page of best practices that result from this session.

Laura Mendelow has a master's degree in organization development, certificate in instructional systems design, and has extensive experience with experiential education techniques. She has been active in the learning industry since 1994 and joined Booz Allen Hamilton in 2002, where she now oversees the OD and coaching programs within learning and development. Outside of Booz Allen, Laura leads the American Society for Training and Development OD special interest group for the D.C. Metro chapter and also provides "time out" group coaching sessions for parents dealing with spirited children to help them reframe and reconnect with their children.

Laura Mendelow
16200 Kimberly Grove Road
Gaithersburg, MD 20878
(301) 325.5123
Email: Laura. Mendelow@gmail.com
ASTD Chapter: Metro Washington, D.C.

Remember Me?

Submitted by Sharon Dera

Overview

This activity reinforces several important maxims about retention, including the notion that repetition really does work.

Objectives

- To discuss ways to improve retention
- To understand why learners or employees retain information

Audience

Twenty to fifty participants

Time Estimated

15 to 20 minutes

Materials and Equipment

- One blank sheet of paper for each participant
- One pencil/pen per participant

Area Setup

Any room setup that provides writing space

Process

1. Distribute a blank sheet of paper and a pen or pencil to each participant. Ask participants to write the numbers 1 through 20 on their papers and then put their pencils down.
2. Tell participants to listen carefully as you read a list of twenty words.
3. Read the following list of words slowly and clearly, beginning with the word "pancake." Continue reading the entire left-side column before moving on. End the list by reading the word "soccer."

Pancake	Birthday	Candy	Football
Vacation	Gifted	Dragster	Payback
Gifted	Gourmet	Olympics	Gifted
Successful	Telephone	Pencil	Cloudy
Sexy	Castle	Airplane	Soccer

4. Ask participants to write down the words they can remember.

5. Allow 4 or 5 minutes. Ask participants to share the total number of words they listed.

6. Read the list of words again and ask the participants to double-check their lists as you read.

7. Ask participants to share the total number of words they had correct.

8. Ask participants to raise their hands if they wrote down the words "pancake" and "soccer." Explain that pancake was the first word and soccer was the last word. Usually, first things and last things are easily remembered.

9. Ask participants to raise their hands if they wrote down the word "gifted." Say, "Gifted was repeated three times." Usually, things mentioned more than once are more likely to be remembered.

10. Ask participants to provide some examples of how they remembered the other words. Explain that, usually, other words are remembered by word association, an emotional attachment, or by visualizing an item.

11. Lead a summarizing discussion about what this tells us about listening and retention. Ask how participants might use this information back on the job.

InSider's Tips

- Use sheets of blank, lined paper for ease of writing.
- The activity is based on word association, retention of information, and the theory that it takes at least twenty-one days of repeated practice to change a habit or behavior.
- You may create your own list of twenty to thirty words that are related to your group, remembering to repeat one word three times.

Sharon Dera, CPLP, has more than seventeen years of experience in needs assessment, human performance, process improvement, and organization development. Her broad experience was acquired by working in the retail, finance, healthcare, government, manufacturing, hospitality, and travel industries in operations, business management, customer service, sales, communications, marketing, succession planning, leadership, coaching, and training. Sharon is owner and CEO of The Proficience Group, Inc., working in partnership with organizations to identify the root cause of performance deficiencies and determine the best solutions/interventions that close performance gaps. The company lends a "fresh set of eyes," exposing possible blind spots. Sharon is currently serving on the National ASTD Chapter Recognition Committee. She earned an MBA from the University of Dallas.

Sharon Dera, CPLP
8948 Random Road
Fort Worth, TX 76179
(817) 236.7594
Email: sdera@charter.net
Website: www.proficiencegroup.com
ASTD Chapter: Fort Worth Mid-Cities

Product Knowledge Scramble

Submitted by Sharon Dera

Overview
Participants work together to quickly match up their product knowledge under the right category in a game that uses both knowledge and action to build on job recall.

Objective
- To review or introduce content in a workshop

Audience
Ten to twenty-five participants who have completed a course, in teams of four or five

Time Estimate
15 minutes

Materials and Equipment
- One blank Header Sheet for each team (see the sample completed sheet at the end of this activity)
- One deck of Product Knowledge Cards for each team (index cards on which products and descriptors are printed)
- A bell or other noisemaker for each team
- (Optional) Small prizes

Area Setup
Any room where teams of four or five can work without disturbing one another

Preparation
Prior to the session, decide what product components you wish to review (or introduce). Create a heading page with categories and places to write information underneath them. Identify various products and some information about each product that you want participants to know and remember. Create Product Knowledge Cards, printing one product or one product descriptor on each card. Copy enough Header Sheets and decks of cards for all teams.

Process

1. Divide the participants into teams of four or five. Assign each team a designated spot and give them a noisemaker.
2. Give one Heading Sheet and one set of Product Knowledge Cards to each team. Ask participants to work as a team to put the product knowledge components on the cards under the correct headings on their sheets.
3. Tell the teams that, once they are certain of the accuracy of their sheets, to signal completion with their noisemakers.
4. Check the winning team's work.
5. Award small prizes to team members if you wish.

InSider's Tips

- For the financial industry, a list of product knowledge components could include the product name, code number, eligibility requirements, feature explanation, benefit explanation, and others.
- For the retail industry, a list of product knowledge components could include the product name, country of origin, UPC code, price, accessories, feature explanation, benefit explanation, and others.
- Keep an answer key available to quickly check the teams' work.
- Although presented as a review technique, the activity could also be used as a before-and-after test, to introduce new information, to have participants place the cards during a lecturette, as an interactive group activity, or many other ways.
- It can also be used to teach other knowledge-based information that has numerous components, such as definitions and appropriate/inappropriate time to use a procedure.

Sharon Dera, CPLP, has more than seventeen years of experience in needs assessment, human performance, process improvement, and organization development. Her broad experience was acquired by working in the retail, finance, healthcare, government, manufacturing, hospitality, and travel industries in operations, business management, customer service, sales, communications, marketing, succession planning, leadership, coaching, and training. Sharon is owner and CEO of The Proficience Group, Inc., working in partnership with organizations to identify the root cause of performance deficiencies and determine the best solutions/interventions that close performance gaps. The company lends a "fresh set of eyes," exposing possible blind spots. Sharon is currently serving on the National ASTD Chapter Recognition Committee. She earned an MBA from the University of Dallas.

Sharon Dera, CPLP
8948 Random Road
Fort Worth, TX 76179
(817) 236.7594
Email: sdera@charter.net
Website: www.proficiencegroup.com
ASTD Chapter: Fort Worth Mid-Cities

Example of a Completed Sheet

Product	Code	Requirement	Feature	Benefit
Business Checking	S71	$200 minimum deposit	No fee on $5,000 average balance	Convenient way to pay bills and manage monthly expenses
Money Market Checking	S4	$1,000 minimum deposit	Dividends earned on daily balances of $2,500	Convenient way to pay bills and earn dividends at the same time

Key Ideas

Submitted by Lori Spangler

Overview

Reading and highlighting ideas make this activity easy to facilitate and an effective tool for learners.

Objectives

- To determine key ideas from a variety of sources
- To expand the input of content from another source(s)

Audience

Four to ten participants

Time Estimate

20 to 30 minutes

Materials and Equipment

- One highlighter marker for each participant
- One white paper or article for each learner (they may be the same or several different articles that discuss the same topic)
- Flip chart and markers

Area Setup

Writing surfaces

Process

1. Distribute a white paper and a highlighter to each participant.
2. Ask them to read the articles and highlight key points that they want to remember or perhaps use in their conversations with clients or employees or in other situations. Allow an appropriate amount of time to complete the assignment.
3. Conduct a round-robin asking each learner to state one key point he or she has highlighted. Continue the round-robin until all ideas have been shared.

4. You may wish to post the ideas, perhaps categorizing them into appropriate groupings such as positive/negative; planning/action; pre/post; one-on-one/teams; or other categories depending on your topic.

InSider's Tips

- The activity is simple to explain and implement.
- Learners can take their highlighted hard copies with them to review after training or to post in their offices.

Lori Spangler is a lead performance consultant at Deluxe Corporation, where she works with a remote sales force, consulting, assessing, and implementing sales training strategies. Lori loves to facilitate training when she can adjust "on the fly" to meet the needs of her learners, either in person or online. In addition to being certified in SPIN Selling, Strategic Selling, and IMPAX Strategic Account Sales, she holds master of arts degrees in adult education and communication.

Lori Spangler
205 Primrose Court
Vadnais Heights, MN 55127
(651) 483.1172
Email: Lori.Spangler@Deluxe.com
ASTD Chapter: Twin Cities

Give Them the BlackBerries

Submitted by Paul Terlemezian

Overview

Participants are asked to use their mobile devices and social networking software to check the facts you present at your session, a surprising but ultimately engaging and effective suggestion to enhance learning outcomes.

Objectives

- To engage the participants early through humor
- To set the tone for sharing relevant knowledge

Audience

From ten to one hundred or more

Time Estimate

5 to 15 minutes, depending on discussion

Materials and Equipment

- None

Area Setup

Any room or activity area

Process

1. At the beginning of any session, ask whether anyone has a laptop, BlackBerry, iPhone, or other communication device. Pause long enough for the participants to reach for their communication devices.
2. Likely the participants will begin to turn them off or check the sound level of their mobile devices, but surprise everyone and say, "If so, please turn them on and feel free to use them during this presentation." Pause again.
3. This time pause long enough for the participants to react and do a double-take.
4. Ask the participants why they think you asked them to turn the devices on. Be prepared for surprise responses and the wise cracks that may follow. Laugh with them.

5. Encourage participants to research and validate or find contrary facts to anything you say during your session. Explain the importance of accurate information in the moment and your sincere appreciation and expectation that they will speak up if they find relevant information on their devices.

InSider's Tips

- This is an effective exercise for use with an audience of managers, executives, trainers, or others who must communicate effectively.
- If possible set up a website page using your preferred social networking software and a twitter tag for their use. Keep these applications open on your laptop or desktop computer during the session and track the activity when you have the opportunity or have an assistant follow the activity for you.
- Design your presentation with the assumption that people have access to immediate verification and communication with others outside the classroom.

Paul Terlemezian retired after a successful career in technology and training with a focus on customer training and business development. In June of 2003, Paul came out of retirement to start iFive Alliances. In addition to developing revenue-producing alliances, iFive Alliances provides consulting services, go-to-market strategies, and keynote speeches on the future of learning as a business. Paul serves on the board of several organizations and founded the TAG (Technology Association of Georgia) Workplace Learning Society, which has a focus on the effective combination of technology and learning in the workplace.

Paul Terlemezian
125 Laurian Way
Atlanta, GA 30328
(404) 252.8330
Email: pault@ifivealliances.com
Website: http://ifivealliances.ning.com
ASTD Chapter: Greater Atlanta

Tell Me About Yourself

Submitted by Kella B. Price

Overview

Participants answer questions about a selected topic related to their training experience or needs as a way to divide themselves into groups for further group activities.

Objectives

- To separate participants into smaller groups
- To learn about participants' interests

Audience

Groups of twenty or fewer

Time Estimate

5 minutes; larger groups may require more time

Materials and Equipment

- None

Area Setup

Any room or activity area

Process

1. Tell participants they will work in small groups based on the answers they give to a question you will pose.
2. Ask the participants a question related to the topic of your session. You can give them a multiple-choice question or allow participants to explain their answers freestyle. Examples of questions include:
   - What did you want to learn from this session?
   - What do you think is the greatest listening obstacle?
   - What is your biggest training challenge in the workplace today?
   - What is the most critical skill in your workplace for employee success?
3. Provide an example by answering one of the questions yourself from your perspective.

4. Next, ask each participant to respond. Divide the participants into groups based on their responses to your question. Ask those who responded in the same way to go to a specific location in the room.
5. When everyone is in a group, assign the task of your choice.

InSider's Tips

- This works well in small groups (under twenty) when you want to have a pleasant way for people to get to know each other. It can also be an energizer.
- If the goal of the activity is to confirm that participants are all different, but can identify commonalities, recap this point at the conclusion of the activity.
- If the goal was to identify different individuals to gain different perspectives on specific content, recap the group "identifier" and their viewpoint at the conclusion of the activity.

Kella B. Price, CPLP, has thirteen years of experience in training and development and talent-management functions. As CEO of Price Consulting Group, she is a trainer and facilitator. Kella has designed training and development tools and published content on diversity, expatriates, stress management, job satisfaction, employee turnover, and virtual training.

Kella B. Price, CPLP
10579 E. 37th Place
Yuma, AZ 85365
(928) 276.3009 or (252) 622.8119
Email: KPriceConsulting@aol.com
Website: www.thepriceconsultinggroup.com
ASTD Chapter: San Diego

Deal with It

Submitted by Tina Pressley

Overview

Groups of players discuss good solutions to problem scenarios and compete to win based on scoring of familiar card games.

Objectives

- To discuss potential solutions for dealing with real situations
- To provide an opportunity to practice skills presented in the training session

Audience

Best for groups between ten and eighteen divided into two teams; with more than eighteen, teams of six to eight

Time Estimate

30 to 60 minutes, depending on the length of discussion

Materials and Equipment

- One deck of playing cards for scoring
- One set of ten or more Scenario Cards prepared with the scenarios on one side and numbered one through ten on the other
- Painter's tape
- (Optional) Prizes for the winning team

Area Setup

A room or space large enough for the teams to work together

Preparation

Before the session, create the Scenario Cards. Identify ten or more scenarios that describe difficult situations or challenges participants face on the job that are related to the training session topic. These scenarios might be dealing with difficult customers for a customer service class or addressing challenging employees for a supervisory class.

An example might be a scenario in which a customer is making unreasonable demands. You might offer this scenario: "A customer purchased a sofa and wants you to load it in the car. When you get to the car you see that the sofa is too large for the vehicle. She insists you put it in the car anyway."

Write the scenarios on one side of an index card, one per card. Follow the scenario with the words, "How are you going to deal with it?" Number the Scenario Cards on the other side with large numbers, 1 through 10 (or however many scenarios you have).

Post these cards on a wall or whiteboard or flip chart with the painter's tape so that the numerals are facing out.

Process

1. Introduce the activity by stating that you can never predict what situation you might face when dealing with customers (employees, people, or others). Emphasize that the activity is designed to help the participants be ready with anything by practicing essential knowledge and skills they have learned during the training session.
2. Divide the participants into teams, and assign them a location in the room (standing or sitting). Ask one team to start by selecting a scenario by number from the wall.
3. Read the card to the teams. Let them know they have 30 seconds to come up with an answer. Say that each team must share its answer with the entire group. The answer is then open for discussion by the other team(s) as well. If the entire group can agree that the answer is correct, the team draws a card from the deck of playing cards. *Note:* Take care that the discussion does not go on too long. If it is obvious that the other team is just being difficult and does not want to agree that the response was correct or adequate, step in and make a judgment call.
4. Repeat this process until all the scenarios have been assessed.
5. Ask the teams to examine their playing cards and show their best hands. You can decide to score by the total point value or use the rules of familiar games such as 21, poker, or blackjack, with the best hand winning the game. Lead applause for everyone in the activity.

InSider's Tips

- The activity is appropriate for anyone who needs to explore solutions to situations in customer service, safety, values, supervisory skills, or other similar topics.
- The activity works best when you have identified difficult, but real situations, ones they will actually face on the job.
- Participants like to be able to see the numbers from where they sit, so post the Scenario Cards where everyone can see them.
- You can adjust the rules. For example, if you think the answer is too short or incomplete, you may ask the other team to respond. Award the correct response as appropriate.

Tina Pressley is an active board member of her local ASTD chapter as the marketing and communications vice president. Tina is a graduate of the University of South Carolina with a B.S. in business/marketing and a minor in computer science. She is the director of training and development at Goodwill Industries Upstate/Midlands South Carolina. Her past experience includes training in retail, communication, motivation, sales, leadership, management, and team building. Tina and her husband are long-term residents of South Carolina and make Fountain Inn their home with their two children, Kita and Zane. Tina loves exercise, reading, developing new training ideas, and working for Goodwill. Tina is also an active community leader in youth sports. She and her husband volunteer as basketball, baseball, football, and volleyball coaches. She is a member of the PTA and president of the Music Booster Club at her son's school.

Tina Pressley
115 Haywood Road
Greenville, SC 29607
(864) 351.0124
Email: tpressley@goodwillsc.org
Website: goodwillsc.org
ASTD Chapter: Upstate South Carolina

Blog and RE-Blog

Submitted by Lisa Haneberg

Overview

Participants revise a blog specific to your training topic and gain new perspectives about their jobs, colleagues, or themselves while encouraging creativity.

Objectives

- To expose participants to different perspectives
- To increase sharing of new and fresh ideas among peers

Audience

As many groups of three to six participants as desired

Time Estimate

35 minutes

Materials and Equipment

- Collect provocative blog posts that address your desired training topic, one per group
- One RE-Blog Worksheet for each participant
- Pens or pencils

Area Setup

An area with tables for participants to sit in groups of three to six and write on the worksheets. Provide clipboards if tables are not available.

Preparation

Search for blog posts that relate to or address the topic covered in your training session. If you have a blog and a post that is appropriate, use this resource. *Note:* A good place to start your search is an Internet tool such as SocialMention.com or Technorati.com. Print out the blog and make enough copies for each participant.

Process

1. Ask participants to form small groups of three to six, preferably mixed so that participants get to know those with whom they work less often.

374

2. Pass out a RE-Blog Worksheet and pens or pencils to participants. Review the instructions at the top of the worksheet.
3. Tell the group they have 25 minutes to create their re-blog post. Provide a countdown warning when 10 and 5 minutes remain.
4. Ask each group to present its re-blog post and then facilitate a brief discussion of each presentation (3 to 5 minutes each). Questions you might use include:
   - What's different about the re-blog?
   - Why is this difference important?
   - What new idea did you hear?
   - What are you taking away from this discussion?

# InSider's Tips

- Let participants know that they do not need to agree with what the blog post they have been given says. In fact, it can be even more interesting when their re-blog post rebuts the original!
- You might need to give a quick primer on what a blog post is, depending on your audience.
- The idea is to spark interest and new thinking and then have each group teach their peers.
- If you have a vehicle for this, offer to help them post and share the re-blog posts.

Lisa Haneberg is a thought leader, consultant, and speaker in the areas of leadership, management, and organization development. She has written thirteen books and has been blogging about management for six years at www.managementcraft.com.

Lisa Haneberg
3063 Portsmouth Avenue
Cincinnati, OH 45208
lhaneberg@gmail.com
www.lisahaneberg.com
ASTD Chapter: Greater Cincinnati

RE-Blog Worksheet

Instructions: Your team will be given a thought-provoking blog post to read and discuss among yourselves. Your assignment is to imagine that you are writing another blog post to capture the team's discussion of this post and topic. Write your "re-blog" post below and be ready to share it with the larger group. Your re-blog post should be no more than three paragraphs in length. Feel free to use bullets and diagrams in your post. You will have a total of 25 minutes to read and discuss the blog post and write your team's re-blog post (for example, take 5 minutes to read the post, 10 minutes to discuss the post within your team, and 10 minutes to work as a team creating your re-blog post).

Re-Blog Post Title: _____

Re-Blog Post Body:

Success Chain

Submitted by J.T. Hostman

Overview
Email is used to connect participants as a support group to monitor their promises to put into practice what they have learned in training.

Objectives
- To put lessons learned in the classroom into real-world practice
- To use the power of the group to recognize, reward, and reinforce individual improvement

Audience
Five to twenty is ideal, but any size will work

Time Estimate
20 to 30 minutes for a group of twenty

Materials and Equipment
- Flip chart
- Markers

Area Setup
None required

Process
1. Toward the end of your training session, ask participants whether they have learned anything they might be able to use to improve their performance on the job. When they (inevitably) say they have, ask for one volunteer to share something he or she will do differently within the next few days/weeks and by what date, based on what he or she has learned. Post the person's name and what he or she will do differently on the flip chart.
2. Congratulate the person heartily (leading the group in a little applause doesn't hurt). Ask who in the room he or she will email to report progress and success.

3. Move to the email recipient and ask what that person will do differently as a result of what he or she has learned and by what date. Post the person's name and what he or she will do differently on the flip chart. Congratulate the person and state, "Once you receive your colleague's email, add your own accomplishment to it and forward it to someone else in the group. To whom would you like to forward your email to report your success?"

4. Continue this same process until everyone in the room has committed to an action and a date by when they will report having accomplished their goals. Tell them that they are going to create a success chain.

5. Ask the last person to email you. Even better, the last person could email the organizational champion for the training event.

InSider's Tips

- This quick reminder helps to ensure effective transfer of learning. It also proves, once and for all, that your training has an impact on real-world performance.

- By the time the process reaches the last person in the line, you will have created a success chain of real-world wins that will not only put learning into action, but also prove to the organization that training is being put into practice. Ask to be copied on the final email so you can collect a record of all the organizational successes, innovations, and cost-savings your courses have contributed.

- Ask a senior-level executive to get involved. Copy him or her on the final link in the chain. This allows the person to send congratulations to everyone who participated.

- This activity tends to work for the same reason Weight Watchers, Alcoholics Anonymous, and other support groups work. People who make a public declaration of their intentions are much more likely to succeed than those who simply resolve to meet a goal. By committing to be a single link in the chain, everyone in the chain is counting on everyone else to fulfill their commitments.

- You may wish to hand out skeleton keys or some such token to each person as he or she makes a commitment as a reminder that this step is the key to success of his or her commitment. You can purchase them from any home improvement store for $1 each.

The Book of Road-Tested Activities

- Want to ratchet it up a notch? Once the process has been successfully completed, have the organization's change champion issue a challenge to see whether everyone can take it to the next level. The person can start the process again in the reverse order, or use the same technique with his or her own reports.

J.T. Kostman, Ph.D., has advised senior-level executives in organizations ranging from the federal government to the Fortune 500 on the development of effective organizational transformation, leadership development, and performance improvement solutions. He is a consultant, coach, and professor. J.T. has a Ph.D. in industrial and organizational psychology, which he earned after a distinguished career as a paramedic, police officer, deep-sea rescue diver, and team leader of an elite scout/sniper reconnaissance team with the U.S. Army. He lives in New York and D.C., where he consults primarily to the defense and intelligence communities.

J.T. Kostman, Ph.D.
313 Wills Avenue
Stanhope, NJ 07874
(703) 403.2555
Email: JTKostman@yahoo.com
Website: www.LSRalliance.com
ASTD Chapter: Metro Washington, D.C.

Take Action

Submitted by Sandi Ruther

Overview
This simple activity connects commitments to those willing to help accomplish them.

Objective
- Enable participants to take immediate steps to implement actions toward their goals

Audience
Twenty to forty participants

Time Estimate
15 to 30 minutes, depending on group size

Materials and Equipment
- Index cards or quarter sheets of paper for all participants
- Pen or pencil for each participant
- Basket

Area Setup
Any setup, but for larger group, a center aisle makes it easier

Process
1. Near the end of a training program or event, explain that taking action is critical to achieving a goal.
2. Give out index cards and pens or pencils and invite participants to spend a few minutes writing down one action that they can commit to take immediately (within the next 24 to 48 hours) to move toward their goal.
3. Have participants write their names, phone numbers, and email addresses on the cards. Collect the cards.
4. Explain that sometimes work and life get in the way of living up to the commitments toward action made during training. Tell the participants that this activity will remind them of their intended actions.

380

5. Explain that you will read the actions from the cards one at a time, but not the names of the people who wrote them. If there are individuals who can help someone make that action happen, those people should raise their hands. Tell these volunteers that their job will be to call and/or support the individual who made the commitment.
6. Hand the index card to the first person who responds that he or she can help.
7. Repeat until all of the cards have been handed out.
8. Instruct the participants to contact the people to whom they offered help. Encourage the participants to connect with each other before leaving the training session or call or email within the next 24 hours to initiate the process.

InSider's Tips

- Suggest participants write down just *one* action. More than one complicates the activity.
- Encourage participants to help each other.
- Make sure everyone writes his or her contact information on the index card.
- Don't force participants; maintain a safe environment.

Sandi Ruther is the founder and principal of ProGold Consulting, LLC, a successful documentation, training, and consulting firm whose mission is to help businesses improve employee morale, operational efficiency, and business profitability by aligning people, processes, and systems. Bringing more than eighteen years of experience in business process optimization, internal auditing, technical writing, technical and business skills training, facilitating, and consulting, ProGold Consulting, LLC, helps clients eliminate organizational roadblocks and implement cost-effective solutions. Sandi is also an expert communicator, delivering dynamic and persuasive keynotes and seminars on the topic "Polished, Not Perfect! A New Definition of Success."

Sandi Ruther
P.O. Box 632156
Highlands Ranch, CO 80163–2156
(303) 593.0025
Email: sandiruther@comcast.net
Website: www.progoldconsulting.com
ASTD Chapter: Rocky Mountain

Dirty Training Room

Submitted by Todd Whisenant

Overview
This activity might be called a "Tale of Two Training Rooms" since the lessons learned about classroom preparation are examined in a graphic (but entertaining) way.

Objective
- To demonstrate appropriate room preparation for a training session

Audience
Ten to twenty-five participants in a train-the-trainer session

Time Estimate
30 minutes, depending on class size and logistics

Materials and Equipment
- "Clean" trash (trash created—*not* trash from trash can), such as empty soda cans, used coffee cups, napkins, and class materials
- Tent cards
- Audiovisual equipment as needed

Area Setup
Two training rooms, preferably *not* next to each other. One room is the one that the trainees have been instructed to go to for the session. This room is "trashed." The second room is meticulous with everything in place and prepared for the training session.

Preparation
If possible, prepare the two training rooms the night before. Get housekeeping or the janitor's assistance, asking them to ensure that they do not clean the "dirty" classroom. If you cannot set up the night before, arrive at least 90 minutes early to prep both rooms. Begin to prepare the "clean" room first, since you do not want participants to catch you before your grand entry.

382

Keep the two rooms apart, preferably out of sight of each other. If necessary, place signage directing participants to the "dirty" room and perhaps place a sign in front of the "clean" room that says: "Do Not Enter—Testing in Progress."

In the "dirty" room "prepare" it as if another group has just used the room, but no one bothered to clean up afterward. Tables and chairs are in disarray. Leave trash such as napkins, crumpled paper, empty soda cans, and used coffee cups on the tables and floor. Leave (or create) notes (not from your training program) on the dry erase board and flip charts. Leave partial, old refreshments on the tables such as stale food, beverage pitchers, melted ice, used plates, or other appropriate trash you create.

The second room should be set with meticulous care with everything in its place. Tables and chairs are properly positioned and clean. All training materials are neatly placed at each seat along with tent cards, pens, and any other materials. The dry erase board should be clean; the flip-chart pad should be fresh; the LCD projector should be on and the first slide already showing. Appropriate refreshments should be displayed in neat orderly fashion; drinks should be at the appropriate temperature; and plenty of ice should be available. The instructor's table is fully prepared and ready for instruction.

Process

1. Do not enter the "dirty" room until 10 minutes after the start time of the training session. A bit of theatrics is needed at this point. Your appearance should be disheveled, with a sense of being rushed, carrying (fake) class materials that appear to be ready to fall out your arms at any moment.

2. Rush into the room, not noting how bad it looks, but simply apologize for being late. As the materials fall onto the front table, look around to see the room and how bad everything is. Begin to apologize for the condition of the room and then excuse yourself and tell participants that you are going to speak to someone about the room situation. Leave the room for 3 or 4 minutes.

3. Return, apologize again for the room, and then announce the class will move to a cleaner room. State the new room location and lead the group to the second room.

4. Greet each participant as he or she enters the "clean" room. Allow everyone time to take in the new environment. Ask, "What do you think happened here?" After the laugher diminishes, debrief on the differences in the rooms using some of these questions:
   - How did you feel in the first room? In the second room? Why?
   - What details did you notice in the second room that you need to emulate in your own training?

- How important are first impressions of a training room?
- Although the setup was slightly exaggerated, why might a room not look its best for a training session? How can you prevent that from happening?
- How does the ambiance of a room affect the participants?
- What's your greatest take-away from this experience?
- What will you add to your training setup list in the future?

5. Comment on any additional ideas regarding the correct way to set a training room, noting various elements and how they affect participant learning.

InSider's Tips

- Trainees may be in disbelief regarding the first room and may try to find another room. You may need to have an assistant (or perhaps security) explain that this is the correct room.
- DO stay hidden (probably in the "clean" room). The entire exercise could be ruined if your presence is known before your entrance into the "dirty" room.
- Many of the participants will no doubt realize what has taken place once they enter the "clean" room. Take note of their body language and facial expressions in both rooms so that you can describe them during the debriefing step.
- Emphasize that the condition and preparedness of the room sets the tone for the learning environment, regardless of the training budget.
- Have fun with the exercise!

Todd Whisenant is the director of human resources for the U.S. Information Technology Group for Campus Crusade for Christ, Inc. He has over twenty years of workplace learning and performance experience, working with several Fortune 500 and nonprofit organizations. His personal experience spans the cable, telecommunication, automotive, financial, retail, photographic marketing, and nonprofit industries. Todd's areas of expertise include customer service, leadership, performance improvement, team building, hiring and retaining, recognition programs, dealing with generations, and communication. Todd has a bachelor's degree in management from the University of Alabama and is certified in human performance improvement and is a certified DDI and AchieveGlobal facilitator. Todd is member of the Central Florida chapter of ASTD and has served as the vice president for communication and president.

Todd Whisenant
3521 Diamond Leaf Lane
Oviedo, FL 32766
(407) 977.8994
Email: todd.whisenant@ccci.org
ASTD Chapter: Central Florida

Chapter 15

Online Learning: Tools to Try

The basic concept of distance learning is not new. In fact, the training profession is moving into its second decade of "practicing" what we now (for the most part) call e-learning. The lingo has changed—webinars, online classes, virtual classrooms—but whatever you call it, learning powered by the digital revolution is here to stay.

However, it is safe to say that many trainers are somewhat reluctant to fully embrace the notion and perfect their design and delivery techniques. But, as Vince Lombardi once said, "Practice does not make perfect. Only **perfect** practice makes perfect."

Most organizations have increased their use of virtual training due to travel restrictions, budget cuts, and an increasingly technology-savvy workforce. Organizations are rethinking how they will continue to meet the learning needs of their employees and are asking their trainers to deliver more content online. Trainers are expected to have the skills to design and deliver virtual training.

Unfortunately, the concept of distance learning (an older term, but inclusive for my purposes here) is still not well understood by either organizations or practitioners. The high hopes for this training often fall short of the quality standards expected in traditional settings. Most of this disappointment is due to a lack of appropriate design and limited knowledge of the skill variations required. Many trainers still believe distance learning (no matter the technology driving the learning) is simply classroom training set to a digital framework. Of course, that is certainly not true.

Cindy Huggett, in *Virtual Training Basics*, convinces us that virtual training is "still training" and requires us to tap into all the good things we do in the classroom. The contributors to this chapter have taken that advice. With a special virtual twist, they have presented good ideas you can include in your next e-learning event.

Tara Denton shares an opening activity that is as good in the training room as it is online. Just as in the classroom, the first few minutes of an online course will set the tone for the rest of the time and Darlene Christopher helps you set the tone right from the start. Joan McGrory explains several ways you can use YouTube to enhance learning for your participants. Virtual role plays? Sure, why not? Darlene Christopher gives you an example. Joel Lamoreaux explains how an exciting idea from kindergarten can be an even better idea online. Paul Venderley shares his version of an online review, complete with a spinner!

You'll enjoy these activities and find ways to use them in your next virtual event.

Twitter Introductions

Submitted by Tara Denton

Overview

Participants follow the lead of Twitter's brevity of language and are asked to provide five-word descriptions of other participants to connect and engage them in the training event.

Objective

- To provide a short introduction that prepares individuals for an active training environment

Audience

Appropriate for any size audience

Time Estimate

5 to 10 minutes

Materials and Equipment

- (Classroom environment) One index card per participant
- (Online environment) Whiteboard with a grid (use line tool). Type each person's name in a square, so each has his or her own personal "square" to "tweet" in. Don't forget to give participants annotation privileges!

Area Setup

No special requirements

Process

1. In a classroom setting, ask each participant to take 1 minute to write a description of themselves in five words (and five words only) on an index card. Tell the participants that they can write a sentence or a collection of words they feel describes them.
2. After 1 minute, ask participants to walk to the a designated place in the room and partner with someone they do not know. Ask them to exchange index cards and prepare to introduce their learning partners.

3. Go around the room and ask each person, in turn, to read the Twitter introduction of his or her partner.

4. In an online setting, ask each participant to find the box on the online whiteboard with his or her name on it. Ask participants to type their five-word Twitter introductions into the squares.

5. In either environment, comment on the diversity in the room and the original choices people made when describing themselves. Take note of the learning and personality styles revealed through the tweets. Comment on the fact that five little words can tell the essence of a person. You can also mention that, when one is forced to simplify, the core of the information is revealed. This can be an important lesson to keep in mind when working on a project.

InSider's Tips

- This activity can be done in an online or classroom environment with equal effectiveness. Its brevity makes it ideal when your workshop is shorter than a day.
- Encourage further creativity for visual learners by asking them to add a drawing or image to their Twitter descriptions.

Tara Denton has designed and delivered learning solutions since 2001. She specializes in building learning products that meet business objectives, facilitating training programs, and coaching others to deliver participant-centered experiences. Tara's learning products have been named as finalists in training product competitions, and her jovial style has made her a repeated speaker and presenter. Tara's flexibility allows her to work on a range of projects, from consulting a Fortune 500 company on an internal certification program to designing and delivering live online courses.

Tara Denton
Life Cycle Engineering
4360 Corporate Road
Charleston, SC 29405
(843) 744.7110
Email: tdenton@LCE.com
Website: www.lce.com/institute
ASTD Chapter: South Carolina Midlands

Virtual Warm-Up

Submitted by Darlene Christopher

Overview
A simple online whiteboard is shown to be a great place to meet and greet in this activity designed to connect virtual participants in a meaningful way.

Objectives
- To introduce participants to the interactive features of the virtual classroom
- To set a tone for a high level of interactivity for a virtual training session

Audience
Any number of virtual classroom participants

Time Estimate
10 minutes

Materials and Equipment
- Internet connection
- PowerPoint slides
- Polling feature
- Any Word document

Area Setup
Any virtual classroom with interactive features

Preparation
In the virtual classroom environment, pre-load PowerPoint slides with simple instructions and screen shots to support the interaction. Pre-load a poll into the virtual classroom. Prepare a Word document or text file with a question that you will copy and paste into chat. Prepare a whiteboard with labeled quadrants.

Process
1. **Introduction:** After welcoming participants and making introductions, show a slide labeled "Interacting in the Virtual Classroom." The order of the steps

below may vary, depending on the features you plan to use. The order of the steps is not as important as making sure you expose participants to the interactive features you plan to use throughout the session.

2. **Post a Poll:** Post an introductory poll with an "easy" question that relates to your content, for example: "How many years of experience do you have with X?" or "How many years have you worked in X or as Y?" Be sure to let participants know whether their poll responses will be anonymous or not. When all responses have been collected, publish the results for all to see, comment on the results, thank the participants for their responses, and move on to the next interaction.

3. **Chat:** Copy and paste a pre-determined chat question from a Word document. For example: "Where are you participating from today? Type the city and state." or "How many employees do you supervise? Type the number." Comment verbally about some (not all) of the responses. If you have a second person helping produce your session, he or she may also respond or comment to the responses via chat.

4. **Icon Status Change:** Tell participants that they can also communicate with you during the session by using the icon status feature (the name of this feature will vary depending on your web conferencing tool). Show a slide with screen shots of the icon status change so you can describe where it is located on the screen and how to enable it. Then ask a question and ask participants to respond by changing their status, for example, "Raise your hand if the audio is clear." or "Change your status to *agree* if you supervise remote employees. Change your status to *disagree* if you do not supervise remote employees." Comment on the results, thank the participants, reset everyone's status to neutral, and move on.

5. **Whiteboard:** Draw a simple quadrant with labels or show an image of a quadrant with labels. Ask participants to use their pointer tools (if your system has one) to point to the box that is the best match. If your web conference tool doesn't have a pointer, ask them to select a box and write their names on the screen. For example, you might ask: "Which region of the U.S. do you support in your work?" then show a quadrant labeled North, South, East, West.

InSider's Tips

- It's critical to introduce participants to the interactive features of the virtual classroom early in a session. The first few minutes of instruction and interaction will set the tone for the rest of the session. Since time in the virtual classroom is precious, it's also important that interactions with participants support your content, rather than interacting for the sake of interacting.
- Rehearse these introductory interactions so they are smooth. A flawless first few minutes of a web conference will set a tone for a professional delivery.
- First impressions count, so figure out what you need to do in order to start your virtual session on time and get through your Virtual Warm-Up quickly, so you can move into the core content.

Darlene Christopher is a learning officer at the World Bank Group in Washington, D.C. She has been designing and delivering virtual training programs for global audiences for more than nine years. She is a regular speaker at ASTD and e-Learning Guild conferences and is the author of the book *Virtual Classroom Essentials* (publication pending). She has a diverse technology background, holding web product management positions in Silicon Valley at Infoseek, Disney Internet Group, and 3Com. Darlene earned a master's degree in international management from the Monterey Institute of International Studies. She is also the director of virtual programs for the Metro D.C. chapter of ASTD.

Darlene Christopher
7742 Desiree Street
Alexandria, VA 22315
(202) 473.6651
Email: darlene.christopher@gmail.com
Website: Webconferenceguru.com
ASTD Chapter: Metro Washington, D.C.

YouTube: A Human Touch

Submitted by Joan McGrory

Overview

Participants have a chance to connect with the instructor (and perhaps even each other) using the most widely available video-sharing tools with the purpose of connecting and engaging learners.

Objectives

- To build relationships between participants and trainers by adding a human element to online course content
- To build rapport, excite, motivate, and add creativity to a class

Audience

Any group of online participants

Time Estimate

10 minutes or under

Materials and Equipment

- A printed outline of the discussion points
- (If stationary recording): Instructor computer with webcam and webcam software and microphone
- (More portable solution): A video camera such as a Flip
- (Screen capture with voice): JingPro ($14.95/year) and microphone (If this choice is used, activity is limited to 5 minutes.)

Area Setup

No special requirements

Preparation

In one take, without edits, in 10 minutes or less, talk to your online students on camera. The message can be a welcome message, a message to clarify common points of confusion, a message to "touch base" by verifying course schedule or chapter/topic/outline or assignment details, excite, encourage, motivate, or a dozen other messages. This communication must be positive and uplifting, as it serves to build rapport and bring your class to life.

Create a login to the website YouTube or else log in with an existing id. Use the YouTube site to upload your video. YouTube will generate a hyperlink to your posted video. Distribute this hyperlink to your participants. Accompany it with the discussion points.

(Optional) If you have an online course management system or class web pages, you may choose to embed your video on an HTML page. YouTube generates the "Embed" code; simply copy and paste the code into the HTML code for your page.

Process

1. Contact your participants by email, sending them the link to your video as a welcome.
2. Provide instructions and invite your participants to briefly record video clips as an introduction to themselves, perhaps suggesting an "NPR Story Corps" style story.
3. Once participants arrive in your training room or your virtual learning class, discuss the results. Be sure to include other participants who may not have created a video introduction.
4. Invite them to discuss other ways the videos could be used before, during, or after the training session.

InSider's Tips

- After the session, invite your participants to briefly record a video clip to recap a concept, to identify confusing points, to stay in touch with the rest of the group, to evaluate the training session, or even to pass on information or perspectives to the next group.
- For instructor videos, always provide the same information in written form. It does not have to be a verbatim transcript, simply talking points along with dates, times, websites, or detailed and/or pertinent information. Provide this in printable format and the participants can follow along as you talk. If you also print the document, then you can point to sections of the document as you talk.

- For supporting evidence, see research by Douglas E. Hersh in The Human Element, Inside Higher Ed (3/29/10) written by S. Kolowich, www.insidehighered.com/news/2010/03/29/lms, and Michelle Meeks of York University in "These Lectures Are Gone in 60 Seconds," *The Chronicle* (03/06/2009), by David Sheih.
- This technique works because the information is provided in multiple formats: written, audio, and video; it is short, focused, and targeted; and it builds rapport and excites, which motivates participants.

Joan McGrory, Ph.D., is an assistant professor for Southwest Tennessee Community College, where she teaches business statistics and leadership and also serves as an advisor for Phi Theta Kappa honor society. For many years, she served her college and community as a computer seminar instructor and earned the position of center director. She developed an online orientation program for the distance education department before moving into a faculty position. She earned a Ph.D. in information systems from Nova Southeastern University. Joan also holds an MBA and a bachelor's degree in electrical engineering from Christian Brothers University.

Joan McGrory, Ph.D.
7776 Juniper Cove East
Cordova, TN 38016
Email: jmcgrory@southwest.tn.edu
Website: http://faculty.southwest.tn.edu/jmcgrory
ASTD Chapter: Memphis

Virtual Role Plays

Submitted by Darlene Christopher

Overview

Participants practice working in a virtual environment and learn important lessons about interacting without traditional visual cues such as body language.

Objective

- To practice giving and receiving feedback for a performance review in a simulated environment

Audience

Ten to twenty virtual classroom participants

Time Estimate

10 to 15 minutes for each script

Materials and Equipment

- Virtual meeting room (such as Adobe Connect, WebEx, LiveMeeting)
- Internet connection
- Prepared slides loaded in the virtual meeting room

Area Setup

Virtual classroom with audio enabled for participants

Preparation

Prepare the role plays you wish to use in your virtual classroom. Keep them simple and short, aiming for four or fewer rounds of comments back and forth.

Process

1. At the point in the agenda when you wish to conduct the role plays, show a slide with text "Scripted Role Play: How to [insert the name of the situation]," for example: How to Respond to Unclear Feedback. Tell participants that the next activity will be a scripted role play wherein they will practice how to respond to unclear feedback in a performance review conversation.

2. Show the next slide with text "Two volunteers needed. Click on Raise Hand to volunteer" (word this slide to match the feature labels used in your virtual classroom tool).
3. Call on the first two people who raise their hands. Assign one person the role of supervisor and one person the role of employee. If you have muted participant phones or microphones, open up the audio for the two volunteers.
4. Assign the roles to the two volunteers. Show the slide with script and ask the volunteers to read it out loud. The script should be labeled with text for the supervisor and text for the employee. Alternate the text so that each person reads twice. For example:
   Supervisor: "You need to improve your interpersonal skills."
   Staff: "Can you give me some suggestions about how I can do that?"
   Supervisor: "You should respect other people."
   Staff: "I feel like I do respect other people. What can I do to let people know that? Would you have suggestions for me?"
   Supervisor: "In meetings you appear disinterested when someone else is speaking. If you look at the speaker or make a comment, you will show respect."
5. Thank the volunteers and debrief the activity. Ask participants questions such as:
   • What are the key learning points?
   • What else could you include in this conversation?
   • How does what you heard fit with your experience with performance conversations?
   • In general, what might you do differently the next time you are in a situation like this?

InSider's Tips

• Without the visual clues and body language of a face-to-face setting, it's difficult to carry out a traditional role-play exercise in a virtual classroom. However, scripting the role play provides a starting point. Often, participants who are reading the script will continue the role play individually but the script helps them start.
• Virtual classroom participants need clear, deliberate instructions. Describe exactly what you want participants to do verbally and with a slide to support your instructions, for example, "raise your hand," "read aloud."

Darlene Christopher is a learning officer at the World Bank Group in Washington, D.C. She has been designing and delivering virtual training programs for global audiences for more than nine years. She is a regular speaker at ASTD and e-Learning Guild conferences and is the author of the book *Virtual Classroom Essentials* (publication pending). She has a diverse technology background, holding web product management positions in Silicon Valley at Infoseek, Disney Internet Group, and 3Com. Darlene holds a master's degree in international management from the Monterey Institute of International Studies. She is also the director of virtual programs for the Metro D.C. chapter of ASTD.

Darlene Christopher
7742 Desiree Street
Alexandria, VA 22315
(202) 473.6651
Email: darlene.christopher@gmail.com
Website: Webconferenceguru.com
ASTD Chapter: Metro Washington, D.C.

Virtual Word Cloud

Submitted by Joel Lamoreaux

Overview

Interacting online teaches important lessons about facing change and other important organizational topics.

Objective

- To help participants quickly "*see*" commonalities and differences in a topic

Audience

Ten to twenty participants

Time Estimate

10 to 15 minutes

Materials and Equipment

- Virtual classroom portal, such as WebEx
- Access to an Internet browser and ability to go to www.wordle.net

Setup

Before you begin, go to your desktop, open your browser, and go to www.wordle.net. Once there, hit the "create" button. You will see a box labeled, "Paste in a bunch of random text." You are in the right place. Leave it for now and return to your virtual classroom.

Process

1. Tell participants to think of ten words they associate with change (or whatever your training topic is, such as customer service, leadership, or personal development), both positive and negative.
2. Ask them to enter those words into the chat box of your virtual classroom. Each must be a single word, separated by a space. Tell them to avoid commas, multiple words, and hyphenated words.
3. You may wish to have a list of ten words of your own to show them as an example. For change, your list might include: fear hope uncertainty frustration promise doubt stability stressful learn grow.

4. As participants begin entering their ten words, edit/copy the lists after about every three people, returning to your desktop and www.wordle.net to paste them into the box. *Note:* You will need to edit out extra words like their names, so that only the ten words for each participant end up in the box.

5. Once all words from all participants are entered, click on the "go" button to create a "word cloud" from their entries.

6. Return to your virtual classroom, and select the option to share your desktop with the participants. Return to Wordle and the entire class will instantly see a creative word cloud that they just made. Tell them that this is a personal representation of how they see change (or your topic).

7. Ask the group which words are the largest, and then explain to them that these were the ones repeated most often. Ask them why they think these would be words many people would use to describe the topic.

8. Ask them about the smallest words, those not repeated and therefore unique to a single person. Ask them why they think this occurred? What words do they see that they did not think of at all? In general, let them open up to whatever observations they can make from the image and the fact that we all see topics the same, yet differently.

InSider's Tips

- The larger your group, the faster you will need to use your mouse, as participants will be waiting for you to finish.
- This activity is an example of how we as human beings see changes in our lives (or whatever other topic you have chosen). The activity will work for any topic when seeing differences makes for interesting observation.
- You can play with color and layout within Wordle to make it even more visual.
- You can leave names in so that they remember who they learned from that day.
- Let them do most of the talking; it is always fascinating what people can pull out of these images.
- You can send the participants a copy (color printout or electronic) as a reminder of their session.
- If any of your participants keep an electronic journal, it is fun to copy/paste their writings into Wordle to see whether any obvious themes appear.

Joel Lamoreaux presently serves employees of Deluxe Corp. from the across the United States and Canada, teaching mostly virtual sessions on various leadership topics. While his formalized education is in journalism and organizational effectiveness, he has developed a life-long appreciation for adult learning and the joy that comes with seeing another person grow and succeed. He gets his "classroom" fix by serving as vice president of programs for the Pikes Peak chapter of ASTD in Colorado Springs, Colorado.

Joel Lamoreaux
Talent Management Consultant for Deluxe Corp.
8245 N. Union Boulevard
Colorado Springs, CO 80920
(719) 528.7302
Email: joel.lamoreaux@deluxe.com
ASTD Chapter: Pikes Peak

Online Review Wheel

Submitted by Paul Venderley

Overview
Skills reviews undergo an entertaining and interactive makeover using this online training tool.

Objective
- To provide an engaging way to conduct a skills review session online

Audience
Webinar participants

Time Estimate
20 to 30 minutes

Materials and Equipment
- PowerPoint software
- Webinar software
- Instructions for Creating an Online Review Wheel

Area Setup
Virtual classroom with interactive features

Preparation
Use the Instructions for Creating an Online Review Wheel at the end of this activity.

Identify the number of topics you will review. Select the questions for each topic. Ensure that the responses can be short. Create a pie chart with all of the topics. Add an arrow to the center of the pie chart, to act as a spinner. Program the "spin" custom animation selection to control the arrow so that it points to a topic.

Insert this "Online Review Wheel" into your slide deck where appropriate or upload it into your webinar program as a separate document that can be accessed whenever needed.

Process

1. State that the group will take some time to review the content of the program. The added nuance is the wheel and the perceived randomness of the questions being asked.
2. Tell the participants that you have an Online Review Wheel and you will spin the arrow to determine from which topic the questions will come.
3. Use the webinar program to trigger the animation that spins the arrow. Ask a volunteer one of the questions from that topic area and obtain responses from other participants.
4. Repeat the process for another topic area. Limit the review to less than 10 minutes to continue to maintain interest.

InSider's Tips

- There may be times during online training that you want to review a specific skill. The Online Review Wheel uses PowerPoint tools to practice soft skills in an engaging way. It provides the illusion of randomness and pulls participants in to what appears to be the "luck of the draw." This activity addresses one of the challenges of synchronous online training.
- Select your volunteers before the activity begins. It speeds up the review.
- Play up the randomness of the wheel. While you know from your notes where the wheel will stop next, your participants won't. Allow the spinner to land on any given topic more than once to truly add a "random" feel to the topic choice.

Paul Venderley is the 2010 president of ASTD Orange County and a senior training specialist for Corinthian Colleges, Inc. Committed to the belief that online training can be just as engaging as classroom training (and that there's little excuse for either to be boring), he seeks to replicate as many classroom-based activities in the online world as possible. He often tries to push the envelope on what's "possible," just to see what happens.

Paul Venderley
2735 E. Viking
Anaheim, CA 92806
Email: performancebydesign@live.com
Website: performancebydesign.wordpress.com
ASTD Chapter: Orange County

Instructions for Creating an Online Review Wheel

Follow these instructions to create the pie chart and program the custom animation.

1. Identify the number of topics for which you will create questions.
2. In PowerPoint, create a pie chart.
   - In the Menu Bar, select Insert.
   - Select Chart. A "Change Chart Type" dialog box will appear.
   - Select Pie Chart.
3. An Excel window will open with a data sample for your chart. Update the spreadsheet to divide the pie chart into equal segments based on the number of topics you have for your review.
   For example, Sales:
   1st Qtr
   2nd Qtr
   3rd Qtr
   4th Qtr
   Note that the default topics PowerPoint adds to this data table are immaterial to the final chart.
4. Close the Excel spreadsheet/data chart. You should see your PowerPoint pie chart.
5. In PowerPoint, remove any labels, titles, or legends included with the pie chart.
6. Expand the chart area to make the pie chart as large as possible. This will be your spinner board. Format the pie pieces as desired.
7. Add your topic titles to the board.
   - It's easiest to use WordArt to create the topic headings.
   - Try the WordArt Text Effect: "Inflate Top" or "Can Top" to shape the topic as an arc.
8. Insert a Block Arrow over your board.
   - In the Menu Bar, select Insert.
   - Select Shapes.
   - Choose a Block Arrow from the Shapes options given.

9. Format the arrow as desired, ensuring that the arrow stands out from all other colors on the pie chart.
10. Create custom animations for the arrow.
    - Select the Block Arrow.
    - In the PowerPoint Menu Bar, select Animations.
    - Select Custom Animation.
    - Click Add Effect.
    - Select Emphasis.
    - Select Spin.
11. The default settings for this animation are 360-degree clockwise, medium speed. You'll want to change those settings to allow your arrow to land on different sections of the pie chart.
    - First, set a 720-degree (Two Spin) Clockwise Spin animation to "Very Fast," immediately followed by a 180-degree (Half Spin) Clockwise Spin animation set to "Fast."
12. Continue to insert custom animation until all topics are covered. The following Custom Animation example should result in each topic being covered once:

    1. Start: On Click
       Amount: 720-degree Clockwise (Two Spins)
       Speed: Very Fast
    2. Start: After Previous
       Amount: 180-degree Clockwise
       Speed: Fast
       Selected Topic: Topic Three
    3. Start: On Click
       Amount: 720-degree Clockwise (Two Spins)
       Speed: Very Fast
    4. Start: After Previous
       Amount: 90-degree Clockwise
       Speed: Fast
       Selected Topic: Topic Four
    5. Start: On Click
       Amount: 720-degree Clockwise (Two Spins)
       Speed: Very Fast
    6. Start: After Previous
       Amount: 120-degree Clockwise (This is a Custom Setting)

Speed: Fast
Selected Topic: Topic One

7. Start: On Click
   Amount: 720-degree Clockwise (Two Spins)
   Speed: Very Fast

8. Start: After Previous
   Amount: 300-degree Clockwise (This is a Custom Setting)
   Speed: Fast
   Selected Topic: Topic Four

9. Start: On Click
   Amount: 720-degree Clockwise (Two Spins)
   Speed: Very Fast

10. Start: After Previous
    Amount: 180-degree Clockwise
    Speed: Fast
    Selected Topic: Topic Two

Chapter 16

Ideas for Your ASTD Chapter

Do you give back to your ASTD chapter? Looking for ways to add spark to your meetings? Here are a few ideas shared by your ASTD chapter colleagues that will surely add some spark and commitment to the next meeting.

If you are not a chapter contributor, now is the time to start. Throughout your career you have most likely received support from others. Now it is time to give back to the profession. You could volunteer to serve on a committee for your ASTD chapter, speak at a local ASTD chapter meeting, mentor someone new to ASTD, run for a board position, volunteer to coordinate a meeting, or dozens of other things. Giving back to the profession is good for your soul and good for your chapter's success. Find a way to volunteer today.

The two contributions in this chapter could not have come from chapters that are farther away! Kenneth Stein from the Space Coast chapter in Florida contributed "A Gift to Use," a quick way to start a meeting that delivers immediate payback. It will have members coming back for more. "Between Meeting Meetings," submitted by Mary Rydesky from the Anchorage, Alaska, chapter, is a great way for chapter members to network and meet other members between meetings. Both of these activities are great and highly recommended for use at your next chapter meeting.

By the way, if you are reading this book, check to see whether anyone from your chapter contributed to this book. The Chapters for Chapters contest invited all chapters to contribute activities that could be published. We were looking for road-tested ideas—those that trainers have tried over and over and that continue to deliver good results every time. We asked and we received many more activities than we expected.

Thank you to every ASTD member who contributed to make this book a success and to all the volunteers who invest themselves into the success of ASTD and your chapter.

A Gift to Use

Submitted by Kenneth R. Stein

Overview
This activity offers many uses beyond its simple structure with give-back opportunities that range from sharing the latest in professional practices to important networking and social connections.

Objectives
- To provide immediately usable information to chapter members
- To provide an opportunity to practice a presentation

Audience
All those attending an ASTD chapter meeting

Time Estimate
10 minutes or less

Materials and Equipment
- As required and provided by each individual presenter

Area Setup
Normal seating as required for the meeting

Preparation
Ask someone to volunteer to provide the Gift to Use at the next meeting. Ensure that the person understands the rationale and that it is meant to be short and practical—no advertising.

Process
1. Open the meeting and introduce the Gift to Use concept for those who might be new to chapter meetings. Explain that the purpose of this activity is to open the meeting with a quick presentation on some topic that the attendees can use immediately. It may be an icebreaker, overview of a book recently read, website, personal success or failure story, or a business lesson learned. It is designed to ensure members leave each meeting with a valuable tool.

Explain that it also is a way to demonstrate the best practice of information sharing. Because it is designed to give chapter members presentation practice without extensive preparation time, encourage anyone who is interested to let you know.

2. Introduce the presenter and as much as the presenter wants you to say about the activity.

3. Support the presenter in any way that you can, answer questions, process handouts, help with introductions. In addition, watch the time. Maintain tight control on the time limit to keep the presenter focused and the activity moving quickly.

4. Lead applause for the presenter and distribute evaluations if desired.

InSider's Tips

- Ensure the topic is immediately usable. Examples of good ideas include: icebreakers, key learning from a book or conference, applicable story with a lesson learned, job aid, or overview of a useful website.

- This is designed as a free-form open dialogue. Participants should be encouraged to use their creativity and imagination to make the information exchange exciting and practical.

- Strictly enforce time limit (we use 10 minutes). Keeps the presentation focused and fast-paced.

Kenneth R. Stein, Ed.D., CPLP, is with the learning organization of the Boeing Company. He has presented programs at American Society for Training and Development international conferences, been involved in live television and talk radio, and participated in numerous learning events. Kenneth is a past president and serves on the board of directors for the Space Coast chapter of ASTD. He is part of the OneVoice Team, winner of the 2009 ASTD Volunteer-Staff Partnership Award. Kenneth has a doctorate in adult education from Nova Southeastern University, is a Certified Professional in Learning and Performance (CPLP), and Senior Professional in Human Resources (SPHR).

Kenneth R. Stein, Ed.D., CPLP
430 Messha Trail
Merritt Island, FL 32953
(321) 704.9384
Email: kstein@digital.net
ASTD Chapter: Space Coast

Between Meeting Meetings

Submitted by Mary M. Rydesky

Overview

This unique take on "pass the hat" pays benefits to everyone in the audience who drops in a card and takes out a potentially valuable and rewarding connection.

Objective

- To increase the personalization of membership as a benefit to local ASTD members

Audience

Two or more

Time Estimate

10 minutes

Materials and Equipment

- Basket
- Blank index cards and pens
- Printed sign that says "Add a Business Card for a Between Meetings Meeting and Networking" on the front and "Take One and Pass It On" on the reverse side. Sign should fit neatly in the basket.

Area Setup

Normal seating as required for the meeting

Process

1. At an appropriate time during an ASTD chapter meeting, show the basket and start circulating it while introducing the concept.
2. Explain that a benefit of local membership is creating relationships with other trainers. Provide a personal testimony of how this helped you. Explain that cards will be added and that the basket will circulate again prior to the end of the meeting. State that there are blank cards should an attendee not have a business card. Each person who put one in will draw one out (randomly),

agreeing to contact that person within two weeks. Contact may be a telephone call or an email. Tell them that meeting for coffee or lunch is encouraged, and making the personal contact prior to the next scheduled ASTD meeting is the expectation.

3. Near the end of the meeting, circulate the basket one last time.

4. Appoint a member to accept the basket at the end of the round and to change the sign to the "Take One and Pass It On" side.

5. Circulate the basket again, telling those who put cards in to pull one out. Repeat the agreement to contact that person and use this as an opportunity to promote the next meeting date and time.

InSider's Tips

- This low-cost tool improves the development of collegial relationships among members. Invite guests to participate, too, to heighten their interest in joining the chapter.

- Make this a feature of *every* meeting so that the chapter becomes known for its commitment to building a friendly network for its members.

- This could easily be adapted for your organization to encourage follow-on learning and networking after a training session.

Mary M. Rydesky has been in ASTD for many years and in Alaska chapter leadership since relocating from Texas in 2003. A well-known trainer and speaker, she currently heads Transition Management, a change management consulting company). Transition Management manages the Alaska Distance Learning Network (www.akdistancelearning. net), providing distance delivery options in support of trainers and businesses wanting a lean approach to training. Mary also runs JarviHomestay Bed & Breakfast in Anchorage.

Mary M. Rydesky
1432 Jarvi Drive
Anchorage, AK 99515
(907) 561.3349
Email: mrydesky@transitionmanagement.us or mrydesky@yahoo.com
Website: www.transitionmanagement.us
ASTD Chapter: Alaska

Activity GPS

Many of the activities in this book could appear in any of several chapters. If you are looking for an activity and cannot find what you want in the chapter devoted to the topic, this Activity GPS will help you locate others that might put you on the road to success. The primary/key topic is listed in the column for each activity. However, each activity may be used for the other purposes as designated with a shaded cell.

Activity GPS table (matrix of activities vs. Training Tools and Training Topics; shaded cells marked with "X").

Title	Page	Minutes	Key Topic	ASTD Chapter Idea	Using Technology	Review and Retention	Participation	Energizer	Opening Action	Icebreaker	Training Technique	Teamwork and Trust	Professional Development	Problem Solving	Personal Development	Working in Organizations	Leadership	Diversity	Customer Service/Sales	Creativity	Listening	Communication
A Cat and a Fridge	139	10–15	Teamwork					X	X			X								X		
A Gift to Use	410	10	ASTD	X							X	X										
Acquainted Antics	109	20–45	Teamwork							X		X										
Activating Enthusiasm	241	20–30	Professionalism										X									X
Answer the Question and Keep the Card	342	20–30	Reviewing			X	X				X	X										
Are You Smiling?	42	10–15	Listening																		X	
Are You This or That?	86	30–45	Diversity							X		X			X			X				
Between Meeting Meetings	412	10	ASTD	X			X				X											
Blog and RE-Blog	374	50–70+	New Tools		X																	
Build a Bridge	162	60+	Teamwork				X					X		X		X	X					X
Capital Team Building	141	30–60	Teamwork				X					X						X				
Conceptualization of You	103	20	Teamwork							X	X	X							X			
Consult the Experts	227	45	Problem Solving									X		X								
Create a Vision	193	30–60	Leadership													X	X					
Creative Storming	69	15–30	Creativity																	X		
Creative Word Toss	73	10–60	Creativity													X				X		

(Continued)

Category		Cultural Networking	Deal with It	Defining a Great Customer Experience	Definition BINGO	Dig It Up	Dirty Training Room	Diversity Quilt	Do You Know How to Listen?	Do You See What I See?	Favorites Poker	Focus Einstein Style	From Seeing to Achieving	Generation Genius	Get Ready for Interviewing
Training Tools	ASTD Chapter Idea														
	Using Technology														
	Review and Retention		■												
	Participation				■		■				■				
	Energizer				■										
	Opening Action				■		■					■			
	Icebreaker														
	Training Technique		■		■	■	■				■				
Training Topic	Teamwork and Trust	■						■			■		■		
	Professional Development					■								■	■
	Problem Solving			■		■				■					
	Personal Development	■								■					■
	Working in Organizations												■	■	
	Leadership												■		
	Diversity	■						■						■	
	Customer Service/Sales			■											
	Creativity			■											
	Listening							■	■	■			■		
	Communication	■							■	■			■		■
Activity	Key Topic	Diversity	New Tools	Customer	Opening	Problem Solving	New Tools	Diversity	Listening	Communication	Teamwork	Opening	Teamwork	Diversity	Professionalism
	Minutes	30	30–60	15–30	7–10	50–60	30	60	30	20–35	15–30	15–25	30–40	30–50	30–40+
	Page	89	371	47	315	222	382	83	32	10	121	301	176	92	263

Activity	Page	Time (min.)	Category
Getting to Know You . . . Getting to Know All About You	277	15	Icebreaker
Give Them the BlackBerries	367	5–15	New Tools
Go for the Win	19	10	Communication
Great Expectations	312	10–20	Opening
Guess What We Have in Common	285	15–20	Icebreaker
Hula Hoop Challenge	172	40–60	Teamwork
I Said I Need to Learn	318	20–30	Opening
I See You Listening	28	30	Listening
I'll Say It Myself	345	10–15	Reviewing
Immodest Interview	287	45–60	Icebreaker
It's Not What You Think	62	15–30	Creativity
Jazzed	329	8–10	Opening
Key Ideas	365	15–30	New Tools
Learning Is Valuable	304	20–30	Opening
Learning Stations	339	30–45	Reviewing
Let Go of Your Fears	321	4–7	Opening
Level the Playing Field	307	20	Opening
Look What I Can Do!	292	10–15	Icebreaker
Make a Wish	310	15–30	Opening
Multitasking Stressors	261	10	Professionalism
No Advice Please	25	10–15	Listening
Objection Resolution	54	15–30	Sales

(Continued)

The following matrix cross-references each activity (columns) against Training Tools and Training Topics (rows). Shaded cells are marked with ■.

Category	Online Review Wheel	Part of the Big Picture	People to People	Perception Reflection	Performance Graffiti Wall	Personality Polaroid	Picture Your Ideal Team	Pipe Dream	Planning with Spaghetti and Marshmallows	Power of Questions	PPT Board Game Review	Product Knowledge Scramble	Purging the Potholes	Puzzled Prospects	Rapid Rate of Change
Training Tools															
ASTD Chapter Idea															
Using Technology	■										■				
Review and Retention											■				
Participation			■								■				
Energizer			■	■											
Opening Action													■		■
Icebreaker															■
Training Technique	■										■	■		■	■
Training Topic															
Teamwork and Trust			■			■	■	■	■						
Professional Development		■			■									■	
Problem Solving		■				■		■							
Personal Development						■							■		
Working in Organizations		■			■					■					
Leadership			■				■	■	■						
Diversity					■		■								
Customer Service/Sales												■			
Creativity									■						
Listening							■		■						
Communication				■		■			■					■	
Key Topic	Online	Professionalism	Teamwork	Communication	Professionalism	Teamwork	Teamwork	Teamwork	Teamwork	Leadership	Reviewing	New Tools	Opening	Professionalism	Opening
Minutes	20–30	20–25	30	10–20	ongoing	45–60	90–120	20–40	30–45	30+	15–25	15	10–15	20–45	5
Page	403	257	154	13	254	131	150	157	165	196	332	361	324	250	299

Activity	Page	Time (min)	Category
Remember Me?	358	15–20	New Tools
Roll of the Die	282	20	Icebreaker
Scenario Cards	230	10–15	Problem Solving
Speedy SMEs	355	30–40	New Tools
Spell It Out!	294	10–15	Icebreaker
Story, Song, Poem, Saying	5	15–20	Communication
Straw Towers	169	45	Teamwork
Stress Symphony	245	10–15	Professionalism
Success Chain	377	20–30	New Tools
Take Action	380	15–30	New Tools
Team Commercial	113	20–30	Teamwork
Team Speed-Dating	105	35–80	Teamwork
Team Think-ING	160	20–30	Teamwork
Tell Me About Yourself	369	5	New Tools
Tell Me Something Good	274	5–20	Icebreaker
The Great Leadership Debate	187	45–55	Leadership
The Penny Story	59	30	Creativity
Think on Your Feet	181	60–90	Teamwork
Three Truths and a Lie	116	45–120	Teamwork
Through the Looking Glass	235	120–180	Problem Solving
Throw Down Your Answer	336	30	Reviewing
Ties That Bind	119	10–15	Teamwork

(Continued)

Activity				Training Topic												Training Tools						
Title	**Page**	**Minutes**	**Key Topic**	Communication	Listening	Creativity	Customer Service/Sales	Diversity	Leadership	Working in Organizations	Personal Development	Problem Solving	Professional Development	Teamwork and Trust	Training Technique	Icebreaker	Opening Action	Energizer	Participation	Review and Retention	Using Technology	ASTD Chapter Idea
Tuscan Summer Evenings	16	10–20	Communication	■				■							■			■				
Tweet! Key Learnings	348	NA	Reviewing												■					■	■	
Twitter Introductions	389	5–10	Online												■	■	■	■			■	
Valuing the Values	208	120	Leadership	■					■	■	■	■	■									
Virtual Role Plays	397	5–7	Online												■							
Virtual Warm-Up	391	10	Online												■		■		■		■	
Virtual Word Cloud	400	10–15	Online												■				■		■	
Vote Trust with Your Feet	200	45+	Leadership	■					■		■		■	■								
We Are All Different	79	20–30	Diversity					■			■			■								
What a Difference a Goal Makes	190	20	Leadership						■	■		■										
What's in a Name?	180	10–15	Icebreaker											■		■						
What's in the News?	51	45	Sales				■								■						■	
What's Under Your Bed?	271	20–30	Icebreaker			■								■		■		■	■			
Whose Snowball?	290	15	Icebreaker											■	■	■		■	■			
Yellow Ball	38	20–35	Listening	■	■																	
You Be the Ethicist	294	90	Leadership						■	■			■									
YouTube: A Human Touch	394	10	Online												■		■				■	
Zoom!	248	15–30	Professionalism						■			■	■	■								

About the Editor

Elaine Biech is president and managing principal of ebb associates inc, an organization and leadership development firm that helps organizations work through large-scale change. She has been in the training and consulting field for over thirty years, working with private industry, government, and non-profit organizations.

Elaine specializes in helping people work as teams to maximize their effectiveness. Customizing all of her work for individual clients, she conducts strategic planning sessions and implements corporate-wide systems such as quality improvement, change management, reengineering of business processes, and mentoring programs. She facilitates topics such as coaching today's employee, fostering creativity, customer service, creating leadership development programs, time management, speaking skills, coaching, consulting skills, training competence, conducting productive meetings, managing corporate-wide change, handling the difficult employee, organizational communication, conflict resolution, and effective listening. She is particularly adept at turning dysfunctional teams into productive teams.

She has developed media presentations and training materials and has presented at dozens of national and international conferences. Known as a trainer's trainer, she custom designs training programs for managers, leaders, trainers, and consultants. Elaine has been featured in dozens of publications, including *The Wall Street Journal, Harvard Management Update, Washington Post,* and *Fortune* magazine.

As a management and executive consultant, trainer, and designer, she has provided services to Outback Steakhouse, FAA, Land O' Lakes, McDonald's, Lands' End, General Casualty Insurance, Chrysler, Johnson Wax, PricewaterhouseCoopers, American Family Insurance, Marathon Oil, Hershey Chocolate, Federal Reserve Bank, U.S. Navy, NASA, Newport News Shipbuilding, Kohler Company, ASTD, American Red Cross, Association of Independent Certified Public Accountants, the University of Wisconsin, The College of William and Mary, ODU, and hundreds of other public- and private-sector organizations to prepare them for the challenges of the new millennium.

She is the author and editor of more than fifty books, including *A Coach's Guide to Developing Exemplary Leaders; ASTD Leadership Handbook;*

ASTD's Ultimate Train the Trainer; 10 Steps to Successful Training; The Consultant's Quick Start Guide (2nd ed.); *ASTD Handbook for Workplace Learning Professionals; The Business of Consulting* (2nd ed.); *Thriving Through Change; Successful Team-Building Tools* (2nd ed.); *90 World-Class Activities by 90 World-Class Trainers* (named a Training Review Best Training Product of 2007); and the nine-volume set of *ASTD's Certification Study Guides.* Her books have been translated into Chinese, German, and Dutch.

Elaine has her B.S. from the University of Wisconsin-Superior in business and education consulting and her master's in human resource development. She is active at the national level of ASTD, is a lifetime member, served on the 1990 National Conference Design Committee, was a member of the National ASTD Board of Directors and the society's secretary from 1991 to 1994, initiated and chaired Consultant's Day for seven years, and was the International Conference Design Chair in 2000. In addition to her work with ASTD, she has served on the Independent Consultants Association's (ICA) Advisory Committee and on the Instructional Systems Association (ISA) board of directors.

Elaine is the recipient of the 1992 National ASTD Torch Award, the 2004 ASTD Volunteer-Staff Partnership Award, and the 2006 ASTD Gordon M. Bliss Memorial Award. She was selected for the 1995 Wisconsin Women Entrepreneur's Mentor Award. In 2001 she received ISA's highest award, The ISA Spirit Award. She has been the consulting editor of the prestigious *Training* and *Consulting Annuals* published by Pfeiffer for the past fourteen years.